It Happened in H'wood

By BILL HALLIGAN
Hollywood, Feb. 4.

It was after 10 when I left the Beachcomber. It's sort of Chinese restaurant where they make a specialty of rum drinks. A zombie may sound like an Igorrote debutante, but it's four ounces of dynamite in a tall glass. Two of them make one very mellow. I had had three.

When I walked out to get in my car I saw a kid about 10 years old sitting on the running board. I thought it funny for a child to be out at that late hour. He had a canvas bag swung around his shoulder and he was selling Liberty magazines.

He said 'Good evening, sir. May I sing you a song?' He sounded like a Harrow upperclass man. I took another look at him. He was wearing a torn jersey and a pair of olive drab shorts. His shoes were canvas sneakers and a toe stuck out. He had the face of a Mike Angelo cherub.

He said, 'Did you say I may, sir?' 'No,' I said, 'I didn't say you may, sir. But now that you suggest it, I will say you may, sir.'

'What would like to hear,' he asked me, 'classical, operatic or popular?' 'Call your shot,' I said, 'and you better be good.'

I leaned up against a convenient telegraph pole and the kid started to sing. He had one of those Christmas carol voices. He sang an aria from 'La Boheme.' As far as he was concerned he might as well be singing from the steps. He had all the — ness of a full voice selling his hit —

Decide Future Of Welles' Pic By This Week

Tale will be told by the end of the current week on the future of Orson Welles' 'Citizen Kane,' it is expected. Although the film is set for release around Feb. 27, no theatre has yet been set for the first date. Shewey is the forecast if RKO does not announce an opening for the film which noon an opening for the film which William Randolph Hearst his life. So closely parallels his life.

Although it appears likely that 'Kane' will be released, danger is said to lay in a rift that has developed within the board of directors over the film. Prex George J. Schaefer, backed by Welles' initial, has been adamant that it be released, while another clique is definitely against it. It can be safely said that the wrangling was furious prior to Schaefer's departure for the Coast on Monday (10) night.

Welles, in the meantime, has repeated privately that he will take legal steps should there be a holdup on the film, as he is a part-owner of it. He made it, on a deal giving him 25% of the gross after production costs are taken into court is something he'd actually go to court is something, however, that would probably hinge entirely on Schaefer's wishes, as the RKO prex and Welles are close friends.

There has been some talk of the picture going out on a roadshow basis in the early dates, which the Welles side feels would be highly desirable. Release chart issued yesterday (Tuesday), in fact, advised branches not to take 'Kane' dates because pic may be sold road as though more may be needed soon afoot for pre-testing the general release. Tests apparently would be only be of the film's drawing power or to determine policy, but to test what Hearst will do.

Welles, As 25% Owner of 'Kane', Would 'Force' RKO to Release Pic

Bovine Justice

Hollywood, Feb. 4.

Killing a toreador is less heinous than killing a bull, under the ruling of the Will Hays office, as applied to the 20th-Fox production, 'Blood and Sand.'

Actual slaying of beef on the hoof, including preliminary bandarillo sharpshooting, is banned, but Tyrone Power, the bullfighter who is runned nix a bull, is permitted to die on celluloid with the approval of the censor.

Orson Welles, it is understood, has prepared to force RKO to release 'Citizen Kane,' no matter what decision of its execs or board of directors. Welles has a 25% interest of the film's net profit and is said to have been advised by his own attorney that he has legal ground for suing RKO to distribute the picture per his contract.

$2.60 Per Share On Par Common Stock in Sight

With January earnings reported to have run ahead of the first month last year, Paramount is expected to show $2.60 per common share for 1940, according to revised Wall Street estimates. Previously figured it would be around $2. Statement is expected out in the next few weeks.

Chief interest in Paramount now centers in the proposed plan of the company to call in the first preferred shares outstanding. Corporate executives are attempting a plan whereby brought in by Mendel Silberberg, Man—

CITIZEN KANE RELEASE DATE NOT YET SET

With release date of Orson Welles' 'Citizen Kane' the day after tomorrow (Friday), not a single playdate, roadshow or otherwise, has been set for the film. That's taken to indicate trouble ahead on the Hearst cate William Randolph his own alleges too closely parallels his life. Hearst is reported bringing much pressure on the RKO directorate to shelve the film.

RKO prex George J. Schaefer paid a quickie plane visit to New York, arriving Friday (21) and leaving Monday (24) after—with important board members—execs of the company.

Lyric, Indpls., Sale May Hasten Olson's Yen for Retirement

Hearst Papers' Anti-'Citizen Kane' Gripe Takes It Out on Welles-CBS

With RKO committed to release Welles' 'Citizen Kane' despite William Randolph now in years from centrate, it's gotta on and make for lesion U.'s...

Welles Suing RKO on 'Citizen Kane' In Effort to Force Pic's Release

Following cancellation by RKO of a press preview for 'Citizen Kane' Orson Welles announced last night (Tuesday) that he would sue the distributing company to force release of the film.

Welles called his daily and trade papers to his Ambassador hotel apartment in N.Y. to inform them that in his own name the two Mercury factions of one Mercury Theatre and that of his company.

MEET PAR PROD. RUSH

---

4 PIX

RKO's Watchful Waiting on Hearst Papers' Further Reaction to 'Kane'

Scare 'Em Off?

Hollywood, May 6.

Motion picture celebs are being bluntly told that they will incur enmity in certain quarters by attending the Coast preem Thursday (8) night of 'Citizen Kane' at El Capitan.

Understood that those who disregard the warning will be tabbed by spotters and reported to headquarters.

RKO Radio is skedding Orson Welles for personals with 'Citizen Kane' in cities where Hearst press is strong.

New York, Chicago and Los Angeles are being used as test arenas for Orson Welles' 'Citizen Kane' and RKO will seek no engagements outside of those and a few other cities until editorial and legal reaction of William Randolph Hearst interests is determined. No selling on the film until 1941-42.

Court test is not anticipated by the distributing company, although a suit on the 'invasion of privacy' charge that Hearstians have suggested will not come as a surprise. RKO fully anticipated, however, that the Hearst press would let loose with a campaign of vituperation.

Hearst papers apparently now figure they can do Welles and the picture more harm by a campaign of silence. They neither mentioned nor printed reviews of the New York opening and apparently have allowed their campaign against Welles as a 'Communist' to lag. Drive, in which papers lined up American Legion and other patriotic groups to make a hue and cry about a Welles Free Company (CBS) broadcast, is felt by everyone in the industry now calculated to bring the picture than anything else.

Reports that RKO is having difficulty getting further dates for the film were denied by salesmanager Andy Smith, Jr. Pic will open roadshow dates in Washington and several other cities later this month.

RCA's 1st Quarter Net Profit, $2,734,572; Sarnoff Reviews Biz

National defense, even though it is reflected in vastly heavier taxes for industrial concerns, was stressed by David Sarnoff, president of Radio Corp. of America, in speaking at the annual stockholders meeting at the RCA Bldg. yesterday (Tuesday). He revealed that RCA had a net profit of $2,734,572 for the first quarter ended last March 31 as compared with $2,312,893 in the corresponding period last year. Consolidated gross income he announced was $34,303,324 or 21% higher than the first quarter of 1940.

Sarnoff pointed out that the profit is the net after providing $1,171,300 in normal Federal taxes and excess profits tax of $124,800, making a total of $1,596,100 Federal taxes in the first quarter, an increase of $1,070,300 or 203% as compared with the initial quarter a year ago. Before provision for Federal...

URGE STRAIGHT 10% TO STOP PRICE CUTS

MO— —DEN

Nazis' New I Said to Be To Cool O

With RKO's co— anent 'Citizen Kane considerable cooling generally held that be released despi William Randolph barricading him porters, there's no the future of the timism of a few greatly subsided siders are willing $100,000 bonfire on 'Kane's' chances cinerator was Me on Monday (3) ducer Orson We paign of showi men. Welles' ar every influential then it could, ho thing of a pu thus force RKO

Welles' ...
N.Y. Herald-Tr ceeded, however Life mag re the clamp on — ings of the fi — by phone to t (Contin—

N. Y. Legiter to House 'Citizen Kane' Day-and-Date With RKO Palace, B'way

With the running Rivoll apparently out as the twin meto to RKO's Palace in New York within the weeks, distributing the next four plan looking over the ideal company RKO house is in each city the picture RKO other continued, one on a two—a reserved seat policy, on a two-a-day, which RK Rivoll,—

already in confusion, into a completely unfathomable mess yesterday (Monday), when he told the Authors Club at luncheon:
'When I get 'Citizen Kane' off my mind, I'm going to work on an idea for a great picture based on the life of William Randolph Hearst.'

WELLES EAST TO TALK 'CITIZEN KANE' FUTURE

Hollywood, Jan. 28.
Orson Welles and his publicity chief, Herbert Drake, left for New York to huddle with George Schaefer and other RKO execs on the future of 'Citizen Kane,' which is, more or less, stymied by threats of blackouts by the Hearst newspapers.

Drake is shoving off for the east with plenty of evidence that there is vast public attention drawn to the picture before its premiere, scheduled for Feb. 14.

FIDLER ASKS $250,000 LIBEL FROM WILKERSON

Los Angeles, Jan. 28.
Damages of $250,000 were asked by Jimmie Fidler, film columnist, in a libel complaint filed in Superior Court last Friday (24) against Wilkerson Daily Corp., publishers of Hollywood Reporter, trade paper, and William R. Wilkerson, editor and publisher. Two causes of libel action were specified, each of which seeks $75,000 compensatory damages and $50,000 punitive damages. Action was filed for Fidler by the law firm of Zagon & Aaron.

Suit was dismissed yesterday (Monday), but will be refiled when

most of the tickets were sold in advance, proven last Friday (24), when the Garden was capacity, despite a snowstorm. The tour's total takings may not top last season because Boston was cancelled when the Garden there demanded 50% of the receipts. Miss Henie and Arthur Wirtz, who jointly present 'It Happens on Ice,' Center, Radio City, expected that with the star opposing her own show the theatre rink revue would show a marked b.o. drop. Instead, takings there went up 20%. Nor was the show's business dented during the 'Follies' engagement.

Bernie Scrams Coast Nitery on the 'Bounce', $6,000 Payoff Dubious

Beverly Hills, Jan. 28.
It was a blunt 'no such' that Ben Bernie tossed at the Victor Hugo nitery when asked to finish out his eight weeks at the grotto. Three weeks were enough, groaned the old maestro, gazing dismally at a reader for $3,000, which he affectionately termed a 'bounceroo.' And if that didn't convince him, there was the
(Continued on page 55)

FLU REISSUE FLOPPING HOLLYWOOD FILMERS

Hollywood, Jan. 28.
Old man flu is putting on a return engagement in Hollywood, slowing up film production and knocking off players, execs, agents and directors with impartial abandon.

Among the victims last week were Edward Arnold

so in or own
Harry Brand, 20th Century-Fox: 'Just saw you in gratulations. You were

Irwin Dash, who publishing a new
The song 'There I Go' took it literally.
While visiting Jack Benny
Jack replied, 'That's the

My mother listens to ask her anything she sings
Anyway, Tschaikowsky and many other immortal is straightened out. That so often.

Lana Turner; Better Olsen and Johnson; Clark Gable. Henny Youngman the station here that

Read an ad in a Los panion to hitch-hiker, a certain vaudeville each other so their eggs I've got field glasses to Eavesdropped at the I am.
Eavesdropped at the detective his telephone number.
As long as I'm leaving now a blotter for the team There's a bookmaker or on how long a marriage

Middleton & Spellme, Bessinger & White Josie Clinton & Co

If you don't like this get stuck like you did.

L.A. to N

Mary Astor.
Jack Benny.
Wallace Beery.
Robert Benchley.

Wednesday, January 22, 1941   VARIETY

H'WOOD BUYIN

RKO, Despite Hearst's Ire, Announces Huge National Campaign for 'Kane'

RKO last week openly flaunted William Randolph Hearst. At the same time it assured the film industry that it has no intention of withholding Orson Welles' 'Citizen Kane' despite the publisher's demand to do so. Film will be released at the end of February.

Studio, which has never taken any official cognizance of Hearst's ire or threats, has announced for the film a national advertising campaign that will be 'one of the most far-reaching ever launched for an attraction by RKO Radio Pictures.

Hearst papers apparently will get their share of the big RKO budget, spite the publisher's edict against publicity for the company or its duct in his publications. Top
RKO said last week
dule is now

Penthouse Blues

Hollywood, Jan. 21.
'A Girl's Best Friend Is Wall Street' might have been a hot title back in the feverish days of 1928, but now the story detours north at Trinity Church and becomes 'A Girl's Best Friend Is Broadway.'

Picture rolls tomorrow (Wed.) at Columbia with Joan Bennett and Franchot Tone in the top spots, directed by Richard Wallace. 'Wall Street' title was ditched after the budget trimming.

HAS HOLD ON OF 20 SHO

Six Plays Definitely chased by Film Com With Stakes in Two and Four More ai tain Buys — Heavy Plunging

HIGH PRICES

to film spark las rea be ds.

WAGE SIS AGAIN

rert to Former Key Workers—Browne's Ad-Phone, From
three owners which attorneys working counsel of approved by
of Goldwyn latter is bour of any further stock interest bought the studio workers on an reverted to the dividends. Switch was ge E. Browne, of Theatrical Stage sident phoned

NTERCEDES

Hollywood, March 18.
proved by plan to put hun-

LOEW'S $500,000 COUNTERCLAIM

Welles' Threat to Raise 'Kane' Puts Him in Spot Between Odlum-Schaefer

Oscaring Their Own

Hollywood, March 18.
William Gargan missed out on an Academy award in the supporting player class but his film work for the past year hasn't gone entirely unrewarded. Last Saturday night he was gifted with a statue of St. Patrick by the Gaelic Society of America for being the 'outstanding' Irish actor.

Femme award went to Geraldine Fitzgerald, who was kudosed with a statuette of St. Bridget.

God Bless America..............Berlin
Yes, My Darling Daughter........Feist
*Down Argentina Way ('Down Argentine Way').....Miller
* Filmusical.

Immediate future for Orson Welles' 'Citizen Kane' is bleak, with indications that RKO planning to give it a brushoff.
Welles' threat of court action causes some other move. Producer's announcement last week that brought no official reaction from RKO. However, George J. Schaefer, RKO pres, is said to have called Welles from Hollywood Saturday (18) and told him:

'I'm coming to New York next week. Don't do anything legal until I arrive. I'll take it up once more with the board of directors when I get there.'

Schaefer is slated to plane into Manhattan tomorrow (Thursday). There's no board meeting scheduled, however, until March 31, which apparently means two more weeks at least in the cans for 'Kane.' Delaying

at 47

When William of the West resigned the tes understand a fortune in

thereafter the oward Hughes n of theatres k to 1930 he k to serve in for RKO and en the late S. withdrew his City

Wednesday, April 23, 1941   VARIETY

GOVT'S 'MORE T

Add: Hearst Vs. Welles ('Citizen Kane'); More Newspaper Attacks

Battle of the Hearst papers against Orson Welles continued on all fronts during the past week as RKO prepared for the roadshow preem of Welles' pic, 'Citizen Kane,' at the Palace, N.Y. May 1 and other cities throughout the country during the month, drumming up an Legion,

tinel here has been going to town in its attempt to discredit Orson Welles for participation in the Free Company's series of Sunday CBS broadcasts. Not only columns, but pieces are devoted daily to attacks upon Commy angles to the situation, Grand Army of the Republic and other patriotic organization leaders given unlimited space on interviews, and proposed actions, played up in the Hearst

BURDENED S BIZ'S NEW

Morgenthau's 'Larg Bill' Warning Ca ready Tax-Loaded men to Flinch Hit Amusement Front

20% GATE

All Film Cos. May Suffer Because Of Hearst's Peeve at Welles' 'Kane'

Hollywood, Jan. 14.
Mia Steady bombardment from the heaviest editorial artillery in the tles The Hearst press is faced by the entire Paran film industry as a result of the fury into which William Randolph Hearst had las been thrown by the revelation musiq that the story of 'Citizen Kane,' Vir Orson Welles' first film, bears All similarity to the life of the publisher.

One Not only has Hearst forbidden any busy thing mention of the distributor, RKO, or Bou Gotts product in any of his papers, but again week the studio publicity department has the ki Careen tipped off that the Hearst paper acers will keep up a continuous posteshellfire against the entire industry. The threat is to put heavy emphasis on high, widescale employment of foreigners in motion picture production to the exclusion of idle Americans. Pot-shots are also threatened against all censorious situations or material in pictures.

Hearst, in addition, is going ahead with his threatened suit for an injunction to restrain RKO from releasing 'Kane,' according to word broadcast by studio officials from Louella O. Parsons, motion picture editor of the Hearst newspapers. Lower street execs declared that was the ultimatum, following a direct question as to the publisher's intention.

Hearst's objection to the release of 'Citizen Kane' is said to be based on
(Continued on page 55)

RKO's Holme Knighted

Randle F. Holme, chairman of RKO's British company, has been conferred a knighthood by the King of England for distinguished service to the crown.

Phil Reisman, RKO foreign chief, received notification in N. Y.

U.S. NEWS VIA AIR TO EUROPE VITAL NOW

Despite the recent publicity concerning short-wave radio propaganda from the United States to South America, the real importance of Yankee transmissions at this moment in history are the news programs in French, German and Italian beamed at Europe. News from the U. S., and especially news of preparations over here to spoil the dictators' pushover campaign, has enormous value just now.

President Roosevelt's inaugural speech will be shortwaved by NBC in French, German and Italian, leaving General Electric in Schenectady to beam the English delivery itself to the British Isles. In Great Britain the BBC will pick-up and longwave the President's address.

EACH TIM 'WILL, WON

Comeback. Barite Grueling 'Ot Saturday as I formance of S Private Meloch self

$500,000 TO

Lawrence Tibbett if somewhat cau through his 'comeback both on the radio and politan Opera but te great artistic risks, b posing to sing the Sat (18) the grueling b of 'Otello.' The result of this dynamic sing
(Continued on

J.J.'s 'Love' For New S Attack o

Quickest operetta n son was 'Night of stopped at the Hudsor day (11) after seven It was a Shubert pro J. was entirely in char which played out-of-t two months to such m ance that the manager not to open it on Bro Showings out of tow panked by a series of tween Shubert and In reported having one reviewer in Bost in Chicago barred

Hearst Opens Blast on RKO-Schaefer; 'Citizen Kane' Release Still Indef

William Randolph Hearst got his first real opportunity last week since his burn at RKO to show how he feels about the company—and stuck the knife in deep. Both the studio and George J. Schaefer, its president, were lambasted mercilessly on front pages of Hearst papers from coast to coast. The news peg was a remote suit against Schaefer and RKO that even the trade papers relegated to inside pages.

Meantime, Orson Welles' 'Citizen Kane,' which it is said Hearst alleges too closely resembles his own life and is the cause of the publisher's ire at RKO, is getting close to its release date and still no engagements have been set for it. RKO maintains that the possibility the film will be roadshow is delaying the opening, but it is known that lawyers have been busy and there's dissension within the company on the course to be taken. Hearst has allegedly demanded that the film be shelved.

Suit that caused the fireworks in the Hearst dailies ended with a $7,000 decision against RKO, won by Joseph N. Ermoleff in Los Angeles court. Ermoleff is a Europen producer who
(Continued on page 18)

MRS. EMLYN WILLIAMS REMAINING IN U.S.

Mrs. Mollie Williams, wife of playwright-actor Emlyn Williams, is remaining in the U. S. indefinitely with their two children. She had planned to return to England after arranging with Herman Shumlin for the production of her husband's 'The Corn Is Green,' at the National, N.Y. But Williams, currently touring the English provinces in his new play, 'He Was Born Gay,' persuaded her to stay in the U. S., at least until after the expected Nazi invasion attempt

Sam Scribner III

Sam Scribner, former showman, has been in the Lawrence hospital, Bronxville, N. Y., for the past week. Veteran, who is 83, was reported ill with grippe, but the hospital declined to verify the ailment.

He is treasurer of the Actors Fund, where it was stated his condition is favorable, and chairman of Theatre Authority.

FDR Birthday Ball Spokesman Denies Actors 'Pushed Around'

Washington, Feb. 13.
Editor VARIETY:
Because Hollywood stars have contributed so generously to the success of the Washington Birthday Ball Celebrations, and because others who are eager to come in the future may get the wrong impression, may I challenge VARIETY's page one story of Feb. 12. to the effect that the guests contributed by the motion picture industry were 'pushed around,' or given unhospitable treatment.

Contrary to the vague charge of Mr. Alan Corelli, that those who made many personal appearances were denied White House luncheon invitations, and the opportunity to participate in other activities, the facts are that all stars were included in every official event on the program, and this included, of course, presence at Mrs. Roosevelt's luncheon in the afternoon, and at the
(Continued on page 55)

BRITISH WAR RELIEF BENEFIT IN N. Y. SRO

Indicated that the 'Carnival for Britain,' benefit show at the Music Hall, Radio City, Friday (21) at midnight, will be over capacity. Over the weekend the theatre advised the American Theatre Wing of the British War Relief that no more tickets

RUBINOFF
AND HIS VIOLIN
on Personal Appearance Tour
until May 15th. Dates in 125 cities.
Management:
PHIL RUBINOFF
Paramount Bldg.   New York City

Music to Suit Audience Mood For 'Fantasia'

Hollywood, Feb. 18.
Recording of three musical numbers to be incorporated in Walt Disney's 'Fantasia' after the initial roadshowings of the cartoon opus are well under way, has been started here by Leopold Stokowski. Numbers will be switched and varied, under present plan, to provide evenings of light concerts or more dramatic compositions to suit all types of music lovers, and incidentally to bring repeat customers to the boxoffice.

Selections to hit the sound tracks under the Stokowski baton are 'Peter and the Wolf,' by Prokofiev; 'Flight of the Bumble Bee,' by Rimsky-Korsakov, and 'Swan of Tuonela,' by Sibelius.

Stokowski has completed music and animation is about two-thirds through on 'Clair de Lune,' by Debussy, which is also planned for insertion in the original picture.

100 Newsreelmen to Use 50,000 Feet Covering Roosevelt's Inaugural

Newsreels are preparing the most elaborate coverage ever given a presidential inauguration when President Roosevelt is sworn in for a third term this month in Washington.

Each newsreel will have 10 cameramen, five or more sound men and technicians, with the five reels represented by nearly 100 men at the inauguration. Approximately 50,000 feet of film will be shot

Joe College Goes Gaucho

Mania for rhumba tempo which has reached heavy proportions in metropolitan centers apparently is reaching the college proms.

Band booking agencies are beginning to sell proms name outfits coupled to Latin tempo dispensers, which work as relief crews much as

Jackie Gleason, M.C.,
To Make

CITIZEN KANE

The Fiftieth-Anniversary Album

HARLAN LEBO

Foreword by Robert Wise

DOUBLEDAY

New York   London   Toronto   Sydney   Auckland

CITIZEN

KANE

PUBLISHED BY DOUBLEDAY
a division of Bantam Doubleday Dell Publishing Group, Inc.
666 Fifth Avenue, New York, New York 10103

DOUBLEDAY and the portrayal of an anchor
with a dolphin are trademarks of Doubleday,
a division of Bantam Doubleday Dell
Publishing Group, Inc.

Library of Congress Cataloging-in-Publication Data
Lebo, Harlan.
    Citizen Kane: the fiftieth-anniversary album / by Harlan Lebo;
foreword by Robert Wise. — 1st ed.
        p.   cm.
    1. Citizen Kane (Motion picture)   I. Citizen Kane (Motion picture).   1990.
II. Title.
PN1997.C51173L4   1990
791.43'72—dc20   90-32471
                                                                        CIP
    ISBN 0-385-41473-0

Book Design by Claire Naylon Vaccaro

FOR MONICA

Contents

Acknowledgments

This book exists only because these people made it possible:

- The librarians who supported the project—in particular, Brigette Kueppers and Raymond Soto at the Theater Arts Library at UCLA, Ned Comstock from the Cinema-Television Library at the University of Southern California, Robert Cushman at the Academy of Motion Picture Arts and Sciences, and Rebecca Cape from Indiana University. These talented researchers and their colleagues provided immeasurable assistance in writing this book, providing insight and support that extended far beyond the normal call.

- Molly Bowler, who added a polish and style to the original manuscript that I could never hope to achieve.

- My agent, Felicia Eth, who believes in me, and my editors, Kara Leverte and Mark Garofalo, who believe her.

- Robert Carringer, who has written often and well about Orson Welles and *Citizen Kane,* for his invaluable guidance.

- Peter Bogdanovich, for graciously giving permission to reprint excerpts from his many interviews with Orson Welles.

- Lou Valentino, a guiding beacon for all who write books about motion pictures, for his generous help in acquiring some of the photographs in this book.

- Bob Sirchia at GTG Entertainment, the former home of RKO-Pathé, for taking us into the back corners of the studio's warehouse to look at the last remaining relics of Xanadu.

- William Alland, Richard Wilson, and Robert Wise, three active participants in the making of *Citizen Kane,* who allowed me to probe their pasts and discover the answers to many of the questions that lingered about the production of this film. These gentlemen helped bring 1940s Hollywood to life for me in a way that no amount of digging through old files could ever accomplish.

• And finally, to my family, my friends, and my coworkers, whose endless patience, amused tolerance, and warm support were the true inspiration for this book. For them, I am especially grateful.

Harlan Lebo
Los Angeles, California
May 1990

Foreword by Robert Wise

Of the many talented people from the crew of Citizen Kane *who went on to excel in motion pictures, Robert Wise, the film's editor, was perhaps the most successful.*

Wise directed several of the most distinctive films of the 1940s and 1950s— including The Curse of the Cat People, The Body Snatcher, The Set-Up, The Day the Earth Stood Still, *and* I Want to Live, *as well as three of Hollywood's biggest blockbusters:* West Side Story, The Sound of Music, *and* Star Trek—The Motion Picture.

Wise broke into the film business at RKO in 1933 as a nineteen-year-old film editing apprentice. By the summer of 1938, he was an editor at RKO. He was nominated for an Academy Award for his editing of Citizen Kane.

* * *

In August 1940, I had just finished editing *My Favorite Wife* when I got a call from my boss, Jimmy Wilkinson, head of the film editing department at RKO. "You know, this Orson Welles—he's making what he calls 'tests' for his new picture, *Citizen Kane*," Jimmy said. "The studio has finally realized that he's actually filming footage for the film itself, so they gave him the go-ahead to make the picture.

"Another editor has been working on the tests," he continued, "but now that the motion picture is actually in production, Welles would like somebody else. You're available, and you're about Welles' age, so why don't you go and talk with him about editing his film."

So I drove from the main RKO studio on Gower Street in Hollywood down to meet Orson at the RKO-Pathé studios in Culver City, where many of the scenes from *Citizen Kane* were being filmed. When I came on the set,

Orson was wearing makeup as the very old Kane—he had been shooting scenes of the picnic at the beach when he slaps Susan. We chatted, and we got along, so I was assigned to *Citizen Kane.*

As Orson shot, I edited the film along the way. We collaborated in much the same way that I worked with other directors at the time. Each day we would review the rushes together. Orson would then describe what he wanted to accomplish with a particular segment, and I would take notes and go back into the editing room to cut the scene. I worked with my assistant, Mark Robson, to assemble the footage, and then Orson would review what we had done; while he had a good idea of what he wanted from Mark and me, Orson never hung around the cutting room to watch us work or direct the editing.

However, I would go down to the set and watch *him.* While I was editing, I visited the set at least once or twice a day to see how the filming progressed. It was fascinating to watch Orson direct—he was simply marvelous at staging scenes and working with actors. Even though he was only twenty-five and working on his first Hollywood picture, he knew exactly what he wanted to achieve in his production. Through his expansive, generous direction, he made his wishes crystal clear to everyone.

What was it like to work on Orson Welles' set? Well, it all depended on what you walked in on. Working with him was never very long on an even keel—it was either up or down: marvelously exciting, stimulating, maddening, frustrating. Most of the time a Welles set was an electric, creative environment.

But I remember one day, while a set was being lit, that it wasn't such a happy atmosphere. About 11 A.M., Orson ordered a tray of food, including a whole chicken, and he sat there on the side of the set observing the work and eating his food while the lighting was changed (he had a right to be hungry —remember, he had probably been in the makeup chair at 4 A.M. that day getting ready for shooting).

Anyway, 1 P.M. came along, and then 2 P.M., and still no call for lunch. By now, the electricians were about ready to drop a lamp on him. Finally, one of his assistants had to tell him, "Hey, Orson, we really should take a break." And finally he called, "Lunch."

But that was Orson. He wasn't unfeeling—he was just caught up in the work. One moment he could be guilty of behavior that was so outrageous that you wanted to tell him to go to hell and walk off the picture, and before you could do it, he'd come up with some idea that was so brilliant that it would leave your mouth gaping open. So you never walked.

With Orson's energy always pouring forth, there was never a shortage of creative spirit on the *Citizen Kane* set. One of Orson's greatest talents was his ability to choose good people to work on his projects (you can put me in that group or exclude me as you like). On *Citizen Kane,* among the crew were famed cinematographer Gregg Toland, art director Perry Ferguson, outstanding composer Bernard Herrmann, and scores of the best artists and technicians that RKO could offer.

Because of Orson's direction, and the people he brought into the project, the filming of *Citizen Kane* was very well planned, organized, and shot from start to finish—I don't think one bit of the continuity was dropped during editing. Much of my editing involved merely taking the marvelous material and putting it in proper shape. But even though so many talented people were associated with *Citizen Kane*, Orson's personal imprint is so strongly stamped on every frame that it would be impossible to consider *Citizen Kane* anything but Welles' picture.

I have been asked many times if we realized along the way that Orson was making a classic film. At the time, we didn't know how important *Citizen Kane* would eventually become—although we could see from the rushes coming in day after day that Orson was indeed getting something very special. But I don't think any of us—including Orson—ever anticipated that we were working on a picture that, down the line, would be considered by many as the best motion picture ever made.

What did Orson expect of us? The term we used in those days was "make it play." Billy Hamilton, my mentor and the man who taught me film editing, said, "Bob, when you put a scene together, just make it play. It may or may not be how the director originally planned the scene, but if you find a way that's better, then just make it play."

That's all Orson wanted from all of us: to *make it play*.

Notes About the Text
and the Photographs

About the Text

This book is the product of research conducted by the author and his colleagues, and includes material drawn from personal interviews, studio files, business memoranda, financial records, factual information found in more than thirty books, and review of hundreds of pages of articles and news accounts that appeared in entertainment industry journals, general circulation newspapers, and magazines from 1938–41—all of this in addition to reams of notes gathered during countless viewings of *Citizen Kane*.

Those participants in *Citizen Kane*'s creation who added their thoughts to the creation of this book—in particular William Alland, Richard Wilson, and Robert Wise—provide a dimension that would have been impossible otherwise. Sadly, most of the cast and crew who contributed to producing the film are gone. However, expressing oneself in print has always had great appeal to Hollywood's creative talent, a penchant which provides readers with a seemingly endless supply of biographies and autobiographies that chronicle the lives of the many talented people who are no longer with us.

Legend blends easily with reality in movies. The passage of time and the frailty of the human ego tend to blur the distinction between fact and perception in the motion picture business, especially when recollections are recorded for posterity long after the fact. Too often, personal accounts are transformed into events as writers want to remember them, rather than a more precise accounting of events as they actually happened.

On occasion, these inaccuracies seep into other publications, where these "findings" are eventually accepted as fact. Therefore, no information assumed to be a "factual account" was included in this book without independent corroboration from at least one additional source beyond the original.

About the Photographs

To select the photographs included in this book, more than two thousand original images and frame stills were reviewed, drawn from the original studio files now housed at the Margaret Herrick Library at the Academy of Motion Picture Arts and Sciences in Los Angeles, the Lilly Library at Indiana University in Bloomington, and the Cinema–Television Library at the University of Southern California. This review narrowed the selection to five hundred photographs, from which the final choice for publication was made.

At the height of their power, Hollywood's major film studios shot hundreds of photographs during the production of its "A" features, including extraordinary off-screen candid shots and images that illustrate many aspects of the studio production process itself. Alexander Kahle, an RKO staff photographer, shot most of the production of *Citizen Kane,* and it is in large part his images that fill the following pages.

Only a few of Kahle's photographs were ever distributed for public use at the time of the film's release. Because of this, many of the photographs included here are being published in book form for the first time.

Citizen Kane: A Recollection

Deep within the confines of a private castle on a man-made mountain in Florida, newspaper publisher Charles Foster Kane lies dying. With his final breath, he whispers, "Rosebud." From his hand slips a glass snowglobe containing a tiny cabin, which shatters on the floor.

A newsreel company prepares a film obituary of Kane. But Rawlston, the owner of the company, is not happy with the newsreel; it captures the highlights of Kane's life, but not its meaning. The story needs an angle, so Rawlston dispatches Thompson, one of his reporters, to discover the meaning of Kane's last word. "It'll probably turn out to be a very simple thing," Rawlston says.

From the recollections of five people, Thompson learns about the key events in Kane's life. In the memoirs of Walter Thatcher, Kane's deceased banker, the reporter reads the story of Kane's youth, and how his mother became a millionaire overnight when a supposedly worthless gold mine given to Mrs. Kane by a defaulting boarder actually contains the "Colorado Lode." Kane's parents sign over custody of both the boy and the fortune to the management of Thatcher's bank.

Kane's wealth grows into the world's sixth-largest private fortune by the time Thatcher's guardianship ends on Kane's twenty-fifth birthday. But of all of his holdings, Kane is only interested in the *Inquirer,* a failing newspaper. Kane takes over as publisher and saves the newspaper, but not without resorting to yellow journalism.

From Bernstein, Kane's general manager, Thompson learns of the early days of Kane's career—and his success in building a publishing empire. Kane writes a "Declaration of Principles," which promises readers that his paper will provide the news honestly, without influence by special interests, and Kane will serve as "a fighting and tireless champion of their rights as citizens and human beings." As a result of his leadership—and scandal-filled stories—the *Inquirer* becomes the biggest newspaper in New York. From Bernstein, Thompson learns about Kane's passion for antiquities and his marriage to Emily Norton, niece of the President of the United States.

Thompson then meets Jed Leland, once Kane's best friend and drama critic for Kane papers, who tells of the deterioration of Kane's first marriage, the rise of the publisher to political power, and his meeting Susan Alexander, a sheet music clerk whom Kane befriends. Kane becomes the leading candidate for governor of New York, but only days before the election, "Boss" Jim Gettys, his corrupt opponent, threatens to expose Kane's "love nest" with Susan unless Kane withdraws. Kane refuses, and the resulting scandal ends both his marriage and his political ambitions. Two years later, his ex-wife and their son are killed in an automobile accident.

Kane marries Susan, and he engineers her career as an opera singer. But Susan, whose voice is average at best, is incapable of singing grand opera. Nevertheless, Kane pushes her forward. Her debut is a disaster; drama critic Leland drinks himself into a stupor rather than write a bad notice about her acting. Kane finishes the unfavorable review for Leland, just as he started it, fires him, and ends their professional association and friendship with a $25,000 severance check.

From Susan, who now runs a nightclub in Atlantic City, Thompson learns more about the horrors of her singing career. The morning after her debut, Susan begs to give up performing, but Kane refuses to let her. Leland returns the $25,000 check torn up in pieces; along with the check, Leland sends Kane's original handwritten text of the "Declaration of Principles," which he had kept, thinking it might one day be an important document. Kane calls the declaration "an antique," and tears it up.

Eventually, the pressure on Susan becomes too much; she attempts suicide, an act which finally convinces Kane to let her stop singing. Kane turns his attention to the construction of Xanadu, a private castle built on a man-made mountain along the Florida coast. But Susan is bored and unhappy at the estate. She longs for life in New York, but Kane refuses to leave their palace. At an overnight picnic, Kane and Susan argue. He strikes her, and the next day, she walks out on him.

Thompson then travels to Xanadu to interview Raymond, Kane's butler. Raymond tells him how, after Susan's departure, in a burst of fury, Kane destroys the contents of her bedroom—but stops his rampage when he discovers the snowglobe. Raymond hears Kane say one word—"Rosebud"—without any clue as to what he means.

Thompson's search ends; he cannot discover what "Rosebud" means. Thompson tells his colleagues—who have come to Xanadu to photograph Kane's relics—that Rosebud may have been "something he couldn't get or he lost. Rosebud is just a piece in a jigsaw puzzle" in Kane's life, Thompson says. "A missing piece."

The reporters depart, and the unwanted remnants of Kane's life are burned. A workman throws a battered sled from Kane's youth onto the flames; across the front of the childhood toy is written "Rosebud."

CITIZEN KANE

1. Before the Beginning

In the balmy July of 1939—the greatest year among many great years in Hollywood—the newspapers of America were crammed with news about the movies. Film fans across the nation scrambled for every scrap about the production of *Gone With the Wind,* which would eventually arrive in December. The premiere of *The Wizard of Oz* was only a few weeks away. In Europe, World War II would erupt with fury in little more than a month, and half of America escaped briefly from the woes of the world at least once a week in the soothing darkness of the movie theaters.

But the biggest single news story in the motion picture business that summer was not a film—it was a piece of paper. Midway through July, RKO Radio Pictures announced that Orson Welles, a young Broadway actor and radio star who had captured the attention of the nation with a single stunning broadcast, had signed the most extraordinary contract in Hollywood history. The world didn't know it then, but the first product of that amazing agreement between RKO and a twenty-five-year-old Hollywood novice—*Citizen Kane*—would soon be acclaimed as the best motion picture ever made.

Only a year earlier, it would have seemed an unlikely goal in Orson Welles' grand plan that he would one day produce, direct, cowrite, and star in the finest film of all time. Welles wanted to expand his creative talents on the stages of Broadway—not on the screens of motion picture theaters.

However, as it turned out, Welles' arrival in Hollywood was the next logical step in a meteoric performing career. Born in 1915 in Kenosha, Wisconsin, to Richard and Beatrice Welles, young Orson was labeled a wonder practically from the moment he could speak—a veritable legend in lore who has been described over the decades, with varying degrees of accuracy, as being able to read at two, adapt Shakespeare, and write plays of his own before he was ten. "The word 'genius' was whispered into my ear at an early age, the first thing I ever heard while I was still mewling in my crib," said Welles. "So it never occurred to me that I wasn't until middle age."

As a small boy, Welles received steady exposure to the arts and entertainers through his mother's involvement in music, the arts, and the friendships maintained by Dr. Maurice Bernstein, his erstwhile guardian, whose feelings for the boy bordered on those of a father. This informal education would instill in Welles a near—sixth sense for performing that was apparent early in his life. By the time Welles entered his teens, he had already developed the stage presence and charming personality of a man far beyond his years.

At sixteen, Welles traveled to Ireland to paint, but when his money ran out, he convinced the managers of the Gate Theatre in Dublin that he was actually a leading Broadway star. He performed roles in *Jew Süss, Hamlet, Death Takes a Holiday,* and several other productions before he moved on to continue his unorthodox teen years, involving himself in other adventures in Europe, Africa, and the United States.

Eventually Welles found his way to Broadway, where in 1934 he began to make good his Irish bluff, in three years advancing from a bold upstart to the most vibrant theatrical star of his day. Welles, at nineteen, stunned the theater world with his commanding presence and artistic leadership, and he appeared in a succession of top-flight plays before he branched out into direction.

Welles then formed a partnership with John Houseman, with Welles directing and Houseman in an administrative capacity—an alliance that was as creatively intense as it was emotionally explosive. In spite of their on-again, off-again personal battles, Welles and Houseman mounted some of New York's most vivid theatrical productions; for the Works Progress Administration's Federal Theatre (a New Deal—era project created to provide work for idle actors), they staged, among other innovative plays, a version of *Macbeth* with an all-black cast, in a stunning Haitian voodoo setting.

In 1937, Welles and Houseman took the bold step of forming their own repertory company and called it Mercury Theatre. It was an ambitious, dynamic enterprise, with plans to mount innovative productions of classical drama. Mercury Theatre even had its own "Declaration of Principles," a statement which vowed that the company would cater to patrons "on a voyage of discovery in the theater" who wanted to see "classical plays excitingly produced."

On a shoestring budget and often surviving from hand to mouth, Mercury Theatre produced several of the most imaginative stage productions Broadway had ever seen, before the frenetic pace and the lure of other less strenuous commitments dimmed its bright light. Mercury's first production in the fall of 1937—a modern-dress staging of *Julius Caesar*—was a visual as well as a theatrical triumph; the play was performed on a stark platformed stage which was painted bright red, while the actors wore business suits, or fascist-style military uniforms dyed dark green.

"The Mercury Theatre which John Houseman and Orson Welles have founded with *Julius Caesar* has taken the town by the ears," said Brooks Atkinson, drama critic for the *New York Times*. "Of all the young enterprises that are stirring here and there, this is the most dynamic and the most likely to have an enduring influence on the theater. It has pitched headlong into the thick of the theater without anything more imposing than a racy enthusiasm for the stage and no apparent ambition to make a fortune."

Soon after *Julius Caesar* came *The Shoemaker's Holiday* and *The Cradle Will Rock*—two more certified hits, which capped Mercury's success. Each Mercury production, as well as Welles' other projects, found him firmly at the helm, ever disorganized and demanding, yet immensely productive, often working as much as twenty hours per day, writing, acting, and directing—a creative whirlwind who set the standard on Broadway for brilliantly imaginative theatrical performances.

But it was Welles' work in radio that brought him to the attention of the world. Welles had performed in hundreds of radio programs since 1934, and he quickly became a broadcasting legend for both his marvelous natural voice and his uncanny ability to play dozens of character parts. Of his broadcasting roles, Welles is best remembered as Lamont Cranston, the mysterious crime fighter better known as The Shadow.

In addition to their theatrical escapades, in the summer of 1938 Welles and Houseman created "Mercury Theatre on the Air" and produced a series of entertaining but low-rated weekly radio broadcasts that aired opposite those titans of the airwaves, Edgar Bergen and Charlie McCarthy.

It was the broadcast that aired October 30, 1938—a seemingly routine adaptation of a science fiction story—that catapulted Welles into national attention. Low-rated though Mercury Theatre may have been—and in spite of the commercial breaks and announcements which stated that the program was merely a dramatic broadcast—the production of H. G. Wells' *The War of the Worlds* still convinced millions of people that Martians had landed in Grovers Mill, New Jersey, and that the United States was quickly being destroyed by the advancing hordes.

"Radio, in those days, wasn't just a noise in somebody's pocket—it was the voice of authority. Too much so—at least, I thought so." Welles said later. "I figured it was time to take the mickey out of some of that authority.

"In my middle-western childhood," Welles said of the days around Halloween, "that was the season for pranks—for soaping windows, putting Farmer Perkins' cow up in the belfry, or at least dressing up in a sheet and spooking the neighbors with a pumpkin head. Well, in that notorious broadcast, I said 'boo' to several million people over a full network, and the punkin' head was a flying saucer from Mars."

What started out as a seemingly routine broadcast quickly stimulated one of the great panics of the twentieth century. With the world's attention firmly fixed on the escalating tensions that would touch off World War II only ten months later, it is not difficult to understand why so many people were willing to believe that Armageddon had come. Millions of people across the country, after hearing the first thirty minutes of the broadcast, believed that the world had come to an end. Thousands abandoned their homes in panic, looking for safe harbor. Leaves were canceled aboard naval vessels. Motorcycle police in New Jersey near the site of the imaginary landing watched in disbelief as hundreds of cars roared past them at ninety miles per hour with no intention of stopping for a ticket.

Welles—who sought only to air a Halloween prank—was stunned by the actual panic the broadcast had caused. "The first inkling we had of all this in the studio itself while the broadcast was still on was when the control room started to fill up with policemen," Welles said. "The cops looked pretty bewildered—they didn't know how you could arrest a radio program—so we just carried on."

Welles was instantly catapulted into the spotlight; the attention of the entire country was focused on this mildly amused twenty-three-year-old, whose Halloween Eve prank had unintentionally given him national stardom. Welles continued to work in both theater and radio, but for the handsome young man with the perfectly modulated voice, it wasn't long until Hollywood beckoned.

The furor over the *War of the Worlds* broadcast had barely settled before rumors began about potential film deals for the young director. Within two months, the talk in Hollywood had Welles slated to appeared in at least two top-flight productions: *The Monster* at Paramount Pictures, and *Napoleon* at Warner Bros. (two projects which were never completed).

Most of the major studios in Hollywood sent out feelers to try to snare Welles. But to land him and lure him to Hollywood, it eventually took the offerings of RKO, one of the smaller of the film industry "majors" and one of the least financially stable. It was perhaps RKO's peculiar financial straits—and its willingness to grant creative freedoms that most motion picture studios would never consider—that made possible the kind of offer that Welles would find impossible to reject.

From its formation in 1928, RKO (which stands for Radio-Keith-Orpheum) had earned a reputation for marching slightly out of step with the rest of Hollywood. Born out of mergings engineered by the financial power-house combination of Joseph Kennedy and RCA Chairman David Sarnoff, RKO was not, in spite of its powerful backers, as productive or profitable as the other "majors" in Hollywood. The quality of RKO's pictures seemed to drift in the wind, depending on the talents of the executives who ran the company. Both the studio bosses and their policies changed frequently, as RKO's board tried to find a leader who would bring to the studio the ideal mix of business acumen and filmmaking ability.

Nevertheless, RKO did manage to produce some of Hollywood's brightest and most enduring hits, such as *The Informer, King Kong, Bringing Up Baby,* and the marvelous film partnership between Ginger Rogers and Fred Astaire in ten delightful and highly profitable musicals, including *Top Hat, Swing Time,* and *Follow the Fleet.*

While RKO did produce an assortment of lasting screen favorites, its batting average for success from year to year remained low. The frequent management changes at the studio produced pendulum swings between periods of high-quality productions and second-rate hokum. For every Fred Astaire–Ginger Rogers musical, there were too many clinkers to keep the studio operating on an even keel.

By 1938, RKO needed yet another new direction, and it turned to George Schaefer to serve as president of RKO Radio Pictures, and its holding company, Radio-Keith-Orpheum Corporation. Schaefer fought to emphasize high-quality pictures based on works of literature, innovative original scripts, and adapted Broadway productions.

While RKO didn't develop the fiscal stability, the prestige, or the creative output of its more formidable Hollywood competition, under Schaefer and others the company did gain something of a reputation as willing to take greater risks and permit its creative talent far more liberties than would other studios. Among the many notables working there in 1939 were Dorothy Arzner, one of Hollywood's few women directors, as well as Garson Kanin, another wonder-boy director from Broadway who, at twenty-seven, already had two hit films to his credit.

It was in this atmosphere at RKO that Schaefer began to court Welles in early 1939. The timing was fortuitous; RKO was looking for a big fish, and Welles was ready to be landed—if the terms were right. In Welles, Schaefer found not only a renegade who could bring new ideas to Hollywood, but also a creative entertainer with national status. In RKO, Welles could envision a willing employer who would give him the setting to let his creative ideas flourish.

As far as RKO and the other studios were concerned, Welles' drawing power represented far more than mere publicity value. Welles' thorough grounding in drama from his childhood remained a strong asset, but his natural physical gifts assured his place as an ideal candidate for Hollywood stardom. At six feet two with dark, transfixing eyes and a powerful voice as well suited to film as it was to radio, Welles radiated the physical presence of a movie idol long before he set foot in Hollywood.

Welles' imposing and potent personality both on and off the screen ensured his status as a leading man who could command film's most alluring parts. The vision of Welles, as Rochester in the 1944 production of *Jane Eyre,* striding boldly across the frozen moors, snow and wind roaring, his cape flying in the gale, provides one of the most vivid star images ever filmed.

The only threat to Welles' screen-idol potential was a gargantuan appetite —routine consumption was an entire chicken and all the trimmings for lunch, or a dinner of two steaks and a quart of ice cream—which kept him, even at an early age, constantly fighting to keep his weight in check.

While Welles certainly had promise as a film actor and director, no one expected his first contract in Hollywood to be anything but a journeyman's entree into the realm of motion pictures. So when in July 1939, Welles and RKO reached an agreement that featured the most astonishing terms ever granted to a studio director—let alone a novice in the business of filmmaking —the news struck Hollywood like a lightning bolt.

Welles' two-film contract spanned dozens of pages of legalese, but the significance of agreement could be boiled down to a single sentence: Welles could produce, direct, write, and star in his projects, or any combination of those roles he chose, and he alone would have virtually complete control of the final film. Welles could shoot what he liked, spend studio money any way he liked (up to $500,000 per picture), and with only minimal input from the studio, make the finished film just as he wanted it.

Considering the business climate in Hollywood at the time, it's little wonder that Welles' contract came as such a shock. In July 1939, the motion picture industry was midway through its best year ever—at least in terms of the quality of the films it produced. The power of the Hollywood studio system and the major film companies' overwhelming creative control over its products were indisputable—a grapple hold on the creative process that few, even the most potent stars and directors, dared challenge.

The studio chiefs maintained nearly complete control over a film's destiny, including its script, casting, production budgets, assignment of technical staff, and the editing of the footage into a final print. Never—at least not until Welles came along—did a mere mortal working within the confines of the studio system maintain such control of the final product.

RKO signed over this power to Welles' novice care. The studio's only substantive involvement in a Welles' project was approval of the story; the studio couldn't even intrude on the finances of the picture, unless the budget exceeded $500,000. (As amazing as it may seem now, in 1939 it was still

Welles preparing designs for Heart of Darkness. *The illustration behind him explains the first-person camera technique, which would have been used for much of Welles' point of view in the film.*

routine for top-flight motion pictures to be produced with budgets of under $500,000; and "B" pictures cost considerably less. For most of the Hollywood studios in the late 1930s, a $1 million production budget was a benchmark figure that studios reserved for projects of special merit. In fact, as Welles soon discovered, at RKO the $1 million figure sent studio executives fluttering in panic.)

To successfully perform the four principal jobs on a film project, then as now, was a nearly unknown phenomenon in Hollywood. Indeed, only the legendary Charlie Chaplin regularly accomplished so ambitious an agenda. But Chaplin, who as an independent producer had owned a motion picture studio a few blocks from RKO, was a filmmaking veteran by the time he took on writing, producing, directing, and starring in his own films. Welles was a rookie, a babe wandering in the jungles of the Hollywood studio system with only a few years of radio and theatrical productions to his credit. It didn't take long for the vultures to descend on him.

Word of the contract was blasted across Hollywood, and opinion was divided between those merely resentful of a brash young newcomer, and others with quite legitimate expressions of concern about giving such freedom to a novice when so many Hollywood veterans were far more restricted. "RKO is going to rue its contract," cried an editorial in the *Hollywood Spectator.* "I would be willing to bet something that Welles will not complete a picture." Said *Daily Variety* columnist George Phair, "A genius is a crackpot on a tightrope. Hollywood is watching Orson Welles, wondering if his foot will slip." W. P. Wilkerson, publisher of the *Hollywood Reporter,* put it more neatly: "RKO president George Schaefer is just plain nuts."

Resentment and distrust compounded when Welles arrived in Hollywood, sporting a beard that was left over from his aborted production of *Five Kings* (an ambitious compilation of five of Shakespeare's plays about British monarchs that Welles still hoped to produce after he completed a stint in Hollywood).

The beard served to alienate some (who considered it a blatant display of Welles' supposed self-absorption with his own "intellectual" stature) and amuse others—Errol Flynn sent Welles the perfect Christmas gift for a whiskered actor: a ham with a beard attached to it.

Clearly, Welles was the hottest subject in town; some in Hollywood loved him, others hated him, but everyone was talking about him. Never had a performer set Hollywood quite so askew.

But while Hollywood rumbled, Welles busily planned his first projects. He was already becoming a quotable Hollywood personality; on his first tour of RKO's studio facilities, he is reputed to have said, "This is the biggest electric train any boy ever had!"

The week Welles signed his RKO contract, the studio trumpeted the deal. "And *what* a picture planned for the first!" the studio's announcements read. In fact, nothing was "set" at all, but Welles was already hard at work developing his first project as arranged with RKO: a screen version of *Heart of Darkness*—Joseph Conrad's novel about an American who creates his own empire in the jungle of Africa.

Mercury Theatre had already performed *Heart of Darkness,* and Welles created an ambitious adaptation of Conrad's novel for the screen that would have relied on innovative camera techniques (including "first-person" camera, which would record the action from the actor's point of view), spectacular tropical sets, and a cast that would have included thousands of extras and a host of featured players, including Tallulah Bankhead.

As ambitious and gripping as *Heart of Darkness* appeared on paper, it was too much for RKO to handle. The estimated budget for the film was more than $1 million, an amount which, as expected, set off alarm bells within RKO—especially in the wake of a new round of studio cost-cutting measures and salary cuts for many employees. In December, Welles and Schaefer met to mull over the problem, and jointly they decided that *Heart of Darkness* would be postponed until Welles got a more traditional picture under his belt.

As an alternative, Welles proposed *The Smiler with a Knife,* an espionage thriller by Nicholas Blake, packed with secret agents and international intrigue—a picture which, at best, would have merely tided Welles over until he found more formidable material.

Welles quickly revamped the story, changed the setting from Europe to the United States, and asked the studio to assign Carole Lombard to star in the production. But Lombard, one of Hollywood's top leading ladies, declined the role. His next choice was Lucille Ball, at the time an RKO contract player with limited box office appeal. But Schaefer, unwilling to risk Welles' first project with a chancy actress in the lead, vetoed Ball for the role before he would grant story approval. Dita Parlo, a delicate Austrian actress who was the biggest star in France, was another Welles' choice for both projects, but the outbreak of World War II trapped Parlo overseas.

Eventually, both projects fell through; *Heart of Darkness* because of the budget problems and other technical issues; and *The Smiler with a Knife* because of difficulties casting a leading lady. (Forty years later, *Heart of Darkness* would eventually come to the screen—the setting shifted from Africa to Vietnam— under the title *Apocalypse Now,* created by a talented but tumultuous director of a newer generation, Francis Coppola.)

Under any other circumstances, the collapse of two film projects in a row would have been considered routine affairs along the often meandering path that leads to producing a picture in Hollywood. However, Welles' agreement with RKO and his presence in Hollywood were anything but routine. Welles may have enjoyed Hollywood's most permissive contract, but his powers of creative control were worthless unless he got a project off the ground. By the time *The Smiler with a Knife* was scrubbed, Welles had been struggling in the Hollywood mire for more than five months, and he didn't even have a script in hand, let alone a project ready to bring before the cameras. In December 1939, he was beginning to feel the heat.

Even before Welles' two projects were canceled, his strongest supporters began to wonder whether he would ever bring a film into production, and his detractors gloated over his failures. The *Hollywood Reporter*'s Wilkerson, one of the most vocal opponents of Welles' contract with RKO, thought it certain that Welles' number was up.

"They are laying bets over on the RKO lot that the Orson Welles deal will end up without Orson ever doing a picture there," Wilkerson said early in 1940. "The whole thing seems to be so mixed up no one can unravel it. You can get better odds that the original Welles announcement, *Heart of*

Darkness, won't ever be done, and can get 50–1 that neither Dita Parlo nor Lucille Ball will ever go into the second announced picture, *The Smiler with a Knife.* The impression is that the current Welles confab with Schaefer in New York may end the whole works.''

For Welles, time was running out; his contract left him with only a few months remaining to get a film under way. Finally, he turned to a project that emerged—not out of greatness, but desperation—during his conversations with Herman Mankiewicz, a screenwriter and one of Hollywood's most notorious personalities.

Mankiewicz, the older brother of producer-director Joseph L. Mankiewicz, was a former writer for *The New Yorker* and the *New York Times* who made the switch to Hollywood in 1926. He had established himself as a brilliant wit, a writer of extraordinary talent, a warm friend to many of the screen world's brightest artists—and one of the most miserable employees in all of filmdom. Mankiewicz produced dialogue of the highest caliber, but in the process, also alienated himself from every studio in Hollywood—some more than once—with his self-destructive and abrasive outbursts.

Mankiewicz's pendulum-swing behavior, Houseman said, "public and private, was a scandal. A neurotic drinker and compulsive gambler, he was also one of the most intelligent, informed, witty, humane and charming men I have ever known.''

Mankiewicz's unvarnished talent had earned him assignments on scripts ever since the closing days of Hollywood's silent era, including such films as *Dinner at Eight, The Pride of the Yankees,* and an assortment of uncredited collaborations with other writers. However, his unique ability to charm or anger as he chose kept him in somewhat limited demand; his drinking problem didn't help either.

But in late 1939 and early 1940, Mankiewicz was steadily employed; he worked for Mercury, writing radio scripts for the "Campbell Playhouse" radio program, a somewhat more subdued but quite comfortable successor of "Mercury Theatre on the Air," which was sponsored by Campbell's Soup. In spite of Mankiewicz's faults, Welles recognized the writer's abilities and trusted him to produce. "Nobody was more miserable, more bitter, and funnier than Mank—a perfect monument to self-destruction," Welles said. "But when the bitterness wasn't focused straight at you—he was the best company in the world.''

In February 1940, Mankiewicz had plenty of time on his hands to let his fertile imagination run wild. While driving in New Mexico in September with fellow writer Thomas Phipps on their way to New York, the car skidded on the wet pavement and rolled.

Phipps suffered a concussion in the accident, and Mankiewicz sustained a

Herman Mankiewicz. "Nobody was more miserable, more bitter, and funnier than Mank," said Welles. "A perfect monument to self-destruction."

triple fracture of his left leg, a hugely painful injury which for months kept him on his back most of the time.

Thus incapacitated, Mankiewicz was only too happy to work with Welles on a film project. The years have fogged the precise origins of the original idea for *Citizen Kane*. However, much later, Houseman recalled that Mankiewicz, during his convalescence, revived a long-simmering idea of creating a film biography in which a man's life would be brought to the screen after his death through the memories and opinions of the people who knew him best. Welles had ideas that meshed well with this concept and considered a newspaper publisher the best subject for the story.

"I'd been nursing an old notion—the idea of telling the same thing several times—and showing exactly the same thing from wholly different views," Welles said. "Mank liked it, so we started searching for the man it was going to be about. Some big American figure, but it couldn't be a politician, because you'd have to pinpoint him. Howard Hughes was the first idea. But we got pretty quickly to the press lords."

In their discussions, Welles and Mankiewicz merged their plans, and created the basic ideas for a film about the life of a world-shaking newspaper publisher, told from the perspectives of his friends and enemies. Welles certainly liked the basic story, and he had little choice but to produce the film; unless a firm project could be developed quickly, his career in Hollywood would be all but destroyed before it had a chance to begin, and the naysayers who had decried the RKO deal would do everything in their power to discredit and force the renegade from Hollywood forever.

So Welles assigned Mankiewicz to work on an original screenplay—not an adaptation as his first two projects would have been. Welles then traveled to New York, and, with a blend of charm and desperate pleading, persuaded Houseman to return to Los Angeles to manage Mankiewicz and his writing schedule.

It was hardly a pretty beginning for *Citizen Kane,* but it was a start nonetheless. On February 19, 1940, Mankiewicz began drawing $1,000 a week to write the script. He was to receive an additional $5,000 bonus on delivery of the completed work. Houseman joined Welles and Mankiewicz in Los Angeles a few weeks later.

It was in this pressure-filled arena—out of an uneasy alliance between a brash new director, a nervous studio, and an erratic genius—that *Citizen Kane* was born. It was, as Houseman called it, "an absurd venture." The birth of the idea may have seemed difficult, but all involved would soon discover that genesis of the script and the production of the film itself would be even tougher.

2. The Script

A MERCURY
PRODUCTION
by

Orson Welles

Within two weeks after Mankiewicz joined the RKO payroll, he and Houseman departed Hollywood for Victorville, about ninety miles from Los Angeles in the desert of San Bernardino County. Victorville, at the time a small agricultural and resort community, was well known in Hollywood—countless westerns had been shot in the nearby scrub country, which spread out for hundreds of miles across inland California. No less than John Ford had recently shot the climactic Indian chase for his 1939 masterpiece, *Stagecoach,* in the vicinity.

For six weeks, Mankiewicz wrote and rewrote. Mankiewicz produced most of the material by dictating to Rita Alexander, the secretary who accompanied the pair from Los Angeles. Houseman contributed some scenes, but his principal task was to review the completed pages and edit them as they went

Houseman and Mankiewicz settled at Campbell's Guest Ranch, an out-of-the-way resort perfectly suited for a marathon writing session. To Houseman, the location was ideal; Welles had agreed in advance that his writers could work undisturbed, but the distance would help shelter them from Welles' influence if he became overanxious to check their progress. The location would also help protect Mankiewicz from the big city and its temptations; even with his leg still bound firmly in a cast, slowing the writer's excesses was a difficult task; among Houseman's more important duties each day was inspecting Mankiewicz's room for hidden stashes of alcohol.

For six weeks, Mankiewicz wrote and rewrote. Mankiewicz produced most of the material by dictating to Rita Alexander, the secretary who accompanied the pair from Los Angeles. Houseman contributed some scenes, but his principal task was to review the completed pages and edit them as they went along. Welles, to no one's surprise, did indeed check in from time to time by phone, but for the most part, the director let Mankiewicz and Houseman work in relative peace.

As agreed, Welles came to visit in early April; he reviewed the nearly one hundred pages of script already written and listened to the writers' plans for the rest of the story. Apparently satisfied with the results, he told RKO that his first film, titled *American,* would be ready to go before the cameras in July. The first public announcement of the project came at RKO's annual meeting on May 27, where Welles himself discussed the project with the shareholders. At that time, and only briefly, the film was titled, *John Citizen, USA.*

Mankiewicz and Houseman sent the first complete draft to Welles in mid-April—a massive 266-page script containing enough material for at least two pictures. The script was numbered through page 325; between pages 212 and 271 was a 58-page gap left for material about Kane's developing relationship with his second wife, Susan Alexander.

Two weeks later, another 44 pages arrived. Mankiewicz and Houseman returned to Los Angeles during the second week in May, and Mankiewicz moved on to MGM for another assignment, temporarily leaving the script for Welles to edit and revise with his own material. Houseman left immediately for New York.

Mankiewicz's script for *American* told the mammoth story of the life and times of Charles Foster Kane, a newspaper publisher whose struggles to be loved and accepted led to his ruin. While the script included the basic story structure that eventually emerged in *Citizen Kane,* the plot also featured a host of twists and side trips—among them murder, corporate espionage, and assassination attempts on the President of the United States—which strayed far from the basic issues.

(Note: the original script and its plot, which follows here, varies greatly from the finished film. A worthwhile comparison, for those interested in such things, is a review of this synopsis, along with a viewing of the film on videotape.)

In *American,* readers are introduced to Kane in the same way as in the film itself. Mankiewicz's script begins with the panorama of the decaying Xanadu, the scene eventually closing in on Kane's bedroom and deathbed. As Kane dies, he whispers a single word, "Rosebud." Clutched in his hand is a snow-globe containing a rustic cabin scene; the snowglobe falls to the floor and shatters.

The action then jumps to a newsreel that covers Kane's life and death (in the original script, this segment is called *The March of Time,* just like the actual newsreels produced by Time-Life). The newsreel captures the highlights and defeats in Kane's life in tremendous detail—including far more information than, ultimately, the film could ever hope to include. "To forty-four million news buyers, more newsworthy than the names in his own headlines, more potent and more bitterly discussed than the world figures he helped to create, was Charles Foster Kane, greatest newspaper tycoon of this or any other generation," read the newsreel narrator.

Here are scenes of Xanadu, Kane's college highjinks, and expressions of the wide swings of opinion about the man: as many people called him "pacifist" as "warmonger," some considered him a patriot, others accused him of treason. The newsreel covers Kane successes—beating the competition with coverage of the armistice ending World War I, and Kane papers' muckraking, among others—and also describes the origins of the Kane fortune in a seemingly worthless gold mine left to a landlady, Kane's mother, by a defaulting boarder. Banker Walter Thatcher recalls to a congressional committee his first visit to meet the young Kane in Colorado, and he reads a statement that describes Kane as a Communist.

As the newsreel ends, the scene cuts to the projection room of the newsreel company, where the reporters explore the subject of Rosebud. Rawlston, the head of the newsreel company, assigns Thompson, one of his reporters, to find the meaning of Kane's last word.

Thompson first visits Susan Alexander in Atlantic City, but she is too drunk to talk with him. He moves to the Thatcher Library, where he reads portions of Walter Thatcher's memoirs, as the first flashback begins. Kane's parents hire Thatcher's bank to assume responsibility for the family fortune, and they sign over custody of their son, Charles, to the bank as well. In the original script, the terms of the agreement are explained in some detail: the elder Kane can see his son only with the specific permission of Mrs. Kane—if he disobeys even once, he forfeits his $50,000 a year allowance forever.

Young Charles, of course, is terrified to leave home. He not only hits Thatcher in the stomach with a sled, but also kicks him in the ankle. Thatcher takes "little Charles" aboard the train, where he cries himself to sleep while Thatcher watches, unable to cope with the boy's pain.

The scene then shifts to Rome in 1890, on Kane's twenty-fifth birthday. Thatcher and Jefferson Parker, the American ambassador to Italy, have come to Kane's Renaissance palace to pay a call on the young man who, within hours, would become one of the world's richest men.

Kane's drawing room is the very model of late nineteenth-century decadence; along with the melange of art treasures, Mankiewicz included among Kane's sophisticated trappings an assortment of pimps, homosexuals, nymphomaniacs, and, in Mankiewicz's words, "international society tramps." Kane makes his first appearance as an adult in *American* while talking to the Duchess della Cordoni, a woman under five feet tall who weighs three hundred pounds. "Amazing woman," Kane remarks. "Always says what she thinks."

Thatcher has arrived in Rome to officially release Kane's estate from trusteeship and present the young man with a detailed list of his holdings.

Kane is offhand about the transfer of power, until he notices that his properties include the *New York Inquirer,* a newspaper Thatcher is trying to sell (in Mankiewicz's draft, the name of the newspaper is spelled *Enquirer*). Kane holds firm and refuses to let Thatcher dispose of the paper, saying, "I think it might be fun to run a newspaper."

Thatcher's memoirs then skip ahead to two years later, when the banker, horrified at the scandalmongering published by the *Inquirer,* visits Kane at the newspaper. Here Thatcher meets Bernstein, Kane's business manager. It is Leland (in early scripts called Brad instead of Jed), who wires from Cuba saying that he can find no war. Kane, in Thatcher's presence, sends back the message, "Dear Brad: you provide the tropical colors. I'll provide the war." (Kane not only publishes rumor and scandal, he also beefs up his Sunday supplements with detective stories featuring a new character from England named Sherlock Holmes.)

Thatcher and Kane spar over the *Inquirer*'s coverage of traction fraud and price gouging ("traction" is the now-outdated term for streetcars). Kane points out that not only is he one of the largest individual stockholders in the Metropolitan Transfer and Street Railroad, but as publisher of the *Inquirer,* he is also the protector of the people's interests. When Thatcher reminds Kane that he is losing a million dollars a year on the *Inquirer,* Kane replies, "at the rate of a million dollars a year—we'll have to close this place—in sixty years."

Thatcher's memoirs then recall his last conversation with Kane—at least, Thatcher writes, "I pray the Lord it *will* be my last." Surrounded by anxious associates, including his son, Thatcher Jr., the elder Thatcher desperately tries to prevent Kane from publishing information which proves that leading investment houses, including Thatcher's, practice unsound business policies.

The story would severely damage the nation's financial enterprises, including Kane's own holdings. Kane, of course, refuses Thatcher's demands, and the banker is mystified. "He's hated me from the moment he set eyes on me," Thatcher tells his colleagues. "You'd think I'd taken things from him—instead of given him things."

Thompson finds nothing about Rosebud in Thatcher's memoirs, so he moves on to New York and a meeting with Bernstein, the aging chairman of the board of Kane's organization. Bernstein too recalls Kane's twenty-fifth birthday in Rome, along with some information that Thatcher didn't know: the *Inquirer* was the sole item on Thatcher's list of holdings that Kane wanted, and Bernstein—who gave up the family wholesale jewelry business to work for Kane—had been on Kane's payroll for six months, preparing for the transfer of power.

Kane's interest in the newspaper business is anything but casual; Kane burns to publish and already he is plotting. Bernstein has been buying new printing presses and is planning to print color comics as well. To cover his expenses, Kane has been duping Thatcher with false expense claims for lavish parties and purchases of masterpieces. "There's nothing easier than taking candy from a kid," Kane tells Bernstein, "unless it's holding on to the *Inquirer* without letting Mr. Thatcher know it's the one thing in the world I care about."

A year later, Leland and Kane arrive at the *Inquirer* for the first time (Bernstein follows close behind with Kane's belongings). Kane meets the staff—a stuffy, outdated bunch—including the editor, Herbert Carter. Kane announces that he will live right at the newspaper offices "as long as I have to."

A scene deleted from Citizen Kane. *Kane, Bernstein, and Leland visit the composing room to remake the pages of the* Inquirer. *When Smathers, the composing-room foreman, points out that the paper goes to press in five minutes, Kane scatters the type across the floor. "You can remake them now, can't you, Mr. Smathers?" Kane says.*

Immediately, Carter and Kane argue about the tone of the paper. "It's not the function of the *Inquirer* to report the gossip of housewives," Carter says. Kane disagrees—"That's the kind of thing we are going to be interested in from now on."

Kane makes sweeping changes on his first day at the *Inquirer*, but he wants something more. He writes a "Declaration of Principles" for his readers, a pledge "to provide the people of this city with a daily paper that will not only present all the news immediately and honestly," but also "a fighting and tireless champion of their rights as citizens and human beings."

The next morning, the new publisher reviews editions of all of New York's papers, ripping the *Inquirer* apart in the process. Carter can stand no more of the insults and threatens to resign—a threat Kane quickly accepts at face value—with "deepest regret."

Kane involves himself in every aspect of the *Inquirer*'s operations. He edits copy, photographs fires, and remakes the paper over and over again. All the while, circulation alternately dips and climbs, eventually growing from 26,000 to 62,000. F. W. Benton, the publisher of the rival *Chronicle*, begins to feel the heat, and offers Kane $500,000 for the *Inquirer*. Kane refuses, "I've never made a penny in my life—maybe I never will—but it's going to be nice to remember that there was someone once who was prepared to give me a profit."

Kane warns Benton that, within a year, the *Inquirer*'s circulation will exceed the *Chronicle*'s 430,000 readers. Benton is unimpressed and shows Kane a photograph of the *Chronicle*'s strongest asset: his editorial council, "the outstanding newspapermen of New York City."

Kane retaliates by hiring the entire council. He poses them for a photograph identical to the one that Benton had—except this one includes Kane beaming in the front row. "None of you has been hired because of his loyalty," Kane tells his new staff. "It's your talent I'm interested in."

The *Inquirer*'s attacks against the "Traction Trust" continue. Kane fights rough; his informants steal carbon copies of letters from the wastebaskets in the transit company offices—incriminating notes to city and state officials that are so inflammatory that Kane's threat to publish them is enough to force the transit company to lower trolley fares and stop pressuring *Inquirer* advertisers. "This new invention—this carbon paper—may prove to be a mixed blessing to the business world," Kane sighs.

By now Kane is thirty, and his doctor has persuaded him to take a long vacation in France. On his return, he has a surprise for his staff: he is engaged to Emily Monroe Norton, the niece of the President of the United States. Kane marries Emily at the White House, and they honeymoon in a tiny cabin in the Wisconsin wilderness—accompanied by an army of Kane's servants to take care of them (a yacht has been dismantled, then shipped to nearby Lake Winnepasca and reassembled for their use).

But the honeymoon is short-lived. When Kane sees a newspaper story about three prominent public figures injured in a train wreck, he suspects that the trio traveling together means that a giant oil swindle is at hand. "If I'm right," Kane tells Emily, "this is the greatest theft that's ever been attempted in America."

Kane wants to cancel the honeymoon, but Emily refuses; the next morning, however, after witnessing Kane's anguish in the night, Emily calls off the honeymoon herself, and they return to warn the President of the scandal.

The President doesn't believe that America is being cheated in a fraudulent oil deal and will do nothing, in spite of Kane's protests. So Kane continues the battle in print for months. As a result of the furor he creates, the Kanes become outcasts from New York society; in the midst of the fray, their son, Howard, is born.

Emily and Kane grow apart; Leland attempts to talk with Kane about Emily with no success, and their relationship grows strained as well. "You can say what you think—and you can fight the whole thing tooth and nail," Leland tells Kane, about the print assault on the oil swindle. "There's no reason why this savage personal note . . ." Leland says, pointing to yet another headline and a vicious cartoon which bitterly attacks the President.

The verbal attacks peak just before the President is severely wounded in an assassination attempt; in the gunman's pocket is a Kane editorial blasting the President's policies.

The President recovers, but the attack deals a severe blow to the Kane empire. Advertisers cancel, vendors refuse to sell his papers, and Kane is forced to resign from exclusive clubs. The incident is nearly too much for Emily, who stays married to Kane only to ease gossip and to preserve his political aspirations. Leland again tries to intercede on Emily's behalf, with no success.

A year passes before Kane's enterprises begin to revive. At the same time, Kane's political stature grows. He becomes an independent candidate for governor of New York to fight the corrupt administration backed by political boss Edward P. Rogers. At the start of the campaign, Kane is the hopeless underdog; but soon his bandwagon begins to roll, and he has a shot at victory. But the election is literally stolen from him, when the Rogers Machine destroys thousands of legitimate ballots to give the election to the stooge candidate. Emily divorces Kane—the election loss and her knowledge of Kane's relationship with singer Susan Alexander are too much (at this point in Mankiewicz's first draft, little is known about Susan).

Emily, Bernstein points out, is no Rosebud. Thompson agrees; he has already tried to contact Kane's first wife (unlike in the final script, she is still alive at this point in *American*), and he shares with Bernstein her lawyer's response to his request. "She regards their brief marriage [ten years] as a distasteful episode in her life, which she prefers to forget."

Since Bernstein can provide no help in the search for Rosebud, the reporter moves on to interview Leland, wheelchair-bound and confined to a convalescent hospital. Leland recalls his early days in New York with Kane— the late dinners, the women, the nights on Broadway. Leland works as the *Inquirer*'s drama critic, but against his better judgment, he goes to Cuba at Kane's request to cover the war that is brewing. "It'll be our first foreign war in fifty years," Kane tells Leland. "We'll cover it the way the *Hicksville Gazette* covers the church social."

Leland finds no war, but Kane creates one. Kane papers carry headlines and stories under Leland's byline about Spanish atrocities in Cuba—none of which actually occurred. Leland returns to New York, outraged and threatening to resign; Kane makes up excuses for the fabricated stories and charms Leland into remaining on the *Inquirer*. Leland returns to drama criticism, but the warmongering continues. "One of these days," Leland says to Kane, "you're going to find out that all this charm of yours won't be enough."

Leland's uneasy relationship with Kane goes on, and they resume attending plays together. While at a play, they bump into Kane's father—now a toupeed dandy—who is visiting New York accompanied by Miss La Salle, a much younger woman (Kane's mother apparently died some time earlier). It is obvious that Kane and his father haven't seen each other in years, and it is equally apparent that the do-nothing elder Kane has no burning desire to see his son. "I've been meaning to drop in and see you," Kane senior tells his son, "but one thing and another . . ."

The group gets together later at Leland's apartment, where father tells son that he's actually married to Miss La Salle. Kane reacts violently at the news and tries to strangle his father before throwing him out of the apartment.

Leland transfers to Chicago when he refuses to cooperate with a new promotion scheme for New York theatrical producers. When Susan Alexander debuts as an opera singer with disastrous results, Leland drinks himself into a stupor, unable to complete his review. Kane delays the review one day—an unheard-of event—and fires Leland, paying him $25,000 severance.

At this point in the first draft of American *comes the fifty-eight-page gap, which would later include material about the first meeting of Susan and Kane and her failed operatic career. The story picks up again during Thompson's second interview with Susan, this time sober, as she describes her life with Kane at Xanadu, the couple's gigantic Florida estate.*

Among the guests in residence for a Wild West party at Xanadu is Jerry Martin, a man much younger than Kane. Jerry and Susan have an affair, a scene partially witnessed by Kane and Raymond, the butler. Kane orders Raymond to kill Jerry—"I thought I saw a rat—a rat that ought to be killed," Kane says after spotting Jerry and Susan in a clinch. Jerry turns up dead the next morning; presumably Raymond does the deed by arranging for the victim to be "accidentally" pitched from his horse. Although Susan doesn't know for certain that Kane arranged the "accident," she does suspect that something was amiss in Martin's death.

Susan and Kane travel around the world by yacht, a trip that lasts a year. "You always said," Kane reminds his wife, "that you wanted to go around the world." Susan is bored on the voyage and continually works on her jigsaw puzzles, both on the yacht and as the scene shifts back to Xanadu. Kane insists on a picnic and camping trip to the Everglades for all of their guests. During the picnic, Kane and Susan fight, and he slaps her. "You'll never have another chance to hit me again," she vows.

The next day, Susan leaves him. When Kane begs her to stay, she begins to weaken, until he tells her, "You can't do this to me." Susan's will returns. "I can't do this to you? Oh yes I can," she says as she walks out.

Susan can't enlighten Thompson about Rosebud, but she suggests that the reporter talk to Raymond, still in command at Xanadu. Raymond recalls the end of the relationship between Susan and Kane, including a statement that the publisher wrote for all of his papers, which announced that the couple had separated "under the terms of a peaceful and friendly agreement." The butler relates how Kane goes to Susan's room before the staff strips it of all her belongings. There he finds the glass snowglobe of a rustic winter scene, which he takes and walks out of the room for the last time.

Now in the depths of the Depression, Kane's fortunes skid downward. The financial disaster that struck the nation—combined with the money drain from Kane's organization caused by the construction of Xanadu—have stripped away his resources, and he goes to Thatcher Jr. for a loan (Thatcher Sr. is presumably dead by this time). Thatcher Jr. agrees to the loan, on the condition that complete financial management of the Kane empire is turned over to his bank.

Even though Kane retains full editorial control of his newspapers, he doesn't agree to the conditions without a fight. "You'll be somewhat disappointed, Mr. Thatcher, I'm afraid, in how little your business control will affect the editorial policies of my papers," he says. Thatcher Jr. replies, "I'll be neither disappointed nor surprised, Mr. Kane. My father told me long ago that there was no connection between your own interests and your own behavior."

But Kane receives one final blow in the script's closing pages. Back at Xanadu, he learns that his son, Howard, has been killed while attempting to take over the Third Regiment Armory in Washington. Kane's staff tries to downplay the story, but Kane writes the coverage himself. "Deprived of the father's guidance to which he was entitled, neglected by everything except the power of money, Howard Kane, only son of Charles Foster Kane, publisher, last night met with a deplorable end," Kane dictates. At the funeral, Kane and Emily sit side by side without speaking a word to each other.

Then, following a few brief scenes which illustrate Kane's declining health, he dies as well.

Raymond has no notions about Rosebud, but he helps Thompson and his staff as they photograph Xanadu and its many treasures. They rummage through the legacy of Kane's life—the art as well as the junk. When Thompson's colleagues ask him about Rosebud, he tells them that he hasn't found the answers, but he has formed a lot of opinions about Charles Foster Kane.

Kane, Thompson tells his friends, "was the most honest man that ever lived, with a streak of crookedness a yard wide. He was liberal and tolerant. Live and let live, that was his motto. But he had no use for anybody that disagreed with him on any point, no matter how small it was. He was a loving husband and a good father—and both his wives left him and his son got himself killed about as shabby as you can get it. He had a gift for friendship such as few men have—and he broke his oldest friend's heart like you'd throw away a cigarette you were through with."

The reporters pack to leave; when one of them picks up his coat, he does not see that he has uncovered some objects from Kane's youth, including an old sled. After the reporters leave, Raymond's workmen begin to burn the unwanted mementos of Kane's life. Among the items tossed into the incinerator is the sled—across the front of it, the word "Rosebud" can be read plainly through the flames.

The script ends with an exterior shot of Xanadu, the incinerator's smoke billowing from a chimney, while the camera pauses for a moment on the "K" emblazoned over the main gate of the estate as the scene fades out.

* * *

Once Mankiewicz submitted his draft of *American*, Welles began the painstaking process of revising and adding to the script. At times, he worked with Mankiewicz on new material and inserts, but at this stage, Welles also deleted entire sections, added substantial material that he had written himself, and reshaped the plot. At a point early in the editing, the film was dubbed with a new title: *Citizen Kane*. Other than at the RKO shareholders' meeting, the project was never again referred to as *John Citizen, USA*.

A multitude of revised drafts of the *Citizen Kane* script were produced (a

count ranging from four to ten, depending on how a "draft" is defined), each one shorter and tighter than the version preceding it. Although Welles had nearly two months to tinker with the script before his production went before the cameras, some of the scenes were written virtually at the last second. When in 1929, Thatcher's bank takes over custody of Kane's bankrupt empire, the version of the scene ultimately used in the film was written by Welles only hours before it was filmed. "Orson wasn't happy with how the scene was playing," said Robert Wise, who as editor of the film visited the set often. "He sent every-

The cast rehearses the brothel scene. The Hays Office ordered the scene cut from the original script, but Welles went ahead and rehearsed anyway, hoping for a reprieve that never came.

one home, and he rewrote the scene overnight. He came back and shot it the next day."

The result was a scene that provided some of the film's most revealing information about Kane's character.

"You know, Charles, you never made a single investment," Thatcher tells Kane as the publisher prepares to sign over control of his companies. "You always used money to—"

"To buy things," Kane says sadly, as he signs the documents, and mutters again, "to buy things. My mother should have chosen a less reliable banker. Well, I always gagged on that silver spoon."

"You know, Mr. Bernstein," Kane says in the scene's closing moments, while acknowledging Thatcher's presence with a nasty look, "if I hadn't been rich, I might have been a really great man."

"Don't you think you are?" Thatcher asks.

Kane replies, "I think I did pretty well under the circumstances."

"What would you like to have been?" Thatcher says.

"Everything you hate," Kane answers, as the scene closes.

However, some of Welles' own scenes didn't survive the final cut. Mankiewicz's original script for *American* included a victory party for the former *Chronicle* staff hired by the *Inquirer*. Mankiewicz envisioned the scene in the *Inquirer* city room; Welles shifted the action to a brothel.

Welles' change to a brothel setting was axed without hesitation by the Hays Office; under no circumstances would the film industry's own Production Code allow a brothel in a motion picture (unless burning it down or some similar "redeeming act" was part of the plot). Yet in spite of the Hays Office edict, Welles was so anxious to include the scene, even though he knew that a brothel was out of the question, that he refused to delete the scene from the script and actually rehearsed on a brothel set.

It was only after a second warning from the Hays Office that Welles finally gave up and moved the setting back to the *Inquirer* newsroom, just as Mankiewicz originally wrote it. But in the days of the Production Code's iron rule, even this relatively staid scene had to be managed carefully: "It will be necessary that you hold to an *absolute minimum* all scenes of drinking and drunkenness," sniffed Joseph Breen, administrator of the Production Code, in his letter granting tentative approval of the final script. "Have in mind that such scenes are acceptable only when they are necessary 'for characterization or proper plot motivation.' "

Welles eventually added his own visual "jab" at the Hays Office, which *did* appear in the final film: when Leland and Bernstein are sorting through statues in Kane's office, the arm of one of the marble antiquities grabs Bernstein in the crotch. The Hays Office staff never noticed.

RKO forced its own changes on the script as well, but the studio's

MOTION PICTURE PRODUCERS & DISTRIBUTORS OF AMERICA, INC.

HOLLYWOOD OFFICE
5504 Hollywood Boulevard
HOLLYWOOD, CALIFORNIA
GLadstone 6111

WILL H. HAYS
PRESIDENT
CARL E. MILLIKEN
SECRETARY

JOSEPH I. BREEN, DIRECTOR
PRODUCTION CODE ADMINISTRATION

July 18, 1940

Mr. J. J. Nolan,
RKO Radio Pictures Inc.,
Hollywood, Calif.,

Dear Mr. Nolan:

We have read the third revised final script dated July 16, 1940, for your production titled CITIZEN KANE.

It would appear, from a reading of this script, that you had not yet received our letter of July 15th, at the time this third revised script was prepared. Because of this, we are handing you herewith a copy of our July 15th letter, in which we set forth the objectionable details which were noted in the second revised script, and which appear to be unchanged in the document at hand.

Very truly yours,

Joseph I. Breen

July 15, 1940

Mr. Joseph J. Nolan,
RKO Radio Pictures Inc.,
780 N. Gower,
Hollywood, Calif.,

Dear Mr. Nolan:

We have read the second revised final script, dated July 9th, 1940, for your proposed production titled CITIZEN KANE, and we are pleased to advise you that the material, except as noted hereinafter, is acceptable under the provisions of the Production Code and suggests no serious danger from the standpoint of political censorship.

There is one important detail in the story at hand, which is quite definitely in violation of the Production Code, and consequently, cannot be approved. This is the locale, set down for scene 64, which is, inescapably, a brothel. Please have in mind that there is a specific regulation in the Production Code, which prohibits the exhibition of brothels.

In all the circumstances, we suggest that the locale in this scene be changed and that there be nothing about the playing of the scene which would suggest that the place is a brothel.

Going through the script, page by page, we respectfully direct your attention to the following details:

Scenes 17, et seq: Here, and elsewhere, it will be necessary that you hold to an absolute minimum all scenes of drinking and drunkenness, wherever these occur. Have in mind that such scenes are acceptable only when they are necessary "for characterization or proper plot motivation."

Mr. Nolan - page 2   July 15, 1940

Page 83: There should be nothing about this scene which indicates that Georgie is a "madam", or that the girls brought into the party are prostitutes. This flavor should be very carefully guarded against.

Page 119: Please eliminate the word "Lord" from Kane's speech, "...the Lord only knows..."

Page 152: The action of the Assistant "patting the statue on the fanny", should be eliminated.

You understand, of course, that our final judgment will be based upon our review of the finished picture.

Cordially yours,

Joseph I. Breen

considerations were focused on issues of finance, not 1940s morals. Budget projections based on early versions of the script indicated that production costs would tip over the $1 million figure. A budget that exceeded the notorious $1 million mark was still out of the question; phenomenon or not, Welles could not be granted such a lavish budget, especially for so risky a venture as an original drama about a subject unproven with the public.

RKO was certainly willing to spend the money when the studio chiefs felt the project warranted it. Other recent RKO productions with $1 million-plus budgets included *Gunga Din* starring Cary Grant plus a cast of thousands, and *The Hunchback of Notre Dame* with Charles Laughton in the title role—both sweeping sagas based on well-known stories that featured stars who were top-ranked box office attractions. But *Citizen Kane* was no *Gunga Din;* if RKO refused to spend more than $1 million on *Heart of Darkness,* it certainly wouldn't commit that much money to *Citizen Kane.*

However, after his experience with *Heart of Darkness,* it is conceivable that Welles deliberately submitted a padded budget for approval, knowing that RKO would want to trim expenses no matter how the original estimates were figured. Nevertheless, resolving the budget issue and identifying ways to trim expenses dragged on for weeks. Sequences were removed to avoid construction of several of the most expensive sets and other cost-cutting measures were accomplished as well. Eventually, RKO and Welles worked out budget reductions that totaled more than $300,000. To the relief of everyone on the Mercury staff, the cuts had little impact on the final product.

By June 18, a final shooting script was ready. This "final" version progressed through several additional revisions, the latest one dated July 16, or more than two weeks after Welles began shooting.

But RKO continued to stall the start date, still nervous about their young renegade director and his spending habits. As the studio later found out, Welles was quite willing to deceive the RKO bosses to bring his film before the cameras.

* * *

Citizen Kane had not yet been released before the debate began to rage over who—Mankiewicz or Welles—was responsible for the script. Mankiewicz felt slighted when Welles added his own name to the screenplay credits, and his resentment cut deeper when Mankiewicz shared the Oscar for Best Original Screenplay—the film's only Academy Award—with the director.

The debate over script credit has grown over the decades, alongside *Citizen Kane*'s rise to the status of film legend. Motion picture fans and scholars alike have written and speculated about the script's true origins, frequently with the fervor of scholars haggling over the most profound scientific mysteries.

The controversy was fueled for decades by conflicting stories from both Houseman (who gives total responsibility for the creation of *Citizen Kane*'s script to Mankiewicz, but credits Welles with the visual presentation of the picture) and Welles (who acknowledges "Manky" for writing the original draft of the screenplay, but also takes credit for writing several key scenes). The continuing debate reveals Welles and Houseman—two powerful, deeply self-absorbed personalities—as incapable, even years or decades later, of objectively viewing how the script developed (Mankiewicz, who died in 1953, played no role in this drama, once his own place in the screen credits was established).

Looking back at Hollywood during the golden age of the studio era, it seems strange that *Citizen Kane*'s authorship ever became a public issue at all. With the motion picture industry near its peak of productivity, screen credit wasn't always granted to the writer most responsible for the script. Several writers could be rotated through film projects as routinely as auto workers on an assembly line; one writer added dialogue here, another filled in action there—yet the on-screen credit was often strictly limited. On *The Wizard of Oz,* for example, no less than thirteen writers, including Mankiewicz, worked on the project over the course of a year, yet the final credit went to only three writers.

The flap over the creation of *Citizen Kane* will no doubt continue as long as critics, fans, and academics study film; settling on an answer that satisfies all movie buffs seems an unlikely proposition. However, of far greater relevance is reaffirming the importance of the efforts that both men contributed to the creation of Hollywood's greatest motion picture.

Clearly, Mankiewicz wrote *American* with Houseman's input; this formed the basic structure of the film. The interviews and flashbacks, the opening newsreel, the hunt for Rosebud, and the "Declaration of Principles" all originated with Mankiewicz and Houseman in Victorville. What *Citizen Kane* would ultimately achieve began with Mankiewicz, who created the foundation for a film unlike any other ever written.

Just as clearly, Welles edited the original draft, added extensive material of his own, and polished the script to a fine sheen. It was Welles' contributions to the script—which gained as much from his deletions as his additions—that transformed *Citizen Kane* into a work of extraordinary personal vision.

When Welles edited *American* and the drafts of the script that followed, he achieved far more than merely crafting new scenes or cutting old ones. From the first, Welles shaped the script to fit his mold for *Citizen Kane,* stripping away unnecessary dialogue and scenes until only the leanest portrait of a man and his motivations remained. To Welles, anything more than that —including much of the material in *American*—was superfluous.

To one degree or another, of course, all directors attempt to structure a script to suit their own personal style. But Welles' contributions to the script transformed the story of Charles Foster Kane from a literal depiction of a man's

Leland's drunken confrontation with Kane. "You just want to persuade people that you love them so much that they ought to love you back," Leland tells Kane. "Only you want love on your own terms—something to be played your own way, according to your own rules."

actions to a terse visual portrait of his thoughts and motivations. While Mankiewicz's original characters told us much, Welles let most go unsaid, instead building the personalities so strongly with heavily edited dialogue and visual statements that their actions speak for themselves. Where Mankiewicz used paragraphs of dialogue, Welles used a line—or sometimes only a look.

For instance, when Susan Alexander and Kane meet, she explains that her mother wanted her to be an opera singer. "My voice isn't that kind," Susan says. "It's just—well, you know what mothers are like." Kane's agonized pause, followed by a barely whispered "yes," tell more about Kane's pain than pages of dialogue ever could.

Perhaps the best illustration of how Welles molded the material appears in the scenes that—in both the original script and the film—reveal more about Kane's actions than any other: Leland's angry confrontations with Kane. In the original script, Leland tells Kane off for his selfish motivations in two separate scenes: the first in the midst of the oil scandal, when Kane's relationship with Emily is collapsing, and later, after the President is wounded. Kane then responds with line after line, justifying his actions.

In the final script, Welles trimmed Leland's comments to their essence, relying entirely on Mankiewicz's original—but by now heavily edited—dialogue. In a few brief lines, after Kane loses the election because of his relationship with Susan, a drunk Leland sums up Kane's motivations for all his actions. "You talk about the people as if you own them, as though they belong to you," Leland tells him in the newsroom of the *Inquirer*. "As long as I can remember, you've talked about giving the people their rights as if you could make them a present of liberty.

"You don't care about anything except you," Leland continues through his drunken stupor. "You just want to persuade people that you love them so much that they ought to love you back. Only you want love on your own terms—something to be played your own way, according to your own rules."

Kane doesn't respond directly to Leland's outburst. Instead of the pages of dialogue that Mankiewicz originally wrote, Welles forces Kane to listen to Leland's tirade without rebuttal. Then Kane picks up a bottle of whiskey and pours a drink for himself. "A toast, Jedediah, to love on my terms," he tells Leland. "Those are the only terms anyone ever knows—his own." Those few words, combined with Welles' tense direction, brings far more power and emotion to the screen than a wealth of dialogue might ever achieve.

Welles left much unsaid, but he also demonstrated how unnecessary it was to say more. In *American*, for example, when Thatcher takes little Charles away from his parents, Mankiewicz includes a scene that shows the boy crying on the train while Thatcher looks on, unable to comfort him during the greatest anguish he would ever suffer. In the film, the scene was deleted; instead, to punctuate the pain of young Kane's departure from his beloved

Colorado home, Welles shows Rosebud lying in the falling snow, while the hollow wail of a train whistle sounds in the distance.

Curiously, although Welles took great pains to trim dialogue to its essence, his favorite scene in *Citizen Kane*—part of Thompson's interview with Bernstein—was not only drawn nearly word for word from Mankiewicz's original draft of *American,* but appears in one of the longest unbroken shots of a single person in the film.

Bernstein tells Thompson why Rosebud could have been a woman from Kane's past, as he remembers a girl with a white parasol from his own youth. "I only saw her for one second," Bernstein tells Thompson. "She didn't see me at all, but I'll bet a month hasn't gone by since, that I haven't thought of that girl." Welles' favorite scene of the film, it was purely a product of Mankiewicz' writing talent. If given a day off from hell, Welles claimed, he'd view this scene over any other from his many films. "All the rest could have been better," he said, "but that was just right."

In the scene, Bernstein tells Thompson why "Rosebud" might have been a woman from Kane's past. "One day back in 1896," Bernstein recalls, "I was crossing over to Jersey on the ferry, and as we pulled out, there was another ferry pulling in, and on it there was a girl waiting to get off. A white dress, she had on. She was carrying a white parasol.

"I only saw her for one second. She didn't see me at all, but I'll bet a month hasn't gone by since that I haven't thought of that girl."

To Welles, Bernstein's soliloquy as written by Mankiewicz was perfection. "If I were in hell and they gave me a day off, and said what part of any movie you ever made do you want to see, I'd say that scene of Mank's about Bernstein," Welles said. "All the rest could have been better, but that was just right."

At the time *Citizen Kane* debuted, it was the material left unsaid—the pared-down dialogue, and the lack of solidly expressed actions—that provided fodder for criticism of the film. Some critics reacted negatively to precisely the tone Welles had sought to achieve. Bosley Crowther, film critic of the *New York Times*, after writing glowing praise for the picture in his initial review, modified his enthusiasm somewhat in a second write-up two days later, in which he cited the "basically vague" theme as the primary reason for his somewhat lessened regard (for both reviews, see Compendium).

For critics accustomed to the traditional straightforward product of the Hollywood studios in their golden era, Welles' less-than-direct approach to storytelling may have seemed quite jarring. However, Welles only showed that the reasons a man does what he does are often not nearly as important as are the consequences of his actions. And, a film need not answer every question or solve all problems; sometimes, as Welles tells his viewers, merely bringing the conflict to the surface is effective enough. Welles' screenwriting techniques and the film that resulted from them may have jolted the Hollywood norm, but history—and the widespread acceptance of his innovations—ultimately proved that Welles was right.

3. RKO Production #281

CITIZEN KANE

Q: *During the shooting of* Citizen Kane, *did you have the sensation of making such an important film?*

A: *I never doubted it for a single instant.*

—Interview with Orson Welles, 1966

With the failures of *Heart of Darkness* and *Smiler with a Knife* well behind him, throughout the spring of 1940 Welles began preparing *Citizen Kane* for the cameras. While work on the script went forward, preproduction work on the motion picture designated RKO Production #281 proceeded at breakneck pace.

Meanwhile, Welles was learning the ways of backstage Hollywood. Contrary to what some thought (and still think), Welles didn't merely walk onto a soundstage and begin shooting without forethought or training. He had already dabbled in film production to produce footage for some of his theatrical productions, and as anyone who saw his productions of *Macbeth* and *Julius Caesar* could attest, his sense for the visual reached far beyond the traditional bounds of the legitimate stage.

True, Welles had never produced a Hollywood film before, but from the moment he arrived at RKO, he began his practical training in earnest. Welles was a regular in the studio screening rooms and viewed all the footage he could obtain. He and his Mercury associates nosed into every corner of the RKO lot, learning the methods of lighting, sound, photography, and the rest of the mystical off-camera machinery which powered the Hollywood studio system.

The script evolved as Welles continued to massage the material. But now he was also a film producer, and in April of 1940 he began a film producer's work: conjuring the incredibly complex blend of artistic expertise and technical wizardry necessary to bring a film script before the cameras.

Whatever liabilities Welles may have possessed as a creative renegade were now overshadowed by his greatest strength: his gift for collaboration. Welles may have had no experience in a Hollywood studio—a boy's biggest

Welles instructs his extras for the scene of the party with the Inquirer *staff, while William Alland positions the cast. Agnes Moorehead, who played Kane's mother, said of Welles, "There was no one quite like him to create excitement."*

electric train—but while he didn't know how to run the locomotive, he certainly knew how to find the right people to lay the track. And once he found them, Welles established a creative bond that produced near-magical results.

RKO, like the other Hollywood studios, housed a corps of craftsmen and technicians that was the hallmark of the Hollywood studio system at its most productive, when a studio operating at its peak could routinely release a fresh feature film every ten days. The studio backed its new young director with the finest talent available; when Welles couldn't find what he wanted on the RKO lot, he looked to other studios to find precisely the right person for a job.

"Orson had no doubt that he knew it all," said assistant producer William Alland. "Yet he was smart enough to appreciate the talent he spotted in others."

The result in *Citizen Kane* was a collaboration unlike anything ever witnessed by Hollywood before, and one it would never see again: here was an intensely creative first-time director bursting with visual ideas, commanding the finest elements of the Hollywood studio system who brought his vision to the screen. Later in his career, during his temporary "exile" in Europe, Welles longed to return to the United States, primarily because he missed that technical partnership. "I am dying to work there because of the technicians, who are marvelous," Welles lamented about Hollywood. "They truly represent a director's dream."

While Welles was a film novice, he was certainly no beginner at casting. Blessed with a keen ability for finding the ideal performer for every role, he had no trouble filling most of the principal parts in *Citizen Kane* by drawing on the treasure trove of talent in his stock company of players from the Mercury Theatre productions and his other projects in New York.

Everett Sloane

For the role of Jed Leland, Kane's best friend, Welles chose Joseph Cotten, a longtime colleague from Mercury Theatre, who had recently completed a triumphant Broadway run costarring with Katharine Hepburn in *The Philadelphia Story*. As Bernstein, Kane's business manager (he has no first name in the film), Welles cast Everett Sloane, who began his acting career in Mercury radio projects. Sloane was better known for his broadcast work in more traditional productions, including a long-running family radio program called "The Goldbergs."

Welles selected Ruth Warrick, a former model and radio singer, to play Emily Norton, Kane's first wife and niece to the President. As Kane's second wife, Welles chose from the Hollywood corps, casting Dorothy Comingore—originally a find of Charlie Chaplin's—in her first major role as Susan Alexander.

Ray Collins, another longtime radio veteran, was signed for the brief but pivotal part of Jim Gettys, the corrupt New York governor who destroyed Kane's political ambitions. Agnes Moorehead, another veteran of Mercury broadcasts as well as other top-flight radio productions of the day, took another short but equally significant part as Kane's mother. George Coulouris, who starred as Antony in Mercury's production of *Julius Caesar,* was cast as Walter P. Thatcher, Kane's humorless banker and guardian. Erskine Sanford, another Broadway veteran, appeared as Herbert Carter, the befuddled editor in charge of the *Inquirer* when Kane took over the newspaper.

For Thompson, the reporter who seeks the meaning of "Rosebud" (and whose face the audience never sees clearly) Welles turned to Alland, a trusted longtime associate. A creative renegade as dynamic in his own way as Welles was in his, Alland originally started his work in Mercury Theatre backstage, doing everything from sweeping floors to stage management. He eventually wedged his way into performing in the Mercury Theatre by literally forcing his talents on Welles, trapping him in his dressing room and reciting the funeral oration from *Julius Caesar.* After the "performance," Welles gave him acting assignments in Mercury productions.

Alland's role as both performer and administrator for Mercury productions continued in Hollywood; besides his role as Thompson, Alland served as a production aide during the writing and planning of the film, as well as the assistant director while Welles was actually appearing in a scene. Alland's soft interview style as the reporter Thompson belied the fact that he could also bring forth a thunderous voice, which he used with great effectiveness as the narrator of the *News on the March* sequence.

Paul Stewart, another Mercuryite who had served as an associate producer for radio programs, was cast as the mysterious and cynical Raymond, the butler "who knows where all the bodies are buried." While Stewart was an ideal choice to play the slimy caretaker of Xanadu, Welles also returned a favor

Dorothy Comingore

Ruth Warrick (left) and Ray Collins.

CITIZEN

by casting him in his first picture. Several years before, Stewart, as an established performer in radio, had helped Welles get some of his first jobs in broadcasting, which led to him becoming one of radio's biggest stars. (Welles needed all the help he could get when he began his radio career. One legend in broadcasting recalls that during his introduction to Knowles Entriken— one of the most important directors at CBS radio—Welles casually emptied his pipe into Entriken's wastebasket and set the trash on fire.)

Filling out the principal cast was a sturdy stable of actors, some of them Hollywood veterans, and most known to Welles either by reputation or personally from theatrical productions. Fortunio Bonanova, cast as Matisti, Susan's singing teacher, had produced and directed films in Europe and actually sang with the Paris Opera before coming to America to appear on Broadway in 1930. While Bonanova had not performed in Mercury Theatre productions, he was an old friend of Welles' from Broadway days, as was Georgia Backus—who appeared in the brief but memorable role of Miss Anderson, the iron-spined keeper of the Thatcher Library ("Mr. Thompson, you will be required to leave this room at 4:30 promptly.").

Other brief roles were filled by a variety of Hollywood character-acting talent. Gus Schilling, once a comedian in vaudeville who was remembered from a tryout for one of Welles' Shakespeare productions, took a small part as the kindly maître d' at Susan Alexander's nightclub; Harry Shannon, playing Kane's father, was perfectly credible as a no-good willing to give up his son for a lifelong annuity; and Philip Van Zandt as Rawlston, the boss of the newsreel company, who sends Thompson on his futile mission to discover the meaning of "Rosebud."

Chosen from the corps of Hollywood youngsters for pivotal juvenile roles were Buddy Swan, who played the sled-wielding Kane as a boy, and Sonny Bupp, who played Kane's son. (The two parts were not, as some assumed on first viewing, played by the same performer, although the two boys do bear a strong resemblance to each other.) RKO's publicity reported that Swan got the job playing Kane at age eight because he once posed for a gag publicity photo wearing a false beard similar to the real whiskers Welles sported on his Hollywood arrival.

To fill a variety of extra roles ranging from stuffy opera patrons to Adolf Hitler, RKO provided Welles with his pick from the masses in central casting. Among those extras granted a precious speaking part was Alan Ladd, then a struggling young bit player who bounced around the Hollywood studios and for a time worked to make ends meet as a grip at Warner Bros. (In RKO's full cast list for *Citizen Kane,* Ladd's first name is misspelled as "Allan.")

In the film's closing moments, Ladd can be seen smoking a pipe and wearing a hat with the brim turned up; he's the reporter who says, "We're

William Alland (left) as Thompson and Paul Stewart as Raymond, two Mercury veterans. In this publicity still, Alland's face appears more clearly than it ever did in the movie. When introduced after the Los Angeles premiere, Alland told the audience, "Perhaps you'll recognize me better like this," and turned his back to the crowd. Note the extra at the foot of the stairs with the pipe and turned-up hat brim: a bit player named Alan Ladd.

Welles reviews the costumes of his extras for the newsreel scenes. The personalities from history in the newsreel included Adolf Hitler, Marshal Foch, and President Theodore Roosevelt.

supposed to get everything—the junk as well as the art," and later, ". . . or Rosebud? How about it, Jerry?" *Citizen Kane* would provide no break into stardom for Ladd—that would come a year later in *This Gun for Hire*—his face, like those of the other reporters, was obscured from view by shadows.

*   *   *

Not only was *Citizen Kane* in large part a re-united family affair, but Welles added personal touches to the script by filling it with references to his friends and associates. The name of Sloane's character was drawn from Dr. Maurice

CITIZEN

Bernstein, Welles' longtime father figure and physician (it was Dr. Bernstein who treated Welles on the set when he tripped and chipped bones in his ankle). Joseph Cotten's character combined the names of theatrical producer Jed Harris and Leland Hayward, agent to many young actors, including Cotten.

Susan Alexander's last name was a tribute to Rita Alexander, the typist who had accompanied Mankiewicz and Houseman to Victorville to write the original script. Ray Collins' character, "Boss" Jim Gettys, Kane's political nemesis, had been listed as Edward Rogers in every version of the script practically up to the day his scenes were shot. At the last moment, the character's name was changed to Gettys, possibly as a tribute to Roger Gettys Hill, the son of Welles' longtime friends Hortense and Skipper Hill.

Immensely talented though Welles' performers were, they also possessed a common trait which was key to Welles' plans: most of the actors were complete novices in the world of motion pictures. Cotten, Sloane, Warrick, Collins, Moorehead, Sanford, Stewart, and Alland had never appeared in feature films. Coulouris, who had been a Hollywood newcomer when he came West to appear in Mercury productions, managed to squeeze in two film appearances before the cameras rolled on *Citizen Kane.* Comingore had appeared only sporadically in bit parts, shorts, and episodes with the Three Stooges; her sole role in a film of note was a brief appearance in Frank Capra's *Mr. Smith Goes to Washington,* in which she played a bright-eyed young socialite who pesters Jimmy Stewart to contribute to a charity milk fund.

The actors' novice status in Hollywood gave Welles the opportunity to mold their performances in ways that most seasoned Hollywood personalities would never accept from a first-time director. "I had the luck to hit upon actors who had never worked in films before," Welles said. "I could never have made *Citizen Kane* with actors who were old hands at cinema, because they would have said right off, 'just what do you think you're doing?' My being a newcomer would have put them on guard and, with the same blow, would have made a mess of the film. It was possible because I had my own family, so to speak."

To the set, Welles brought a nearly unending supply of inspiration and encouragement for his actors. "I give them a great deal of freedom and, at the same time, the feeling of precision," Welles recalled twenty-five years later. "It's a strange combination. In other words, physically, and in the way they develop, I demand the precision of ballet. But their way of acting comes directly from their own ideas as much as mine. When the camera begins to roll, I do not improvise visually. In this realm, everything is prepared. But I work very freely with the actors. I try to make their life pleasant."

For once, Welles was modest. His gift for directing, and for drawing from his actors dynamic performances that transcended much of their other work, provided the most important reason why, during the course of Welles' career—even after financial or critical disasters—actors of the highest stature sought to work with him.

Charlton Heston—who in 1957 insisted that Welles star opposite him and direct *Touch of Evil*—perhaps best summed up Welles' gift for guiding actors: "He makes it enormous fun," Heston said. "He persuades you that every shot you're doing happens to be the most important shot in the whole picture and the key to your role, and he then proceeds to get you to agree to that by cajolery and imagination."

In spite of his commanding directorial presence on the *Citizen Kane* set, never, throughout the production, did Welles forget that he too was a novice at the curious business of making motion pictures. Welles, said Agnes Moorehead, "trained us for films at the same time that he was training himself. All of us were learning."

Not only was Welles intent on bringing out the best in his stars, he was equally serious about publicly acknowledging their talent. The credits, which appeared at the close of the film only after obtaining waivers from an assortment of organizations representing both technicians and talent, include cameos of each leading performer in a highlight of a scene from the picture. Within the first month after *Citizen Kane*'s premiere, Collins, Comingore, Cotten, and Warrick were all signed to studio contracts, and others weren't far behind.

Finally, and certainly most important, Welles cast himself to play Charles Foster Kane. Welles was by no means obligated to star in the film; his contract with RKO, and its virtually unlimited creative control, allowed Welles to star in *Citizen Kane* if he chose, or cast someone

Welles and Erskine Sanford take a break from their confrontive scenes.

else in the starring role instead. Even before production began, it was clear that the role of Kane was going to be one of the choice parts in film history. But with this plum came a tremendous burden—the success or failure of *Citizen Kane* depended almost entirely on the power of that single performance.

Not only would Welles have to deliver the performance of his life, but he had to assume the massive task of preparing himself artistically in addition to the crushing pressure of both producing and directing his first film. As difficult as it is to imagine now—decades after Welles brought film's most acclaimed role to the screen—there was actually concern at RKO that the studio's new young phenomenon might have bitten off more than he could chew.

However, those in the Mercury fold knew, as did Welles himself, that there wasn't the slightest doubt that the whole package would work. For the man who pulled off a sensational modern-dress version of *Julius Caesar* and scared half of America with a Halloween prank—and now fortified by a supremely talented cast and the backing of a powerful Hollywood studio—bringing Charles Foster Kane to the screen would seem like child's play.

* * *

While casting and script revision continued, Welles was also forming the creative team that would give *Citizen Kane* its visual style: himself, cinematographer Gregg Toland, and art director Perry Ferguson.

Throughout the preproduction of *Citizen Kane,* the trio met each morning to plot out the photography and set design and establish down to the finest detail, the visual elements that would combine to bring *Citizen Kane* to the screen. They reviewed the script scene by scene, carefully developing the camera angles and design elements that each shot would require. Then the three would separate—Welles to rehearse his actors and polish the script, Toland to work with his camera team and lighting experts, and Ferguson to coordinate the set design and construction.

By the time the production had progressed to the stage that final storyboards were produced, all the planning for nearly every shot—camera angles, set designs, and the flow of action from one scene to another—was ready to be included in the detailed drawings (see the illustrations in this chapter). Long before the project went before the cameras, Welles knew how every important sequence of his filming would look when it was shot.

It is important to note that Welles and his creative team didn't aspire to create new photographic techniques—instead, they developed their cinematic plan for *Citizen Kane,* and then dipped into the catalog of film techniques to achieve their desired effects.

Before a cinematographer could be assigned to Welles by RKO, the

Welles portraying Kane at the height of his power.

.ONG SHOT SHOWS SPEAKER'S
LATFORM AND PICTURE OF
ANE WELL LIGHTED WE

TRAVEL IN WITH WALKER

TRICK UNTIL WE GET TO

.ANE AS HE FINISHES SPEECH
OOKS OFF AND SEE THAT

EMILY AND KANE JR. HAVE
GONE WE DISCOVER THEM

AT ONE OF THE ENTRANCES
WAITING FOR KANE AS

UT TO SHOT OVER KANE'S
ARRIAGE THRU BUSINESS OF
JTTING KANE JR. ABOARD AND

CARRIAGE PULLS OUT AND A
HANSOM PULLS IN AND THEY
GET IN WE GO TO

INTERIOR AS THEY HAVE
THEIR RIDE IN SILENCE

GARDEN.

CLOSE UP OF KANE - CUT TO

CLOSE SHOT OF EMILY AND
KANE JR. IN BOX - BACK TO

HE COMES UP AND JOINS
THEM   THEY ARE IN TURNF

JOINED BY SOME WELL
WISHERS AS THEY LEAVE WE

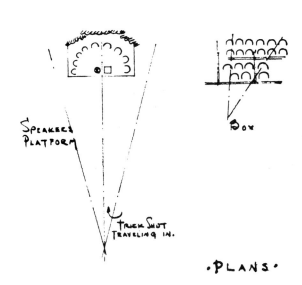

SPEAKERS
PLATFORM

TRUCK SHOT
TRAVELING IN.

·PLANS·

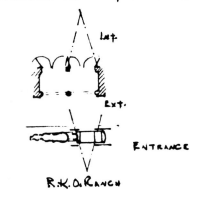

BOX

Int.

Ext.

ENTRANCE

R.K.O.RANCH

A storyboard used for Kane's campaign speech. Toland's photography, Ferguson's production design, and Welles' direction were so well coordinated that by the time the production planning reached the storyboard stage, even the most precise camera angles and flow of the action were already determined.

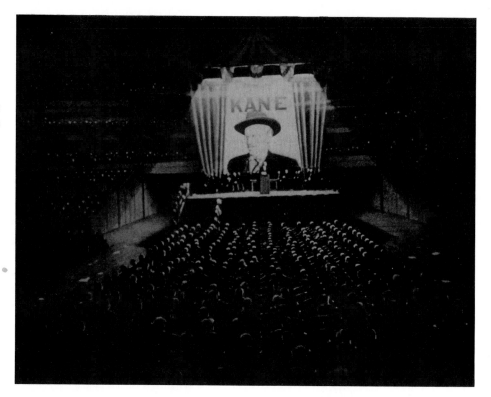

Kane's campaign speech as shown in the film. See pages 54–55 for storyboard.

director knew who he wanted to shoot his film. Gregg Toland, already a legend in Hollywood for his innovative photography, was known as a creative artist who brought an imaginative eye and an innovative mind to the sets of such films as *Wuthering Heights* and *The Grapes of Wrath*. "Toland was the best director of photography who ever existed," Welles said. "There has never been anyone else in his class."

Although Toland was perfectly capable of working quite successfully within the more traditional confines of the studio system—and often did—he appreciated and respected the most individualistic directors in Hollywood, such as Howard Hawks and John Ford, and sought to work with them as often as possible.

However, in 1940, Toland was under contract to independent producer Sam Goldwyn and, at first, seemed out of reach to Welles. But Toland had seen Welles' *Julius Caesar* in New York and was dazzled by the production. To Toland, Welles was a director who knew what he wanted and was willing to give his photographer free rein to get it. And because he was a newcomer to Hollywood, Welles wasn't bound by the dictates and standardized practices of the studios.

So when Toland called Welles and offered his services, Welles grabbed him. Goldwyn agreed to lend Toland to RKO for what would soon become the crowning achievement among many jewels in an already brilliant career.

Welles made it clear that perfecting the cinematography was the critical element in realizing his vision for *Citizen Kane*. "From the moment the production began to take shape in script form," Toland recalled, "everything was planned with reference to what the camera could bring to the eyes of the audience."

The mutual admiration between Welles and Toland was immense, and so was the product of their creativity. "Orson and Gregg respected each other, and they got along beautifully," Alland said. "No matter what Orson wanted, Gregg would try to get it for him."

From the first, the partnership worked marvelously; Welles served up his endless stream of ideas about the camera angles and shots he desired, and Toland developed a cinematic plan to bring the director's desires to the screen. The vision for *Citizen Kane* may have originated with Welles, but Toland— among many other things—helped bring the creative process into focus, and added not a little of his own creative spirit as well.

"In spite of the fact that Welles' previous experience had been in directing for the stage and for radio," Toland said soon after *Citizen Kane* was released, "he had a full realization of the great power of the camera in conveying dramatic ideas without recourse to words."

From Toland's point of view, *Citizen Kane* was not only well-timed artistically, but technically as well. New developments in both lighting and film —in particular the release of Kodak's new Super XX black-and-white film stock in 1938—opened vast new horizons for cinematographers, allowing them to shoot with less light and achieve greater contrast and depth to the image.

Toland and Welles were willing to try nearly anything to work toward the visual style they hoped to achieve. Few Hollywood cinematographers— even those of Toland's stature—got the opportunity to swing out with more than the occasional experiment. Toland, because of his ongoing work with directing innovators, got more chances than most. But with Welles and *Citizen Kane,* the skies were the limit.

"During recent years, a great deal has been said and written about the new technical and artistic possibilities offered by such developments as coated lenses, super-fast films, and the use of lower-proportioned and partially ceilinged sets," Toland wrote in 1941. "Some cinematographers have had, as I did in one or two productions, opportunities to make a few cautious, tentative experiments with utilizing these technical innovations to produce improved photo-dramatic results.

"Those of us who have, I am sure, felt as I did that they were on the track of something really significant, and wished that instead of using them

Welles and cinematographer Gregg Toland.

Toland shoots Kane's return to the Inquirer *(this take was not used in the film).
Here, Welles barely avoided yet another on-set accident, as he missed by inches
tripping over the rail for the dolly track.*

conservatively for a scene here or a sequence there, they could experiment free-handedly with them throughout an entire production.

"In the course of my last assignment, the photography of Orson Welles' picture, *Citizen Kane,* the opportunity for such large-scale experiment came to me."

Welles and Toland outlined a twofold mission for the cinematography in *Citizen Kane.* "Its keynote is realism," Toland said. "As we worked together over the script and the final, preproduction planning, both Welles and I felt this, and felt that if it was possible, the picture should be brought to the screen in such a way that the audience would feel it was looking at reality, rather than merely looking at a movie."

Of no less importance, was the creation of a visual flow for the picture, a seamless blending from one scene to the next. Welles, said Toland, "instinctively grasped a point which many other far more experienced directors and producers never comprehend: that the scenes and sequences should flow together so smoothly that the audience should not be conscious of the mechanics of picture-making."

Time and again, Toland and Welles plotted photography and direction to achieve this seamless quality in the scenes. The diverse elements of the story are woven together with a variety of techniques, such as cinematic bridges of sound or music that link one scene with the next, and camera angles or visual elements included in adjoining scenes which link the action from shot to shot.

The most impressive of this seamless flow of cinematic storytelling connects Leland's recollections of Kane's rise and downfall in politics. The scene begins with Leland, as an old man, talking with Thompson about Susan Alexander, as he describes the first night she met Kane.

Susan, who is cured of a toothache by Kane's good-natured antics, winds up singing an aria for her new friend, and she plays the piano at her dingy boardinghouse while Kane listens. The shot dissolves to Kane listening to Susan sing and play the same music, but now in a different location—this time in a far more comfortable apartment, no doubt provided by Kane. As Susan finishes her performance, she turns to Kane, and he applauds his approval.

The sound of Kane's clapping for Susan bridges into the next scene, where the applause is now directed at Leland campaigning for Kane in a backstreet rally. Leland trumpets Kane's merits, and the shot concludes with Leland shouting that Kane was the candidate "who entered this campaign . . ."

". . . with one purpose only," roars Kane in the next scene, which has shifted to a huge auditorium at the climax of his campaign. In only a few seconds of film, Toland and Welles showed the progress of the campaign from a minuscule grass-roots effort to power politics on a massive scale.

Welles, on the crane in work clothes, directs the filming of a sea of bundled Inquirers.

KANE

Following the speech, Kane and his wife Emily are blackmailed into visiting Susan's apartment, where Gettys tries to force Kane from the campaign. When Kane refuses to withdraw, Gettys and Emily leave, and the scene ends with a shot of the front door of Susan's apartment. The shot freezes, and the apartment door becomes the lead photograph on the election day front page of Kane's competition, the *Chronicle*.

A newsboy holds the *Chronicle* with the banner headlines about Kane. He offers a copy to Leland, who declines it as he walks through the swinging double doors of a saloon. The clatter of the saloon doors melds into the roar of the printing presses at the *Inquirer* the night of the

Welles inspects a shot through a test viewfinder while Toland looks on.

CITIZEN

election, where Bernstein is forced to choose between two potential headlines for the evening's edition. He chooses "Fraud at Polls."

This shot of the "Fraud at Polls" headline blends into a copy of the actual newspaper a few hours later, shown lying in the mud in front of the *Inquirer*. Leland, now drunk, steps past the tattered newspaper and into the building to confront Kane.

The next shot shows the headline "Kane Marries Singer," which dissolves to the New Jersey courthouse where Kane and Susan are married. They drive off on their honeymoon, with Kane telling reporters that it "won't be necessary" to build an opera house for Susan to get the opportunity to perform. The shot then jumps to another headline, "Kane Builds Opera House."

The background music over the headline carries over to the next scene, as Susan frantically prepares for her operatic debut. The action eventually winds up in the newsroom of the *Chicago Inquirer,* where Kane discovers Leland, passed out in a drunken binge after trying to write the dramatic notice of Susan's performance. Kane finishes the review for Leland and then fires his former friend. As he walks out of the *Inquirer* for the last time, the shot dissolves to Leland as an old man, as he concludes his recollections.

"Direct cuts, we felt, were something that should be avoided wherever possible," said Toland. "Instead, we tried to plan action so that the camera could pan or dolly from one angle to another whenever this type of treatment was desirable.

"These unconventional set-ups impose insurmountable difficulties in the path of strictly conventional methods of camerawork. To put things with brutal frankness, they simply cannot be done by conventional means. But they were a basic part of *Citizen Kane* and they *had* to be done!"

But there was more to Toland's assignment than solely shooting Welles' picture. In many respects, Toland, himself only served as a mentor to the young director, not only responding to his vision, but giving him gentle lessons about the workings of Hollywood. By coaxing Welles through many of the basics of film production, Toland also helped transform him into a movie director.

"Orson would rehearse a scene as he would do it for the stage, then Gregg would explain to him why it could not be done for the screen in the same way," said Ralph Hoge, a longtime associate of Toland's and key grip on *Citizen Kane.* "Gregg was careful to take Orson aside and explain these things in private. Orson was easily convinced on matters he was unfamiliar with—but not in public; you couldn't convince him of anything in front of other people."

Welles recalled Toland's patient treatment as well. "He was quietly fixing it so as many of my notions as possible would work," Welles said. "Later he told me, 'That's the only way to learn anything—from somebody who doesn't know anything.' "

Toland's tutoring began early in the production when Welles, by his own admission, was having difficulty with some of the filmmaking fundamentals.

"I said, 'There's a lot of stuff here I don't know,' " Welles recalled. "And Toland said, 'There's nothing I can't teach you in three hours.' It was Toland's idea that anyone can learn [the fundamentals of film direction] in three hours, and he taught it to me in three hours. Everything else is if you're any good or not."

Toland relished the challenge of Welles' approach, in spite of the pace and the demands. After he wrapped up *Citizen Kane,* Toland lamented, "I must admit that working this way for eighteen or nineteen weeks tends to spoil one for working under more conventional conditions."

Welles never forgot Toland's role in the success of his first motion picture; forty years after the film was released, Welles was still singing Toland's praises. "It's impossible to say how much I owe to Gregg," Welles remembered. "He was superb." He and Toland also shared the same frame in the film's credits. Just below Welles' name in the closing credits is that of Gregg Toland.

*   *   *

Teamed with Welles and Toland was art director Perry Ferguson, one of several talented designers working at RKO under Van Nest Polglase, director of RKO's art department (because Polglase administered RKO's art department, he received top billing in the screen credits over the art director who did the actual work). Ferguson, with the art direction of such films as *Bringing Up Baby* and *Gunga Din* to his credit, was, like Toland, fascinated by stretching the limits of the Hollywood way of making films; in *Citizen Kane* he saw an opportunity to push the boundaries of his craft.

Ferguson took Welles' suggestions and transformed them first into detailed sketches, and then into scale models that Welles could view with a tiny periscope from any angle. Once the director was satisfied with the design, the sets were constructed on stages at RKO's main studio on Gower Street in Hollywood, and at the RKO-Pathé lot on Washington Boulevard in Culver City (also housed on the RKO-Pathé lot were David O. Selznick's production facilities, where *Gone With the Wind* had been filmed the year before).

The sets for a film such as *Citizen Kane* would have been a tremendous challenge, even without Welles' elaborate photographic dictates. The picture called for more than one hundred sets spanning nearly eight decades of American history, from middle nineteenth-century America through pre–World War II urban New York and Florida. The range of settings produced by Ferguson included turn-of-the-century mansions, slum streets, a lavish bedroom for Kane's second wife (complete with childlike stencils of cute little animals), dingy newspaper offices, the stage at a political rally, a private castle, a host of doorways, staircases, corridors, and a re-creation of backstage at an opera house—both in rehearsal and in performance.

In addition to the traditional box formation that is the standard configuration for Hollywood sets, Welles wanted an additional element: ceilings for virtually every shot (although curiously, none of the scenes involving Thompson interviewing other characters have ceilings in them).

"I suppose that closing the top of the set was the real revolution we caused," remembered

A typical example of Ferguson's designs, and set dressing by Darrell Silvera. Richly appointed and realistic, right down to the magazines on the chairside rack, this set appears on screen for only a few seconds. Note also the statue on the side table next to Kane, a smaller version of one of the massive statues that stands next to the fireplace in the great hall at Xanadu.

CITIZEN

The fireside statues at Xanadu were changed from
scene to scene to note the
passing of time.

Welles. "It's disastrous to let a cameraman light a set without a ceiling—it's artificial."

Adding ceilings to motion picture sets was not new in Hollywood—the innovation came in the frequency and variety of their use. Besides adding a look of completeness to the sets, they also provided Welles with the ability to shoot up from very low angles, an option he used extensively. The ceilings were not merely flat surfaces over the drama below. Ferguson varied them with every manner of texture and treatment—beams, filigree, stained glass, even skylights partially shaded with makeshift curtains to shield the reporters in the newsroom from the midday sun. Each ceiling, even the simplest, included a different touch; for example, when Leland and Bernstein are unpacking statues in Kane's office at the *Inquirer,* a plain ceiling is pierced by a single long shadow that slices across the top of the frame.

Beyond the often-discussed success of the ceilings, Ferguson's set designs —achieved in conjunction with set decoration department head Darrell Silvera and his staff—stand out for the extraordinary level of detail that filled every frame of the picture. The sets were crammed with paintings, period furniture, and all manner of personal mementos—far more than could ever be absorbed in a single viewing.

The sets also included subtle clues that span the decades of the film, items which during a single viewing would pass unnoticed by everyone except those on the set who knew they were there. For instance, in Susan's second apartment (where Kane, sitting cozily in a large rattan chair, listens to her hapless singing), standing on an end table next to Kane's chair, is a foot-high copy of one of the sculptures that later appears life-size on the left side of the fireplace at Xanadu.

Earlier, in her first apartment, while Susan laughs at Kane wiggling his ears at her, the camera picks up the ill-fated snowglobe, which would survive Kane's destruction of her room at Xanadu and inspire Kane to remember Rosebud—the same snowglobe that falls from his hand and shatters when he dies. The snowglobe sits on Susan's dressing table and props up a photo of a child—a portrait no doubt supposed to be Susan as a little girl—a choice tidbit that sends its own message about the importance of youth to Susan, a trait she and Kane unknowingly share.

At Xanadu, the statues by the fireplace change with the progression of the years. Ferguson and his crew must have been particularly fond of those fireside statues; one of them is included among dozens of statues in Kane's office when Leland is sorting through artwork, and they are also featured prominently among the items in the closing shots, when the newsreel crew is photographing Kane's relics.

In one of the final shots of the film, as Toland's astounding crane shot travels over the flotsam and jetsam of Kane's life, the camera clearly frames several items that have been seen before—among them the ornate steel headboard that Kane brought with him on his first day as publisher of the *Inquirer*, when he planned to live in the editor's office. Next to the sled on the junk pile is a tattered bundle of decaying newspapers—properly aged to show the passage of the years—lying on its side. Viewers can't see the front page, but it is unquestionably one of the bundles of *Inquirer*s with Kane's "Declaration of Principles" emblazoned across the front that appeared in a mountain of newsprint early in the picture—and perhaps here a subtle reference to the decay of Kane's standards.

To give Toland the setting he required for his cinematic voyages into depth of focus, Ferguson first needed to provide depth of set. Each stage employed designs that provided vivid settings for the photography—often for the briefest of shots. For Susan Alexander's second apartment, Ferguson produced not one room but two; the front room where the action takes place is complemented by the entrance to an equally detailed room to the rear. The shot lasts only a few seconds, and the action is focused entirely on Kane or Susan—yet the impact of the richly appointed set is not wasted.

Toland's praise for Ferguson matched his enthusiasm for working with Welles, and the cinematographer made special note of the art director's budget sense. "His camera-wise designing of the settings not only made it possible to obtain many of the effects Welles and I sought," Toland said, "but also made possible the truly remarkable achievement of building the production's sets for about $60,000, yet gave us sets which look on the screen like a much larger expenditure."

All of Ferguson's design efforts—the ceilings, the attention to the tiniest detail—were well worth the extensive planning. Among the less often noted elements of *Citizen Kane* is the picture's intense realism; virtually every scene is dressed, lit, and shot so realistically that a viewer can easily feel like a peeping tom, peering into a man's real life.

But Ferguson had more to consider in his task than creating design innovations. RKO's ongoing pressure to shrink production budgets—even for its wonder boy's project—kept Ferguson on his toes to not only produce the sets Welles wanted, but to keep the price tag as low as possible. The final *Citizen Kane* budget showed total set costs of less than $100,000—about $78,500 for the set design and construction and another $21,200 for labor and related costs—a bargain by any Hollywood standard of the 1940s, and dirt cheap when the final results were viewed.

Ferguson, Toland, and Welles, spurred by RKO's financial restrictions, economized in a variety of ways. The budget pressure, and the resulting careful cost-conscious plottings actually contributed to the visual style of *Citizen Kane*

Backstage at the debut of the opera Salammbo. *The effect of the choreography of frantic extras implies hundreds of people in the scene—yet only a handful are used.*

by forcing the threesome to consider innovative visual options that at other more lavish studios, they would not have been forced to employ.

The judicious use of extras and sly camera angles implied a cast of thousands, but actually included only a handful of people in even the most elaborate shots. Scenes that seemed to include hundreds or even thousands of actors in them were accomplished by using special effects, carefully plotted swirls of movement by the extras, or both. The shots of Kane's campaign speech—Kane on the podium, his wife and son in the audience, the flurry of action outside of the auditorium—contains only a few players in

any *individual* shot, but the overall impact is one of thousands of people appearing in a whirlwind of action. The "audience" in the meeting hall is actually a matte painting, pricked with holes so light would shine through and give the illusion of motion to the "crowd."

During Susan's operatic debut, the screen seems filled with mobs of frenzied people from the staff and company of the opera production; the impact is achieved by carefully plotting the rushing of actors across the stage at five different distances from the camera—some only a few feet from the lens, blacking out the scene. What seems like hundreds of people filling

Susan faces the "audience" in her opera debut. The spectators are never shown here, only implied by the skillful combination of lighting and photography.

the frame is actually no more than twenty; the resulting visual impact of the intricately choreographed small groups of actors provided a far more stylized look to *Citizen Kane* than would more traditional surgings of teeming mobs.

RKO's background material on *Citizen Kane* claims that the picture included 28 principal players, 89 bit players, and 796 extras. If accurate, those numbers could have represented only the sum total used for all of the various shots over the course of the entire eleven-week shooting schedule. While Kane's party in the city room of the *Inquirer* features upwards of sixty people, no other single sequence in *Citizen Kane* includes more than thirty performers, and some of the "crowds" show as few as five.

Toland could match Ferguson at economizing. Some of the best shots in *Citizen Kane,* which show how to plot a shot with astounding impact while saving money in the process, provided lessons to every cinematographer in Hollywood. Toland displays the best use of his artful yet cost-saving photographic technique in the scenes of Susan's disastrous debut as she described it to Thompson.

In this second flashback of the film, which shows the premiere of the opera *Salammbo,* Toland photographed the scene from behind Susan as she faces the audience while the curtain rises. The shot shows Susan, small and terrified, as she stands alone in the center of the stage facing the dark abyss of the opera hall punctuated by banks of spotlights, and the unforgiving spectators beyond.

Yet the "audience" is only implied—viewers cannot see anyone through the blaze of lights but the performer. The shot is so effective that many viewers remember "seeing" the audience in the shot.

* * *

Almost exactly eleven months after he signed a contract to produce films for RKO, Orson Welles was prepared to shoot *Citizen Kane.* But while the young director may have been ready to bring his vision before the cameras, RKO was not. Budget problems not only forced economizing on the set, but ultimately made necessary a large dose of Wellesian chicanery before the cameras could roll.

Late in June, Toland's camera plotting and Ferguson's set construction had progressed to the point that Welles could start shooting his picture. Welles had already been rehearsing his principal players steadily for several weeks, both in meetings on the set and in less formal gatherings at Mankiewicz's home.

Welles conducted detailed off-set rehearsals of every scene—a rarity in those days of Hollywood's factorylike production—and for several key passages, recorded the rehearsals for detailed review.

But RKO, still leery of the budget which Welles was reluctant to trim, wanted to hold up principal photography until all of the issues were resolved to the studio's satisfaction.

Welles, straining at the leash, found a way to counter RKO's stalling tactics. On June 29, he began to shoot "tests"—film logged in the studio's records as "experimental" footage that was, in reality, shots completed for final print. Eventually, RKO management figured out what Welles had done, but by the time they discovered the ruse, he appeared to be making steady progress, and the studio allowed him to proceed. So *Citizen Kane*'s actual start date was June 29—a month before the "official" studio date, and began with the projection room shots during which Rawlston orders Thompson to find Rosebud. (The scene was shot by cramming cast and crew into an actual projection room at RKO on Gower Street.)

Soon after, Welles shot Thompson's first visit to interview Susan, her suicide attempt, and several other sequences. All of these shots are listed in RKO's log as "Orson Welles Tests." So by the time the official "first day" of filming, July 30, Welles already had more than a dozen final shots in the can.

These early scenes—the first Welles ever completed as a feature film director—showed just how far the collaboration between Welles and Toland had progressed. Overlapping dialogue, casual conversation, lightning-fast interchange—all were apparent and vibrant in Welles' first bold steps as a motion picture director. The shots are crisp and imaginative: actors bathed in light or submerged in darkness, the eerie haloing of spotlights behind Rawlston when he gives the orders to find out about Rosebud, and many other stunning moments. The cameras had barely started to roll, and already Welles showed the talents of a Hollywood veteran—it was apparent that he was living up to his reputation for breaking all the rules.

In spite of the difficulties that RKO had already encountered with Welles, the studio was anxious for him to succeed and eager to showcase its young prodigy. For the first official day of shooting, the studio invited the press to watch Welles at work. Reporters were treated to the filming of some of the most inconsequential shots of the picture, including, among others, the newsreel footage of Kane's marriage to Emily on the White House lawn. After the event, the *Motion Picture Herald* carried a blurb about the session titled "Silence! Genius at Work."

Once production swung into high gear, Welles ran a closed set and kept access to rehearsal and takes as tight as possible. Only cast and crew absolutely necessary to the production, those with a "need to know," or invited guests such as columnist Louella Parsons and director John Ford, were welcome.

Welles' secrecy was not intended to keep details of the film out of the press, in spite of what some later said when the forces of William Randolph

```
                    ORSON WELLES TESTS
                    as of July 2, 1940


HEART OF DARKNESS                              $            $

#1  Sound and Photographic -               2,676.06
      Robert Coote, Dolly Haas, Gus Schilling,
      Everett Sloan                             23.79   2,699.85

#2  Process Glass Shadow Effect


CITIZEN KANE                                    344.75

#1  Photographic -
      Orson Welles                             251.28

#2  Photographic -
      Orson Welles - 50 years of age           398.26

#3  Photographic -
      Orson Welles - young                      711.56

#4  Sound and Photographic -
      Jo Cotten, Ruth Warwick, Orson Welles

#5  Sound and Photographic -                    848.39
      Evelyn Meyers - Age 22
      Orson Welles - Age 44

#6  Sound and Photographic -
      Orson Welles - Age 33 - 44 - 64
      Ruth Warwick - Age 22 - 42               671.71
      George Coulouris - Age 54
      William Alland - Richard Baer

#7  Sound and Photographic -
      Orson Welles - Age 44 - 65
      Linda Winters - Age 22 - 41              780.91
      William Alland

#8  Sound and Photographic - Int. Projection Room
      William Alland, Period 1940    6/29        528.22
      Three Bit Players                          225.00
                                                 55.80 OT
                                                804.80

#9  Sound and Photographic - Int. Living-Room & Cafe
      Linda Winters - Age 28 - 42    7/3
      Orson Welles - Age 45               1,038.00 (Budget)
      Gus Schilling, William Alland, Irving Mitchell  5,573.08
                                          1,376.79
                                              $8,272.93

                    TOTAL
```

The tests that weren't tests; the budget sheet that itemized costs for the "experimental" footage that Welles shot to get his film into production. Numbers one through seven are, indeed, tests; number eight, filmed June 29, 1940, is the projection room scene of Rawlston ordering Thompson to find Rosebud—the first shot of the actual production. Number nine includes a meeting between Kane and his second wife, Susan ("Linda Winters" was then the stage name of Dorothy Comingore), as well as her first drunken encounter with Thompson. "Welles wanted to get going, so he fooled RKO into thinking that he was just testing his ideas," said editor Robert Wise. "Eventually, they figured him out, and they let him go ahead."

The scene in the projection room. Actors and the film crew crowded into a real screening room at RKO to film Welles' first scenes of the production.

Welles rehearses the dancers for the "Charley Kane" number.

Form- No. C-34—25M

R K O Radio Pictures, Inc.   **SHOOTING SCHEDULE**   DATE 7/19/40

PICT. No. 281 _____ TITLE CITIZEN KANE _____ DIRECTOR Orson Welles

Trosper

		ESTIMATED		ACTUAL	
		DATE	DAYS	DATE	DAYS
Start Rehearsal					
Holidays 1	Start Photography	July 30			
	Finish Photography	Oct. 19			70+1=71

DAY	DATE	DESCRIPTION OF SET OR LOCATION	ACTOR'S NUMBER	Set No.	LOCATION OR STUDIO	DAY OR NITE
Mon.	7/29	Cast Report to Still Dept.				
Tues.	7/30	Ext. N. Y. Street & Drugstore & Cheap Apt. House - 1915	1-8-B-X	34	Studio	N-S33
		Int. Susan's First Apt. Bedroom - 1915	1-8	35	"	N-S34
Wed.	7/31	" Susan's First Apt. Bedroom - 1915	1-8	35	"	N-S34
Thurs.	8/1	" Susan's First Apt. Bedroom - 1915	1-8	35	"	N-S34
Fri.	8/2	" Kane's N. Y. Home Living Room - 1917 - 1918	1-8-25	29	"	D-S45
		" Kane's N. Y. Home Susan's Room - 1920	1-8-27	28	"	D-S47
Sat.	8/3	" Madison Sq. Gardens - 1916	1-6-11-19-B-X	31	"	N-S35
SUNDAY						
Mon.	8/5	Int. Madison Sq. Gardens - 1916	1-6-19-B-X	31	"	N-D27
Tues.	8/6	Ext. " " " "	1-6-11-19-B-X	80	"	N-S36
		Int. Carriage - 1916	1-6	32	"	N-S37
Wed.	8/7	Int. Hallway - Susan's 2nd Apt. - 1916	1-6-8-20-B-X	33	"	N-S38
		Int. Susan's 2nd Apartment - Living Room - 1916	1-6-8-20-B-X	33	"	N-S39
Thurs.	8/8	" Susan's 2nd Apartment - Living Room - 1916	1-6-8-20-B-X	33	"	N-S39
Fri.	8/9	" Susan's 2nd Apartment - Living Room - 1916	1-6-8-20-B-X	33	"	N-S39
Sat.	8/10	" Susan's 2nd Apartment - Living Room - 1916	1-6-8-20-B-X	33	"	N-S39
SUNDAY						
Mon.	8/12	Ext. Town Hall in Trenton -1917	1-8-B-X	14	RKO Ranch	D-S42
		" " " " " "	1-8-B-X	14	" "	D-D18
		Door of Newspaper Office- Sign - (News Digest Shot)		14	" "	D-D28
		Ext. N. Y. Street - 1916	B-X	14	" "	N-D24
Tues.	8/13	Int. Kane's Tent - Everglade's Camp - 1932	1-8	40	Studio	N-S51
Wed.	8/14	Ext. Everglade's Camp at Xanadu (PROCESS) - 1932	B-X	39	"	D-S50
		" Xanadu Terrace - 1929 - (News Digest Shots) (PROC.)	1-8-B-X	68	"	D-D20
		Int. Kane's Car - Xanadu - 1932 - (PROCESS)	1-8		"	D
		Int. Kane's N. Y. Home - Breakfast Room - 1901	1-6		"	D
Thurs.	8/15	Int. Chicago Opera House - 1919	1-2-8-11-B-X	22	"	N-S43
Fri.	8/16	Int. Opera (THAIS) - Stage Shots - 1919	8-B-X	23	Pathe	N
		" Grid of Theatre - 1919	8-X	81	"	N-S43A
		Int. Chicago Hotel Room - 1919	1-8-B-X	82	Studio	D-S46
		" Kane's N. Y. Home - Breakfast Room - 1902	1-6		"	D
Sat.	8/17	" Chicago Inquirer City Room - 1919	1-2-3-B-X	13	"	N-S15
SUNDAY						

Form C-34-A—25M

NAME OF CAST AND NUMBER

NUMBER	CHARACTER	NAME	Days Work	Days Idle	Total Days	DATE START	DATE FINISH
1	Kane	Orson Welles	40	19	59	7-30	10-8
2	Bernstein	Everett Sloane	22	6	28	8-12	9-12
3	Leland	Joe Cotton	22	2	24	8-12	9-10
4	Thatcher	Geo. Coulouris	7	10	17	8-29	9-17
5	Thompson	Wm. Alland	13	11	24	9-9	10-4
6	Emily	Ruth Warrick	10	1	11	7-30	8-10
7	Junior		4	0	4	9-13	9-17
8	Susan	Dorothy Comingore	18	37	55	8-1	10-3
9	Mrs. Kane	Agnes Moorehead	4	0	4	9-13	9-17
10	Kane, Sr.		4	0	4	9-13	9-17
11	Hillman	Dick Baer	12	13	25	8-3	8-30
12	Carter	Erskine Sanford	5	1	6	8-31	9-6
13	Smathers	Ed. Hemmer	1	0	1	9-6	9-6
14	Rawlston	Phil Van Zandt	2	0	2	10-4	10-5
15	Raymond	Ed Barrier	8	4	12	9-19	10-2
16	Bertha Anderson	Georgia Backus	1	0	1	9-18	9-18
17	Mike	AL EBEN	5	4	9	8-21	8-30
18	Miss Townsend	Ellen Lowe	2	0	2	8-27	8-28
20	Rogers	Ray Collins	4	0	4	8-7	8-10
23	Narrator	Bill Alland	6	0	6		
25	Matiste	Bona Nova	1	0	1	8-16	8-16
28	Georgie		4	0	4	8-20	8-23
30	Horses & Carts						
31	Bits & Extras						

Portions of the original shooting schedules for Citizen Kane. *"Studio" refers to RKO's main lot on Gower Street, "RKO Ranch" is the company's outdoor facility in Encino in the San Fernando Valley, and "Pathé" is the RKO-Pathé lot on Washington Boulevard in Culver City. In the column labeled Actor's Number, "B" stands for bit players, and "X" means extras. While the schedule was altered radically to accommodate routine production delays and Welles' ankle injury, this early version provides a vivid example of the frenetic pace of the production.*

Hearst tried to suppress the film. Instead, Welles was merely ensuring that the film would progress as he saw fit, without interference from the studio. (In spite of Welles' contract, several dissenting RKO executives would have been only too happy to meddle in Mercury Theatre's operations).

For the most part, Welles' plan worked; RKO executives kept their noses out of Welles' project. But when they did intrude, Welles made it clear their presence was unwelcome. One RKO legend recalls that when studio executives dropped in to see how production was going, Welles calmly stopped shooting, divided his crew and actors into softball teams, and played a game until the intruders departed.

RKO was not completely in the dark about progress on *Citizen Kane.* Schaefer and others had a pretty good idea of how the project was going, thanks to cut-and-dried production reports from the set, as well as some covert information obtained from RKO technicians working on the film. When Welles' idol, John Ford, visited the young director on the set, Ford actually pointed out a "spy" among the RKO crew so Welles would know who was doing the informing. But if RKO managers planned to keep a close eye on Welles' work day by day, they were out of luck—Welles successfully shut them out entirely.

* * *

Throughout the summer and early fall of 1940, Welles rehearsed and shot *Citizen Kane.* Toland's team kept the photography and lighting in order, and Ferguson's crew of designers, painters, and carpenters stayed barely one step ahead of the shooting schedule.

At the center of production was Welles—always in the fray answering questions, making requests, being measured for costumes, and generally coaxing, encouraging and demanding the best possible work from all. It was, in many ways, a production much like any other Welles project: endlessly frenetic, exhausting, enlivening—a creative exhilaration for everyone involved. For more than a few, their work on *Citizen Kane* was the most productive of their lives. "There was no one quite like him," said Agnes Moorehead, who would later appear in another Welles project, *The Magnificent Ambersons,* "to create excitement."

Not only was the creative pressure tremendous for all involved, the physical demands were even more challenging. Eighteen-hour days were typical, twenty hours at a stretch were routine, and more than a few times, Welles and his cast and crew worked straight through one day and into another without stopping.

It was on a late summer night that Welles filmed one of the movie's most

Welles takes a break from rehearsing the breakfast scene to show Ferguson how he wants the flood of headlines announcing Kane's death to pass before the camera. Each newspaper is pulled off the stack with a flourish and a flutter of pages.

KANE

A fatigued Joseph Cotten and Welles take a break during filming.

CITIZEN

important shots—in which Cotten, supposedly drunk, tells off Kane for his selfish ways.

"The thing you don't do when faced with a drunk scene is to get drunk," Cotten recalled. "Orson and I came to the conclusion that fatigue would be akin to the kind of numbness that too much drinking can bring. So we started shooting after dinner, having completed a full day's work that day. I had nothing to drink, but by three o'clock in the morning, I *was* drunk. I felt so heavy-footed and tired that I didn't have to act drunk at all.

"I was so tired that I did a tongue-trip. I had the line, 'You said yourself you were looking for someone to do dramatic criticism,' but the words came out: 'dramatic crimitism.' The line remained in the picture." A close study of Welles' pleased expression in the same shot shows the slightest hint of surprise at the delivery of the line.

Welles was still going strong as the sun rose. "I remember that the eight o'clock whistle blew and the sound man cracked, 'That's an interference we don't generally have on a picture,' " Cotten recalled.

"After Orson called an end to shooting, the prop man brought out a silver tray with drinks," Cotten said. "The big stage door was open and we saw the sunshine outside. Someone suggested, 'Why don't we go outside and have our drink?'

"There we were—Orson, Aggie Moorehead, Everett Sloane, Paul Stewart, myself and others—sitting around in the morning sun and having drinks. I'll never forget actors from other pictures walking down the street and seeing us. I can just imagine what they were saying: 'Those actors from New York! Imagine them sitting around in the morning drinking Scotch and sodas off a silver tray!' They didn't know that we had been working for twenty-four hours straight."

With Welles acting in many sequences while directing at the same time, he was frequently in no position to watch the action from behind the camera. The task fell to Alland, when he wasn't rehearsing or appearing as Thompson, to back up Welles as his eyes and ears off camera (with Kane dead by the time Thompson enters the picture, Alland and Welles never appeared together).

"I didn't pass artistic judgment," Alland said. "I merely checked to see if Orson was getting what he wanted. After each scene, he would glance at me. If I smiled, the take was okay. If I remained pokerfaced, he'd shoot it again."

A Welles production had certain givens, including the amount of accidental physical damage that Welles managed to inflict on himself. Only days into production, while rehearsing Kane's confrontation with his political rival, Gettys—a shot in which Kane runs down a staircase while screaming, "I'm going to send you to Sing Sing"—Welles tripped and fell heavily on his left ankle, chipping the bone.

For several weeks, Welles directed from a wheelchair and was forced to reschedule several scenes, shooting around himself while he mended (Welles can be seen limping slightly in his first appearance in the Great Hall at Xanadu). The date that a photograph was taken on the set can practically be determined by the condition of Welles' foot: first in a cast, then in a sock, later in a sandal, and finally in a shoe again.

An even more spectacular injury to Welles occurred during the filming of Kane's destruction of Susan's bedroom at Xanadu in a final fit of anger after she leaves him. With four cameras rolling, Welles, heavily made up and padded to appear more than sixty, destroyed the entire set with his bare hands, throwing suitcases, tearing quilts, ripping books from shelves, and breaking a large assortment of makeup and perfume bottles.

The attention to detail in Susan's room was extreme; Ferguson's crew used real perfume in its original bottles—Chanel No. 5, Joy, and Ashes of Magnolia, among others. Their scent filled the air on the set in the path of Welles' destruction. "Each time, he threw himself into the action with a fervor I had never seen in him," Alland said. "It was absolutely electric; you felt as if you were in the presence of a man coming apart."

While shooting one of two takes of the scene, Welles severely slashed his left hand, and the cut was so deep that it required immediate stiches. Welles' injury may have been wasted; it's impossible to tell for certain whether that take was used in the film; perhaps only a brief moment from that particular take was used.

However, spectators who witnessed the shot noticed Welles suddenly stop swinging with the injured hand when he gashed himself, which is precisely what happens in the final print after Welles scatters the bottles on the makeup table. While it's unclear whether Welles is actually shown injuring himself—no blood can be seen—it is clear that near the end of the shot, when he sees the tiny snowglobe and calms himself, Welles abruptly pulls his left hand out of camera view.

Welles, of course, was barely slowed by either injury. The fact that he injured himself at all, let alone twice, came as a great relief to everyone in Welles' camp—much to the surprise of Hollywood reporters. The Mercuryites knew a successful Welles production was always marked by their fearless leader damaging himself to greater or lesser degree with a slip, a major gash, or, in one case, a fifteen-foot fall onto his chin through a trapdoor in the Mercury Theatre stage floor.

Earlier in Welles' career, one accident involving another actor was no laughing matter. While directing and starring as Brutus in Mercury's production of *Julius Caesar,* Welles nearly killed actor Joseph Holland during the assassination scene, when the quite real and deadly sharp hunting knife he had

Welles rehearsing his reaction to Susan's operatic debut. William Alland (left foreground), an assistant to Welles who also appeared in the film as Thompson, the reporter, became Welles' eyes and ears while Welles appeared on camera.

used without incident to "stab" Caesar in dozens of performances slipped cleanly and painlessly between Holland's ribs and severed an artery near his heart.

Welles had insisted on using a real knife for the coup de grace—as opposed to the rubber weapons used by the other assassins—because of the added "realism" the blade added to the action. Holland recovered without lasting damage.

On the *Citizen Kane* set, one other "accident" was clearly the result of Welles' directorial demands. Welles shot take after take of Rosebud being thrown into the Xanadu incinerator, while Paul Stewart as Raymond the butler delivers the film's final line, "Throw that junk in." After the ninth take, the Culver City fire department rushed onto the set; apparently, the inferno became so hot that the flue caught fire, and it appeared that the studio was ablaze (the extent of the inferno varies greatly, depending on the story-teller—the intensity of the flames ranging from a small fire inside the flue, to at the other extreme, the roof of the stage actually ablaze).

The firemen took no chances with "the movie people"—they were still leery after David Selznick's shooting of the burning of Atlanta for *Gone With*

Kane destroys Susan's bedroom. "Each time, he threw himself into the action with a fervor I had never seen in him," said William Alland of Welles' performance. "It was absolutely electric."

the Wind eighteen months before, when fire crews stood helplessly watching the largest controlled fire in motion picture history roar hundreds of feet into the sky, while they prayed the inferno wouldn't burn out of control—a disaster which fortunately never happened.

* * *

Off camera, perhaps the most interesting issue on the set was the continuous transformation in physical appearance of the principal players, who aged as much as fifty years during the course of the film. The makeup was the product of Maurice Seiderman, who Welles called, "the best makeup man in the world." For his work on *Citizen Kane* alone, he most assuredly deserved the title.

"Maurice is an alchemist," said Welles during production. "Without that medieval Russian, the picture could never have been made."

Seiderman did not achieve the acclaim of some of his counterparts at other motion picture studios, such as Ben Nye or the Westmore family. However, working over bubbling experiments in a tiny shop on RKO's back lot,

Using a bust of Welles as a base, makeup artist Maurice Seiderman prepares neck wattles for Kane at age seventy.

Cotten (left) struggles mightily against his ill-fitting contact lenses to perform with William Alland as Thompson.

A very bald Everett Sloane, head shaved to accommodate the requirements of Maurice Seiderman's makeup, watches Welles check costumes.

Seiderman singlehandedly created some of the most astonishingly realistic makeup ever to appear on film. Seiderman aged the principal characters of *Citizen Kane* across the entire span of their adult lives—not merely adding superficial wrinkles, but transforming every aspect of the actors' physical appearances with specially designed wigs, neck wattles, body fat, crabbed hands, and an incredible variety of aged ears, noses, chins, and facial bags.

Concocted from a combination of latex molds, traditional theatrical body paint, and specialized chemicals of Seiderman's own creation, the makeup produced astounding physical transformations. Even under close-up inspection, it was difficult to detect where the makeup ended and the actor's real features began; for added realism, Welles' makeup included Seiderman's painstaking addition of individual pores on the latex surface—each calculated to match their position on Welles' own skin.

While Cotten, Coulouris, Comingore, and Sloane all grew old during the film, it was Welles whose transformation was shown most spectacularly—in twenty-seven stages. The process of altering Welles' full physical appearance for the film started with a complete body cast, with Welles immobilized in coatings of hydrocolloid (a jelly substance) covered with plaster. While Welles lay frozen into position, Seiderman gleefully tortured his subject by reading from books the actor hated.

Then, using the molds, as well as a separate cast of Welles' head, Seiderman created the array of body pads and a total of seventy-two assorted face pieces for Kane—among them sixteen different chins alone—as well as ears, cheeks, jowls, hairlines, and eye pouches to be used at various stages of the publisher's aging from twenty-five to seventy-eight.

Both Welles and Cotten were supplied with contact lenses veined with tiny lines of paint and filled with a milky substance to simulate the rheumy-eyed look of the very old; Cotten's lenses—which were fitted on him by a doctor on short notice after Welles hurt his ankle and filming had to be rearranged—were so uncomfortable that they left him nearly sightless during the first takes of Leland reminiscing as an old man (the lenses were refitted more successfully for later retakes).

Modifying real human features played a role in weaving Seiderman's magic spells as well. Sloane's balding head was no simulation; instead of being fitted with wigs and skullcaps to show a receded hairline as he aged, his head was partially shorn, leaving only a few strands of hair on top—note the shots of Bernstein early in the film, such as when Thatcher and Kane quarrel over the *Inquirer*'s articles about the "Traction Trusts." Then, for his interviews with Thompson, when he portrayed an old man, Sloane's head was shaved completely. The inconvenience reportedly earned the actor an additional $2,400.

To age parts of Comingore's own skin from that of a young lady of twenty-one to that of a woman approaching middle age, Seiderman applied a mysterious solution to her skin that actually wrinkled it—although only temporarily.

Seiderman's processes were durable yet precise; once, when Welles suffered from a cold while shooting, Seiderman found that his hand-concocted adhesives wouldn't stick firmly to the actor's face. Seiderman discovered that because of Welles' illness, the acid balance of his perspiration had changed just enough to throw off the effectiveness of the adhesive preparation.

Unfortunately for all involved, the makeup was no less an ordeal because

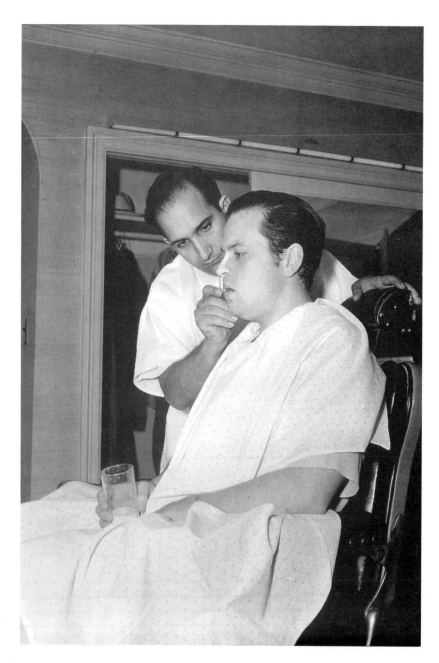

Four A.M. Seiderman prepares the twenty-five-year-old Welles for a four-hour makeup session that will add nearly fifty years to his face and body. The first step is the ever-present prosthesis to fill the length of Welles' nose.

of its brilliance. The most complex applications required as long as four hours for Seiderman to apply. Welles was often in his makeup chair as early as 3 A.M., depending on the extent of the aging required, eating a typical Wellesian breakfast of four eggs and a dozen strips of bacon while he enjoyed watching Seiderman work (Welles, an old hand at stage makeup, had dabbled in the craft since he was a boy, and thoroughly appreciated the makeup man's artistry). The shooting schedule was even more grueling for Seiderman. Working full-tilt in the wee hours of morning, and on call every day to do repairs,

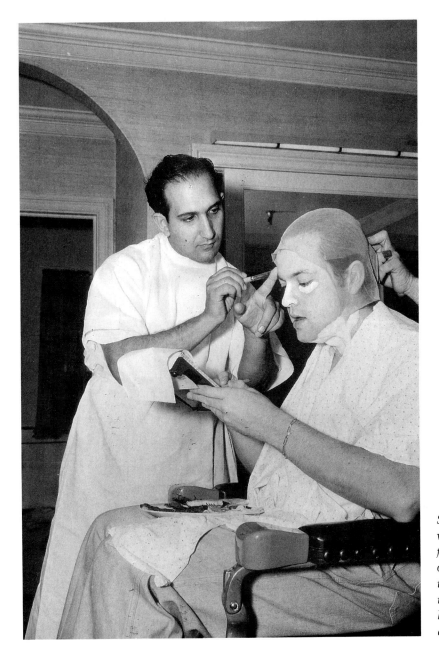

Seiderman first adds a neck wattle, and then laces on a fine mesh net. Welles carries on without missing a beat, taking notes about production while eating a typical breakfast: four eggs and a dozen strips of bacon.

he often slept on a cot in his laboratory so he could be ready for the next day's schedule.

The results of Seiderman's efforts were miraculous and thoroughly convincing, even under the unforgiving glare of Toland's head-on lighting. For Welles, who was often heavily padded as a man forty years his senior while he directed on the set or met with his technicians, wearing extensive makeup became second nature; at times he remained in makeup for as long as twenty-seven hours. Not once during an actual take did his makeup fail.

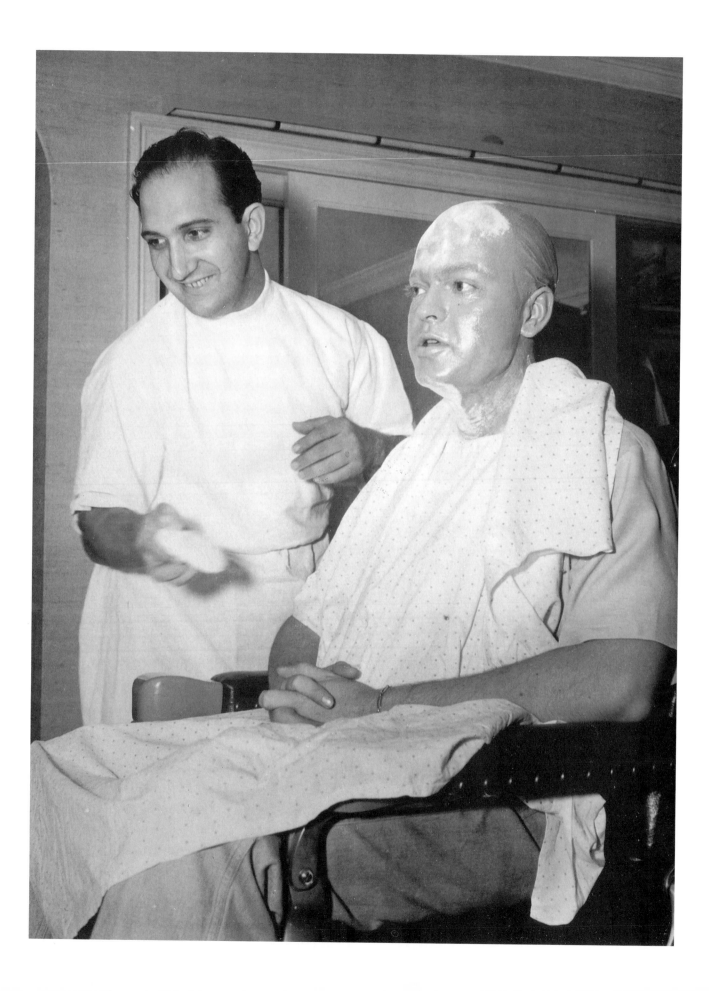

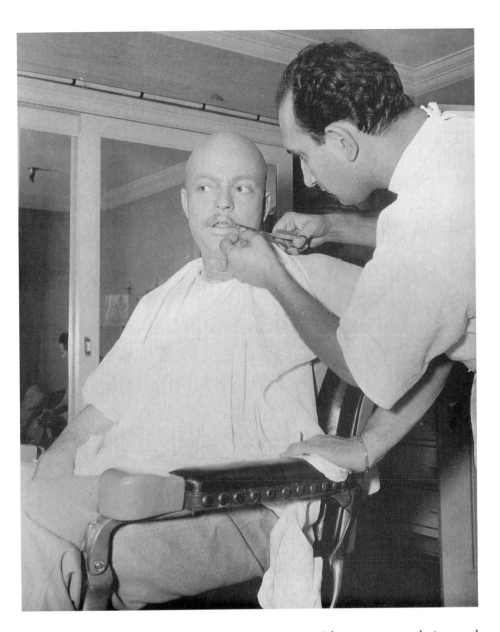

After more powdering and detailing, Seiderman glues on a mustache.

Seiderman adds a latex face appliance, already constructed, to give the appearance of age.

95

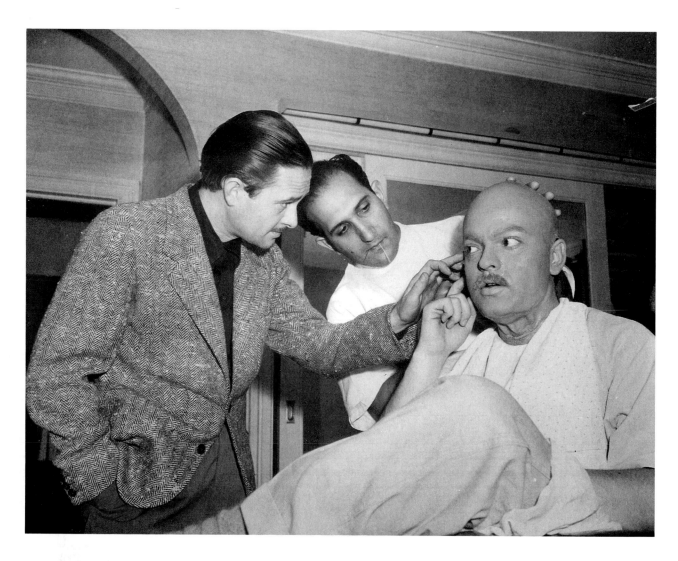

Cinematographer Gregg Toland stops by to check on Seiderman's progress. Note the difference between Welles' real eyes here, and the milky contact lenses added in later stages of makeup, which gave him the rheumy stare of an old man.

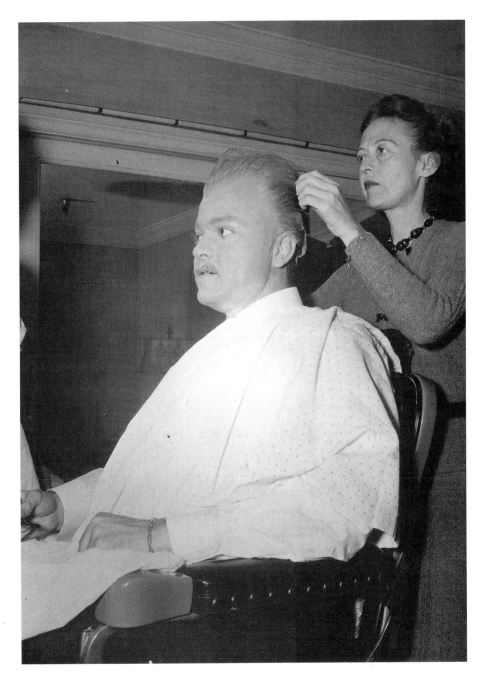

On goes a wig.

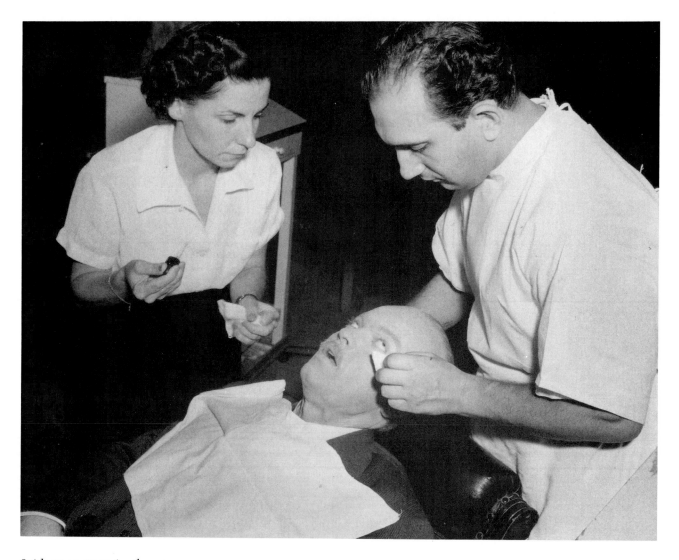

Seiderman pops in the contact lenses.

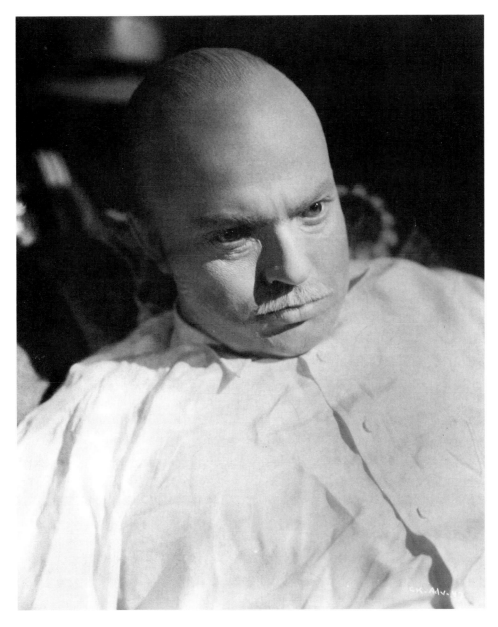

Four hours after the makeup session began, Welles, appearing seventy, emerges ready for a take.

Seiderman's makeup was complemented nicely by the costumes of Edward Stevenson and his staff, who produced clothing to reflect the fashion trends of more than seventy years, including thirty-seven changes for Welles alone. Stevenson and Seiderman, no doubt at Welles' request, wisely avoided dating the characters with stuffy turn-of-the-century fashions and hairstyles. For the nineteenth-century sequences, none of the principal characters looked "in period"—no fancy mustaches or overly rigid clothes—features that did dominate the original storyboards for the film.

During planning of the costumes, Dorothy Comingore provided an additional technical hurdle; she was pregnant when she signed to appear as Susan Alexander. However, Comingore's condition posed no problem for Welles. "It's all the better," he told her. "You're hired. If you start in it, it'll really prove to those bums that I'm going to finish the picture on time."

Comingore began to work almost immediately after signing her contract. Her first scenes show her meeting Kane when she was still quite slender; later, when she was noticeably pregnant, Toland relied on discreet camera angles or carefully positioned props to hide her condition. In her later appearances, working on jigsaw puzzles in Xanadu's Great Hall or being interviewed at her nightclub, she is either sprawled over the hearth in a long dressing gown, or sits square up against a table.

In the shot at Xanadu when Susan confronts Kane in her bedroom and had to be shown standing, she carried a muff and wore a fur stole over traveling clothes to hide her impending child (her daughter was born on January 4, 1941, two and a half months after principal photography was completed).

The logistical issues of using complex makeup and elaborate costumes created challenges of their own during the shooting. With Welles growing younger or older by decades depending on the scene, the production schedule practically revolved around his physical appearance. If the makeup wasn't planned perfectly, shooting could be delayed by hours while Welles returned to the makeup room for another session with Seiderman. For all his genius, Seiderman could do nothing to shrink the time required to prepare the actors.

To match the requirements of filming to the needs of the makeup, Welles and Seiderman planned with surgical precision the shots and their makeup requirements. For example, the breakfast table sequence—which in less than three minutes of film shows the decline of Kane's marriage over nine years, while both husband and wife age accordingly—was shot over two days, and the sequence was filmed in reverse order, with Welles in middle age during the first takes. As the shots were filmed, Seiderman removed the makeup layer by layer, until only the base makeup and Welles' nose prosthesis remained.

Welles wore a prosthesis to fill out the length of his nose in the film (in fact, Seiderman's work was nearly as extensive on Welles as a young man as

Dorothy Comingore, dressed as Susan Alexander for her opera debut, in a costume by Edward Stevenson.

Comingore, several months pregnant when the scenes of Susan leaving Kane were filmed, was filmed wearing traveling clothes and holding a muff to hide her condition.

when he is shown as a doddering septuagenarian). Sensitive throughout his career about his natural nose, which he considered a bit too pug for his otherwise powerful features, with few exceptions, Welles appeared on film with a prosthesis to give his nose a stronger line.

"Norman Mailer wrote once that when I was young, I was the most beautiful man anybody had ever seen," Welles recalled years later. "Yes! Made up for *Citizen Kane!*"

When the film debuted, Welles acknowledged Seiderman's contributions to *Citizen Kane* with full-page advertisements in both the *Hollywood Reporter* and *Daily Variety,* tributes in which Welles called Seiderman "the best makeup man in the world." Seventeen years later, Seiderman and Welles would take on no less a makeup challenge during the production of *Touch of Evil,* when the master makeup artist would reshape, discolor, and add mounds of padding to the actor—who even without extra layers by this time weighed more than three hundred pounds—to create the grotesque persona of Hank Quinlan, the murderous police detective.

*   *   *

Seiderman's makeup was only one indication that the Welles set was unlike any other in Hollywood. At every turn, the cast and crew alike were experimenting with new or improved techniques that their demanding director required to complete his vision for *Citizen Kane.*

The unconventional sets presented intriguing technical challenges, not the least of which was lighting. With full ceilings, there was no room for banks of powerful overhead lights which are the staple of Hollywood productions. With the occasional exception of a tiny spot, backlighting, or an overhead fill, every shot in the picture was lighted from the floor—nearly all from the front or the sides of the set—using as main light the double-arc broadside lamps developed primarily to shoot light-hungry Technicolor film. (Viewers can see the effects of the lighting by looking at the shadows, which stretch across the floors as if the scenes were shot outdoors at daybreak or sunset.)

Beyond the enhancements to artistry and realism that ceilings added to the production, they also provided technical benefits. The ceilings, nearly all of which were made of muslin stretched over frames, were acoustically transparent, so the sound technicians could place their microphones just above the roof and eliminate the ever-present curse of the cinematographer: microphone shadows—or even worse, the microphone actually peeping into the frame. Normally, Toland said, "One must always be on the lookout lest the mike or its shadow get into the picture. In this position, the microphones were always completely out of camera range."

Welles wore extensive amounts of makeup even while playing Kane as a man his own age. "I was the most beautiful man anybody had ever seen . . . made up for Citizen Kane," said Welles.

Toland's camera crew prepares to shoot Joseph Cotten and Everett Sloane at Kane's party for the staff of the Inquirer; the spotlight next to the camera is scarcely two feet from Cotten's face.

Lighting actually makes an intentional appearance in the picture. For Kane's party in the city room of the *Inquirer,* which celebrated the publisher's pirating of the *Chronicle*'s "greatest newspaper staff in the world," lights required for the shots became part of the scene.

To illuminate more than half of the set—a sequence that includes a long table flanked by rowdy newspapermen, a brass band, and sixteen dancing girls—Toland used a twenty-foot-long strip of footlights just to the left of the actors seated at the table.

From some angles, viewers can see the row of lights on the floor—Welles took no pains to hide the lights, and their appearance in the shot makes them seem like props for the party—

which they are. Welles whistles to summon the band, and then smoothly steps over the row of lights when the dancing girls arrive. Just before Kane says to Leland, "Are we going to declare war on Spain, or are we not?" the lights kick on, illuminating both performers and the ceiling as well. Later in the scene, the entire row of lights is visible on screen, and they blaze directly into the camera while Kane is parading with the dancing girls during the singing of the "Charley Kane" song.

To photograph some of Welles' most dramatic sequences, Toland positioned his camera below floor level; for several shots, holes were cut in the stage floor to bring the camera low enough to meet Welles' exacting demands (some sets

The strip of footlights for the party scene at the Inquirer.

were constructed on platforms as much as six feet above the stage floor so camera pits could be cut as needed). Among the shots that required this sort of carpentry are Kane's postelection confrontation with Leland, and Kane's destruction of Susan's room.

Some shots required complex off-camera choreography to meet the intricate requirements of the staging. Welles wanted to open the sequence of Kane's mother signing away his guardianship to Thatcher's bank by filming young Charles playing in the snow as seen through the window of the set; the camera would then pull back to show the boardinghouse with the adults inside discussing young Kane's fate while still showing the boy through the window outside.

To film the scene required perfect timing of camera movement, actors' performances, and cooperation from a breakaway trick table that was designed to snap into place as a camera dolly rolled back across the set past it. "It was," said Toland, "a complex mixture of art and mechanics."

Over and over again the shot went awry, with either equipment failing or actors miscuing. It took four days before Welles and Toland were happy with the results. The final take used in the film was terrific, but not perfect. If viewers listen carefully, they can hear the camera dolly back across the set and the table lock into position—the "clunk" of equipment just barely audible above Moorehead's footsteps across the board floor.

By using deep focus and careful staging, Welles and Toland created what stands as the most important photographic element of *Citizen Kane:* the placement of actors in positions on the set at angles and distances from each other far beyond the norm for a Hollywood film. Toland's careful photographic techniques allowed the camera to record objects at a range of twenty inches or several hundred feet with equal clarity, and Welles took every opportunity to place his characters, not according to standard Hollywood practices, but wherever the action should take them. The result produced scenes that were not merely innovative for innovation's sake, but demonstrations of how unconventional staging could enhance the action.

No shot shows better what Welles strived to accomplish than the scene in which Kane signs over control of his empire to Thatcher's bank during the Depression. As the shot begins, Bernstein, on the right side of the frame, reads aloud from the conditions of the agreement, his face only inches from the camera. To the left, Thatcher sits across the table. Kane is off camera to the right. When Kane enters the scene, he paces toward the rear of the set while he listens to Bernstein read, traveling more than forty feet away from the camera before he returns to the table to sign the documents. Throughout the entire shot—which appears without a cut—all three actors remain in crisp focus.

Later, when Leland and Kane argue after the doomed election, both actors wander across the *Inquirer* newsroom throughout the scene, at some points

The floor lighting is visible in camera range to the lower left. Note also the overhead fill light; Toland couldn't always accommodate Ferguson's seamless ceilings with lighting from the front.

The shot of Kane as a boy playing in the snow, a sequence that pulled the camera back through the set to pick up the action of Kane's mother signing over custody of the boy to Thatcher's bank. The shot required precise timing of actors, crew, and a camera dolly. The rolling dolly reveals itself in the film, by its just-audible rumble.

more than thirty feet from each other, at others only inches apart. One shot begins with the camera lens at floor level and Leland in the far right corner of the screen. At first, the only part of Kane visible is his foot and pant leg, which cover the left-hand side of the screen before he walks into view.

One of Toland's favorite examples of his own photography was his shot of the *Inquirer* staff members with a loving cup they present to Kane on his return from Europe. As Bernstein reads the inscription, his face is barely a foot from the camera. The cup is about three feet from the camera, and the extras surrounding it are placed at distances from three feet to ten feet

Toland and Welles line up the shot of the postcampaign confrontation between Leland and Kane. Several shots were filmed from angles so low that holes were cut in the set floor to accommodate camera and crew.

Welles lines up the beginning of the complex shot of young Kane in the snow.

away. Almost hidden by an actor's sleeve is a copyboy more than fifty feet from the camera who yells "Here he comes!" just before Kane enters the room. In spite of the extreme depth, Toland said, "the loving cup was in such sharp focus that the audience was able to read the inscription from it."

Toland used the same technique of grouping faces on screen in several films, among the most fondly remembered is his photography in *The Bishop's Wife,* which lovingly captures the rosy faces of the Mitchell Boychoir singing a Christmas hymn under the direction of angel Cary Grant.

One of *Citizen Kane*'s most famous deep-focus shots was actually an illusion accomplished in the camera. To shoot Susan's attempted suicide, Welles

Toland's deep-focus photography at its best in the scene in which Kane signs over control of his financially troubled empire to Thatcher's bank: Bernstein, only inches from the camera, Thatcher at midrange, and Kane as much as forty feet from the camera.

KANE

envisioned a shot with three separate points of interest: in the foreground, only inches from the camera, Susan's medicine and spoon; behind them, Susan lying in bed, breathing weakly and barely lit; in the far background, the door, which Kane breaks through.

To shoot the scene, Toland didn't use deep focus—he used math. The exact length of the scene was calculated in advance. Then, with Susan and the background dark, the close-up of the medicine and the spoon was lit and filmed. Without moving the camera, the film was counted backward to the exact point when the scene started and shot again—this time with Susan and the door lit, and the foreground dark. So effective is the photography that for many years most observers (including several critics who analyzed the shot) assumed it was a single take which had required complex lighting and deep focus.

* * *

On October 23, 1940, almost four months after shooting began—or about three months, according to RKO's official start date—Welles wrapped principal photography for *Citizen Kane.* In spite of injury, inexperience, and the extraordinary nature of the production, Welles finished only eleven shooting days behind schedule. But with nearly three months of editing, special effects, music, and other postproduction yet to come, work on *Citizen Kane* had just begun.

* * *

Whatever cinematic elements could not be accomplished for *Citizen Kane* with cleverly designed sets or innovative camera angles were added in postproduction through an array of special effects. Considering that *Citizen Kane* is first and foremost a relatively straightforward drama, the number of effects required for the film is surprising; by some estimates, as much as half the footage required optical wizardry in one form or another—matte paintings, back projections, optical printing, and models—to accomplish the effects that Welles required. In fact, viewers can assume that virtually every exterior shot —Xanadu, the *Inquirer* office building, Kane's campaign speech, the caravan of cars along the beach going to Kane's picnic, and many others—were completed with optical effects, and many tighter shots were handled the same way as well.

The RKO camera effects department, headed by Vernon Walker, completed the effects for *Citizen Kane;* assigned to various aspects of the work were effects cameraman Russell Cully, montage effects expert Douglas Travers, matte artist Mario Larrinage, and optical printer Linwood Dunn (Dunn was already a legend in Hollywood for his invention of the Acme-Dunn optical printer, which could produce a variety of on-film effects). Cully and Dunn used matte paintings, back projections, and other optical tricks with great impact in *Citizen Kane*, to add doorways, entire buildings, and in general to give the film a far more lavish look that would only have been possible without effects for double the production's cost. The exteriors of Xanadu, for example, didn't exist; they were the creation of RKO artists who produced a painting of the castle which was fitted optically to other images of the Kane estate.

Many of the slickest effects were accomplished with a standard Hollywood technique called a "wipe," which permits the butter-smooth transition from real action to special effect and, if necessary, back to real action again. In the Thatcher Library, the *Thinker*like statue of Walter Thatcher is a model; as the camera pans down from the statue, an unseen wipe provides the transition from the model to the real action below it.

The same effect was also used with perfection in one of *Citizen Kane*'s most memorable scenes. When, in Susan's debut as an opera singer, the camera rises through the opera house's rafters to show two stagehands—one pinching his nose at her performance—a wipe takes the shot from the live action of Susan's performance, to a model of the rafters, and back to live action for the shot of the stagehands.

Some special effects shots weren't originally planned, but were needed to keep production moving along. Originally, the scenes shot of Joseph Cotten as an old man were supposed to be filmed on an elaborate hospital set. But because Welles injured his ankle, the shooting schedule was shuffled, and Cotten's scenes were advanced so far up in the production schedule that the set wasn't yet built. Cotten and William Alland did the scene against a blank wall; the eerie hospital background and wheelchair-bound patients were added later with a series of slides projected onto a screen.

However, one of the most oft-mentioned special effects in *Citizen Kane* wasn't intentional at all. When Susan walks out on Kane, the scene opens with an abrupt shot of a screeching cockatoo. The cockatoo—which appears on screen for only a moment—has no eye; the background of the Florida coastline shows through plainly where the eye should have been. The missing eye, the meaning of which was long a subject of speculation among film writers and students, turned out to be only the result of an accident in the special effects lab.

* * *

Not the least of *Citizen Kane*'s merits was the depth and complexity of the sound. Welles' background in radio clearly had taught him how sound can drive home even seemingly innocuous scenes. In his radio programs, Welles

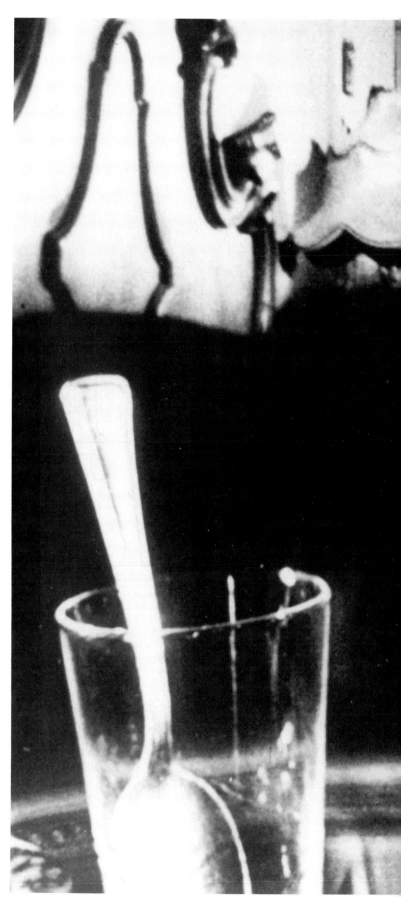

Susan's suicide attempt. The depth of focus for the scene was accomplished by first lighting and shooting the glass and spoon in the foreground; the film was then rewound and reshot, the second time with the rest of the scene lit, and the foreground dark.

The special effects used to depict Susan's opera debut take the shot from live action . . .

. . . to a model of the opera hall rafters . . .

took extraordinary steps to capture just the right combination of sounds for a particular scene. (On one occasion, to achieve just the right echoing tone, two actors had to perform lying down in a bathroom stall at CBS and perform with their heads wedged under a toilet.)

From the nearly imperceptible tinkling of crystal wind chimes in the background of the shot of the snowglobe at Kane's death, to the booming cannonade of Kane's campaign speech, *Citizen Kane* is awash in carefully blended individual sounds, all crafted for the audio track by Bailey Fesler, James G. Stewart, and Harry Essman.

Careful listening reveals a marvelous melding of sound and action; the abrupt clank of a typewriter, the echo-filled conversations between Kane and Susan in Xanadu, or the solitary steamship whistle sounding under Leland's interview with Thompson that shows the hospital is near the river. Some individual sounds were heavily manipulated, such as the rasping crackle of Welles whispering the dying word "Rosebud," an effect achieved by blending two separate soundtracks of Welles uttering the word.

The more intricate sound sequences were handled just as carefully as the makeup or the scoring. To create the auditory power of Kane's speech— Welles' goal was for the scene to "sound like Madison Square Garden with 10,000 people in it"—Stewart worked nearly a month, first combining dia-

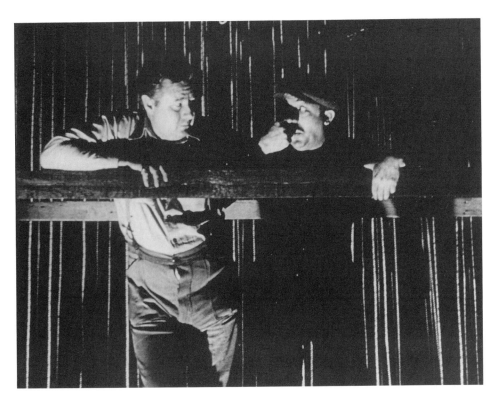

. . . and back to live action again.

logue together with rerecordings of the same speech with echo added. He then added applause, laughter, cheers, and cries of acknowledgment, all blended smoothly into one sequence.

The carefully constructed sound served not only to complement the action, but, with direction from Welles, also enhanced the plot. As Boss Jim Gettys leaves Susan's apartment building with Kane screaming "I'm going to send you to Sing Sing" behind him, the last word of the sentence is drowned into insignificance by the mere "beep-beep" of a car horn.

*   *   *

Editing Welles' footage into a final print was accomplished by Robert Wise, an RKO staff member assigned to the production. With a film as carefully planned and photographed as *Citizen Kane,* it would seem that Wise's role in postproduction would be limited. Nevertheless, to assemble all the diverse elements involved in such an elaborate production into a rough cut required several months of work.

Welles, as was his style with all of his other trusted technicians, made his requests of Wise and then let his editor work unencumbered by a hovering producer-director-star. "The process of editing was pretty much the same with Orson directing as it was with my other projects," said Wise. "He told me what he wanted to achieve, but he didn't hang over my shoulder."

Two of Wise's editing contributions were particularly memorable. The newsreel sequence about Kane's life, called *News on the March,* was created in cooperation with RKO's own newsreel department. The sequence meshed 127 pieces of film; to give the footage a tattered look on screen, Wise and assistant Mark Robson copied some segments repeatedly to simulate age, or dragged them across a concrete floor to actually inflict damage on the negative.

"Mark and I would be in our cutting room, running pieces of film through cheesecloth filled with sand to age it for the newsreel," Wise said. "People who didn't know what was going on would see us at work and say, 'these guys are crazy.'"

The result was a true-to-life imitation of an actual *March of Time* newsreel. The smooth intercutting of old and new footage not only thoroughly summarizes Kane's life, but also sets the stage for later flashbacks and abrupt shifts of content that fill the rest of the film.

News on the March was perhaps too realistic—when *Citizen Kane* eventually screened in Italy following World War II, Welles recalled that many theater patrons booed, hissed and shook their fists at the projection box, because they thought the newsreel material was actually bad photography.

Wise also edited one of the most talked-about scenes of the picture, the

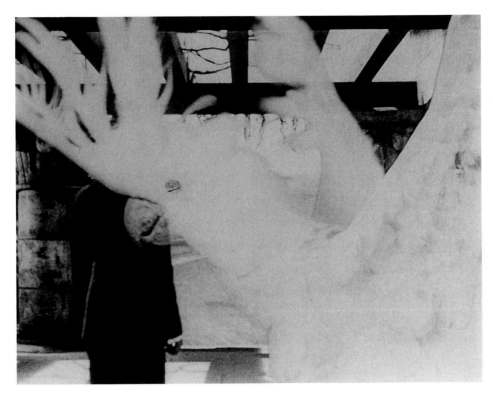

The screeching cockatoo, with its missing eye.

breakfast table montage, which captures the rapid decline of Kane's first marriage, beginning with the innocent mutual adoration of newlyweds and ending nine years later with the stony silence of the irreconcilable couple. Wise worked for six weeks, on and off, to complete the editing of this single scene, shifting the sequence of film segments, dialogue and swish pans to achieve just the right tempo for the action and the failure of Kane's marriage.

*   *   *

To score his film, Welles called on Bernard Herrmann, a colleague from their days together at CBS. Herrmann had served as music director for "Mercury Theatre on the Air," and Welles persuaded him not only to produce a traditional film score, but one that required the difficult task of including authentically re-created moments of grand opera as well.

Herrmann composed and recorded for nearly three months, supervising the recording of a forty-five-piece studio orchestra on the RKO lot. The full-bodied sound, which seems much more akin to that of a full symphonic orchestra nearly three times that size, was achieved through Herrmann's careful orchestration and directing.

The generous time allowed for scoring and recording was rare in Holly-

The heavy "wear-and-tear" look to some of the film in the newsreel sequence was produced by intentionally inflicting damage to the film, including dragging it across a concrete floor or rubbing it with sand. "People would walk by," said editor Robert Wise of observers who watched this "aging" the film, "and say, 'these guys are crazy.'"

wood. "This not only gave me ample time to think about the film and to work out a general artistic plan for the score," Herrmann recalled, "but also enabled me to do my own orchestration and conducting."

Although Herrmann was given the luxury of time, the challenges were still extreme. Because scenes of the opera were such an integral part of the plot, Herrmann began work early in the film's production. (The opera segments, Herrmann recalled, were composed in the style of the "19-century French-Oriental operatic school.") Dorothy Comingore's performances of Herrmann's arias were sung by Jean Forward, a soprano from the San Francisco opera. Herrmann structured the score so Forward, otherwise a fine singer, was forced to sing above her range, straining the performance so Comingore, as Susan, sounded painfully weak-voiced.

For the rest of the score, Herrmann worked on the film one reel at a time, as it was being shot and cut. "In this way, I had a sense of the picture being built, and of my own music being a part of that building," Herrmann said. "Most musical scores in Hollywood are written after the film is entirely finished, and the composer must adapt his music to the scenes on the screen. In many scenes in *Citizen Kane,* an entirely different method was used—many of the sequences being tailored to match the music."

Herrmann composed a four-note theme for Kane (the theme is heard in the first bars of music in the film). He also composed a haunting theme to evoke the secret of Rosebud (this passage plays in several variations throughout the first scenes of *Citizen Kane*, most distinctly as the camera pans up the fence bordering Xanadu, and after the light goes out in Kane's room just before he dies). The theme for Rosebud, Herrmann said, "is heard again and again throughout the film under various guises, and if followed closely, is a clue to the ultimate identity of Rosebud itself."

Herrmann's background in radio and his familiarity with the split-second requirements of timing a broadcast came in handy when Welles' frequent tinkering with the film forced changes in the score and the soundtrack.

"Most composers would go right through the roof if you made any changes in the film after the music was written," recalled editor Robert Wise. "We gave Bernie his cues and then later we found out that Orson wanted to make some changes in the film. I was expecting big problems, but Bernie would make those adjustments and changes right from the score so fast it didn't seem to faze him—that must have come from his days in radio. He would look at the score and say, 'Well, let's see—we can drop from bar four to bar eight, and pick up here,' and it was done."

Herrmann's composition was hailed as a masterpiece of film scoring. From eerie woodwinds playing through the mists of Xanadu to the snappy horns of Manhattan, Herrmann's themes provided gentle background or crashing overtones as needed, always complementing the action perfectly. There are tender moments as well; as Susan recovers from her suicide attempt, the street music playing outside the hotel is a gentle honky-tonk version of her operatic solo.

In addition to powerful dramatic elements in his score, Herrmann inserted many humorous moments as well. His lovely lilting sweep of the "Rosebud" theme heard behind young Charles playing in the snow stops abruptly with the "plunk" of violin strings when the boy's snowball hits the boardinghouse sign. When Thompson departs the Thatcher Library with the crack, "Goodbye everybody, thanks for the use of the hall," the blat of trumpets is more sarcastic than any horse laugh.

Herrmann did not compose the "Charley Kane" song, which acts as the publisher's theme song throughout the picture. The music was taken from the Mexican song, "A Poco No," and new lyrics were written by lyricist Harry Ruby. However, Herrmann did use the song extensively in his score, combining the light melody with some of the film's most dramatic and breathtaking music.

Herrmann's experience on *Citizen Kane* opened Hollywood's doors for the composer, who ultimately became one of the most distinguished artists in film. He produced innovative scores for more than thirty pictures (including

The breakfast table montage, in less than three minutes of film, shows the deterioration of Kane's first marriage.

Bernard Herrmann

seven of Hitchcock's best), in addition to carrying out more traditional composing and conducting assignments around the world. But *Citizen Kane* was Herrmann's first and—in many ways—best experience in Hollywood.

"I had heard of the many handicaps that exist for a composer in Hollywood," Herrmann said. "One was the great speed with which scores often had to be written—sometimes in as little as two or three weeks. Another was that

Herrmann composed this theme for "Rosebud." The theme crops up throughout the film and provides musical "clues" to Rosebud's identity.

the composer seldom had time to do his own orchestration. And again—that once the music was written and conducted, the composer had little to say about the sound levels or dynamics of the score in the finished film.

"Not one of these conditions prevailed during the production of *Citizen Kane.*"

* * *

Early in January—after five months of scriptwriting and planning, an eighty-two-day shooting schedule, and nearly twelve weeks of postproduction, the first rough prints of *Citizen Kane* were ready to view. The film was, indeed, still rough—it was shy some special effects and final takes of several scenes, bits of music, and a few lines of dialogue which needed to be relooped. Nevertheless, the studio was ready to schedule the premiere of its newest picture—the release date for RKO Production #281 was set for February 14, 1941.

4. Conflict

Hollywood harbors no secrets. In 1940—as now—it was nearly impossible to slow a movie industry rumor mill, and the whisperings late that year had a lot to do with the goings-on behind the closed doors of Orson Welles' set.

The rumblings began early. Welles never intended to keep secret that his picture portrayed the life of a newspaper publisher. But he was only midway into production when the rumor began to spread that the film was a near-factual exposé of one of the most powerful men in America, William Randolph Hearst, a media giant of his age whose empire at the height of its power included twenty-six newspapers, sixteen magazines, eleven radio stations, and five news services.

As a result of the scuttlebutt, Welles and *Citizen Kane* wound up a pawn in an age-old back-stabbing game. Columnists Louella Parsons and Hedda Hopper, two not-so-friendly rivals in the Hollywood gossip mill, but each a loyal supporter of Hearst, used the young director as yet more fodder in their continuing battle in print and behind the scenes. Each columnist showed just how cruelly she could wield her power in the entertainment industry in attempts to discredit and suppress the film.

Although both writers had been among Welles' most ardent supporters when he first burst on the Hollywood scene, now, independently of each other, they would do everything in their power to become his judge, jury, and executioner. Parsons and Hopper managed to whip Hollywood into a frenzy over the release of *Citizen Kane,* creating a tornado of public and private pressure that would eventually inflict massive damage on the film's popularity and financial success.

Of course, in the first few weeks of 1941, whether or not *Citizen Kane* actually depicted William Randolph Hearst made no difference; Louella Parsons believed it, Hedda Hopper believed it, and Hearst's legion of lawyers, editors, and informants most certainly believed it. The Hearst organization—with or without the old man's blessing will be forever unclear—made a monumental effort to stop *Citizen Kane,* first by trying to destroy the film, then by working to suppress distribution, and finally by attempting to ignore its existence. The pressure soon became so extreme that there were moments when *Citizen Kane* was in grave danger of never being seen, and winding up, negative and all, in the incinerator.

From the first, all Hollywood knew that something unusual was brewing on the Welles' set. With reports of Welles' flair for the spectacular preceding him, it didn't take long for Hollywood insiders to speculate that the fictional story Orson Welles was cooking up over at RKO might not be so fictional after all.

As early as September 1940, with Welles barely a month into production, rumors about *Citizen Kane*'s possible links to Hearst appeared in the national press. The September 16 edition of *Newsweek* reported that "The script of Orson Welles' first movie, *Citizen Kane,* was sent to William Randolph Hearst for perusal after columnists had hinted it dealt with his life. Hearst approved it without comment."

The *Newsweek* article included no attribution that might have identified who gave the script to Hearst, or if indeed this "approval" actually occurred. Most likely, the story developed when reporters, who visited the set from time to time, began to piece together bits and pieces about the plot, and based on sketchy information, concluded that the film was about Hearst. The leaks were aided by RKO executive J. R. McDonough—openly an opponent of the Welles unit—who, without permission, sent a copy of the *Citizen Kane* script to RKO's New York office and then didn't control its distribution. The script was copied and eventually leaked to reporters—". . . exactly," said Welles in a list of grievances about mistreatment by RKO managers, "what we were trying to prevent."

Three months later, with the film nearly complete, the rumor began to spread. Two days before the end of 1940, the *Hollywood Reporter* broke the news that *Friday* magazine, a highly sensationalized, bile-injected scandal sheet, was ready to print the first story about the plot of *Citizen Kane.*

"The Orson Welles interests are concerned about it," wrote publisher W. R. Wilkerson. ". . . seems most of the dope on this hushed-up yarn was dug up in New York by *Friday* editors who knew Mercury players returning from parts in the flicker."

Welles and his staff were well advised to be concerned. *Friday,* with sensational headlines splashed across its cover and a rabidly fascist-baiting stance, called itself "The Magazine That Dares to Tell the Truth." Its oft-stated credo under publisher Dan Gillmor was "Problem Number One is the fascist drive against the American Democracy." With headlines like "Does Basketball Kill?" and "Ford's Secret Gestapo Exposed," the weekly magazine, during its short run in the early 1940s, chewed up and spit out whatever and whoever it liked, often with little regard for the truth.

Apparently, the magazine's conspiratorial diggings extended to young Hollywood directors, because seemingly without provocation or reason, *Friday* did everything it could to ruin Orson Welles.

Friday didn't carry its story about *Citizen Kane* until January 17, 1941, so it wasn't the first publication to reveal points about the plot. However, what the magazine did print was a photo feature about *Citizen Kane*—but instead of showcasing the film and its stars, it published a sheer hatchet job in a point-by-point "exposé" comparison between Welles' story and the life of William Randolph Hearst.

As it turned out, *Friday*'s writers hadn't even previewed the film or visited the set before they prepared their article. The writers, who obviously had no love for either Welles or Hearst, printed seven photographs and captions that "revealed" how plot points of *Citizen Kane* virtually matched Hearst's life, conveniently making up most of their facts about both the film and the real-life publisher as they went along.

The story accompanying the photos was even worse and was loaded with slurs about Welles and his work habits. "Orson Welles' first motion picture, *Citizen Kane,* had better be strictly colossal, or Hollywood will give him the old heave-ho back to Mars where he came from," the story began. "He came two years ago and it has taken him that long to produce a picture. Most of the time, Orson was amusing himself. His imported casts grew beards and cut them off, or dyed their blonde hair black, as Orson's newest idea succeeded its predecessor."

When *Friday* eventually got around to talking about *Citizen Kane,* it drilled home the point that Welles kept a closed set because he had something to hide—namely that his film was about Hearst. "There was only one [copy of the] script," Friday pointed out. "Orson wrote it and has been sleeping with it under his pillow."

Friday saved the worst for last. The article closed with this capper: "Louella Parsons, Hollywood's correspondent for Hearst, has been praising Welles lavishly, giving *Citizen Kane* a terrific advance build-up. When informed of these outbursts of praise, Welles said, 'This is something I cannot understand. Wait until the woman finds out that the picture's about her boss.' "

The *Friday* article did a marvelous job of reinforcing what people were already starting to believe. But even before it appeared, storm clouds were beginning to rise against *Citizen Kane;* the timing of the *Friday* article would only add to the tempest.

On January 3, barely two weeks before the article hit the newsstands, Welles showed the film for the first time to those outside the studio. The trade press called it "a small group of friends," but the small audience also included one extremely interested and angry reporter: Hedda Hopper, the nationally syndicated columnist whose articles appeared locally in the *Los Angeles Times.*

Welles hadn't invited Hopper, even though he had promised her months before that she would be included in their first audience. From the first, Hopper had been among those who publicly supported Welles. More than a year before, she had stoutly defended Welles when the rest of the motion picture industry was screaming about the huge mistake RKO had made by signing him.

"Too bad Orson Welles isn't an Englishman," Hopper wrote in September 1939. "If he had been, Hollywood would never have given him such a run-around. We reserve that for our own citizens. Mr. Welles doesn't scare easily and I'm thinking he'll make Hollywood sit up and beg for mercy."

But when Hopper saw a note about the screening in the *Hollywood Reporter,* she certainly recalled Welles' promise. Her angry phone call to Welles' office generated an immediate and apologetic telegram, which once again renewed his offer for the columnist to attend the first screening.

"Dearest Hedda," Welles began, "I owe you the biggest apology of my life and here it comes. Drake [Herbert Drake, Mercury's publicist] said, 'The magazine people—*Look* and *Life*—have to make their deadline, so we must show them the picture no matter how bad or incomplete very soon.' I said, 'Must we?' He said, 'We must.'

". . . [I] fully realize I have broken a solemn promise that you'd be the first to see *Kane.* Please understand and forgive. Come tonight if you must, but it still stinks. Many shots are missing or only tests are cut in and we need music like Britain needs planes. Love, Orson."

That night, Hopper and five others became the first people outside Welles' inner circle to see *Citizen Kane.* To Hopper, there was no question that Charles Foster Kane was in reality William Randolph Hearst. "What I saw appalled me," Hopper recalled years later. "It was an impudent, murderous trick, even for the boy genius, to perpetrate on a newspaper giant."

Hopper warned Welles that he would never get away with what she thought was such an obvious slander against Hearst. Welles insisted that his film would stand on its merits, no matter what Hopper assumed. Then Hopper took the first step in ruining whatever chance for early success *Citizen Kane* might have had: she called Hearst and told the publisher that *Citizen Kane* was actually a thinly disguised story about him.

Hedda Hopper. "It was an impudent, murderous trick," she said of Citizen Kane.

Although Hopper worked for Hearst's competition, she had always been friendly with the publisher. But Hopper's "friendly" call accomplished more than just warning a close associate of trouble ahead. Not only did Hopper tattle on Welles, she also took the opportunity to twist a knife into her old rival, Louella Parsons, motion picture editor and columnist for Hearst's International News Service.

Parsons too had been a Welles supporter from the beginning, more so even than Hopper. From the day Welles arrived in Hollywood, Parsons tracked his every move in her column, and she provided plenty of solid backing to the young director when he was on tenuous footing during the failures of *Heart of Darkness* and *The Smiler with a Knife*.

In a column in October 1939, on Friday the 13th, Parsons said, "If Mr. Welles makes a great picture, I'll be the first to say so. If he makes money we will all have to eat our words, and I for one will do it gladly, for we need good pictures. Furthermore, we cannot deny that Welles is a brilliant young man." On New Year's Eve 1939, in her summary of a year called the best in motion picture history, Parsons said, "Orson Welles wins the honor of being the most discussed personality to come to the films in 1939."

Earlier, when Parsons was invited to the first official day of shooting on the *Citizen Kane* set, she gushed, "I can hardly wait until tomorrow at 5 P.M. to see the great Orson Welles in action." When it turned out she had to miss the press party because of other commitments, she caught up with him three weeks later on the set during the filming of the opera scenes. Parsons devoted a full column to Welles, which in the *Los Angeles Examiner* was topped with a photo of Welles in costume as a middle-aged Kane. Parsons described him as a "remarkable young man," "a brilliant youth," and "a genius."

In spite of all the accolades, when, early in the film's production, Parsons too heard the rumors that *Citizen Kane* was about Hearst, she confronted Welles with the issue. "When I heard that the film he was making was about Mr. Hearst," Parsons said in her memoirs, "I called him to ask if this was so."

" 'Take my word for it,' he said. 'It isn't. It's about a completely fictional publisher.'

"I took his word, and so informed the Hearst editors, who kept insisting that it did concern Mr. Hearst."

Years later, Parsons was still bitter about what happened next. By allowing Hopper to attend the first screening of *Citizen Kane*, Parsons said that "Orson pulled one of the classic double crosses of Hollywood."

What Welles could have gained by "double-crossing" Parsons, the most powerful columnist in Hollywood, is anybody's guess, but what made Parsons even angrier was Hopper's phone call to Hearst. By telling Hearst about the film, Hopper not only tipped off Parsons' boss, but she also showed Hearst that Parsons had been duped.

"As the story was reported to me," Parsons recalled, "Hopper said, 'Mr. Hearst, I don't know why Louella hasn't told you this picture is about you.' Mr. Hearst thanked her."

Then Hearst himself talked to Parsons—an event that Hopper described in these words: "Across the cerulean Hollywood sky the clouds obscured the sun, yes, and the moon too. Mr. Hearst called Louella, and when she gathered that I had seen the picture and that it did, in fact, have much to do with her boss' life, her sky fell right down around her ears."

Parsons didn't recall the conversation with quite the same Technicolor melodrama. Parsons simply said, "Mr. Hearst called me and asked that arrangements be made for me and two of his lawyers to see *Citizen Kane.*"

She did precisely that. On January 9, Parsons saw the rough cut of *Citizen Kane,* in the company of Hearst executive Oscar Lawler and A. Laurence Mitchell, a Hearst attorney.

Louella Parsons' belief that Welles was a "boy genius" would change abruptly after she saw his first film.

"I must say now, so many years later, that I am still horrified by the picture," Parsons later wrote. "It was a cruel, dishonest caricature. It was done in the worst of taste. The boy genius certainly used all his talents just to do a hatchet job."

Parsons walked out of the screening room before the film was over—although her chauffeur stayed long enough to say, "You made a right fine picture, Mr. Welles." The columnist had witnessed a film that, as far as she was concerned, slandered one of the men she admired most, and even worse, she had been humiliated by her chief rival in the process. Parsons never spoke another word to Welles. Her relationship with the "brilliant young man" was over.

However, Parsons was by no means finished with Welles' picture. She lashed out with a vengeance and spent months trying to coerce everyone of importance in the industry who would listen to her to suppress the film and prevent it from being booked into theaters.

Parsons moved fast. That same day, most likely with no guidance from Hearst's lawyers, Parsons called George Schaefer's office at RKO in New York and threatened, noted a nervous secretary, "one of the most beautiful lawsuits in history if they release *Citizen Kane.*"

The Hearst machinery moved swiftly as well, this time most certainly with the lawyers' assent. Within hours, the whole organization was on the alert and in action against RKO, Welles, and *Citizen Kane.* On January 9, all mention of Welles and his film were banned outright from Hearst publications. Even worse for RKO, all of the studio's other films were expelled from Hearst papers—both in advertising and in articles.

In some cities, the order took effect with incredible speed. Many Hearst papers, including the *Los Angeles Examiner,* dropped reviews of *Kitty Foyle,* a Ginger Rogers hit and one of RKO's most important films of the year, from late editions that same day.

Parsons wasted no time keeping the trade papers informed of pressure against RKO. On January 10, *Daily Variety* carried the details of the ban under the headline, HEARST BANS RKO FROM PAPERS. To further strengthen the threat, all of the motion picture studios were put on notice that they too would suffer for Welles' crimes.

"As a result of the fury, Hearst papers will keep up a continuous shellfire against the entire industry, using employment of foreigners instead of 'idle Americans' as ammunition," wrote *Variety.* Five days later, the same publication moaned that "All film companies may suffer because of Hearst's peeve at Welles' *Kane.*" When two days later, *Friday*'s story appeared, the magazine might as well have poured gasoline on an inferno that was already out of control.

Threats to seek an injunction against the picture and to stop its distribution were rumored endlessly, but never took solid form. Meanwhile, RKO stood solidly—for the moment—behind Welles and his picture. "There is no serious consideration," George Schaefer told reporters, "to withhold *Citizen Kane* from release."

But with Parsons' prodding, a threat in more diabolical form sprang up in Hollywood. Parsons encouraged Louis B. Mayer, production chief at MGM, head of the most formidable studio in Hollywood and arguably the most powerful man in Hollywood, to bluntly suggest a power play that would have ended the irritant of *Citizen Kane* forever. Mayer, through his bosses in New York, proposed that the Hollywood studios—other than RKO—should form a fund to buy the negative of *Citizen Kane,* along with all of the prints, and destroy them.

Mayer asked Nicholas Schenck, president of Loews, the holding company for MGM, to meet with Schaefer in New York. "Louie has asked me to speak to you about this picture," Schenck told the RKO president. "He is prepared to pay you what it cost, which he understands is $800,000, if you will destroy the negative and all the prints."

Schaefer didn't say yes, but he didn't say no right away either. "Such an extraordinary suggestion coming from a man in your position must be carefully considered," he replied.

But Schenck corrected him, for the record. "The request comes from Louie," Schenck said. "Not me."

The RKO board was divided about how to handle *Citizen Kane.* Schaefer and others, of course, were set to release it; but once trouble started, several others on the board were strongly opposed to the film ever being viewed by the public. Mayer's offer didn't help to solidify support.

But there were bigger issues at stake that few outside of RKO knew. Two of the principal stockholders of RKO were the Rockefeller family and industrialist Floyd Odlum, chairman of the Atlas Corporation. As part of their vast holdings, both the Rockefellers and Odlum held large interests in Chase National Bank, one of Hearst's principal lenders. "The owners of RKO, therefore, have an interest in the financial stability and solvency of Hearst," *Variety* reported. But the newspaper also reported that Odlum was neutral on the issue of *Citizen Kane* and would leave the decision to Schaefer.

But the long-awaited lawsuit never came. Parsons recalled that Hearst himself prevented his company from taking actual legal action. "I don't believe in lawsuits," Parsons reported Hearst saying. "Besides, I have no desire to give the picture any more publicity."

Strangely, with all of the public fuss over the suppression of *Citizen Kane,* this conversation recalled by Parsons is the only public acknowledgment that

Hearst himself knew that his organization was taking action against RKO, Welles, and *Citizen Kane.* Hearst's only request on record was the one that asked Parsons and the attorneys to view the film. There is no other evidence that the publisher personally gave orders to take action against Welles. As far as anyone knows, or has ever admitted publicly, Hearst never discussed the issue with anyone. "But then," as one of his associates said nearly a half-century later, "making a direct request wasn't how Mr. Hearst would have done it anyway."

Of course, with coverage of Hearst vs. *Citizen Kane* often assuming the aspect of a day-to-day battle royal in the non-Hearst press, it would have been impossible for the publisher not to notice what was going on—thus approval by his silence amounted to, in fact, an endorsement of his organization's actions.

An actual suit would have been risky business for either side. To win, the Hearst companies would have been forced to prove malice or damages, both of which were extremely unlikely. This was especially true for Hearst, one of the most public of public figures—a man who openly lived with his mistress, Marion Davies, while still legally married to another woman. In the harsh light of a courtroom, there was absolutely nothing factual—or more to the point, nothing potentially libelous—that could specifically link Kane to Hearst.

On the other hand, RKO could hardly afford to be involved in a legal action that, if lost, would have worsened the company's already shaky financial footing. Tying up the film in litigation would be victory enough for Hearst, potentially leaving it unreleasable for years. A far greater weapon against RKO was the continuing threat of a lawsuit which hung over the studio and any exhibitor who showed the film—a nasty prospect which lingered long after *Citizen Kane* premiered.

Finally, on January 22, RKO did fight back. Schaefer brought Welles to New York to meet with RKO's board and make his case for the film's survival.

To fend off attempts within the motion picture industry to force RKO to shelve or destroy *Citizen Kane,* Schaefer screened the film in New York for the corporate heads and lawyers of all of the studios' holding companies. Editor Robert Wise flew to New York with a work print of the film—a harrowing two-and-a-half-day journey through midwinter blizzards in a two-engine plane.

With Welles in attendance, Schaefer showed *Citizen Kane* in the private projection room at Radio City Music Hall, the goal being to drum up support for the film. However, RKO's president knew only too well that the picture might just as easily be scuttled.

"The idea of the screening was to show the picture to all of the big bosses so they could make a judgment as to whether they should tell RKO to shelve it or release it," Wise recalled.

Before the screening, Schaefer, Wise remembered, let Welles have his say. "Orson talked to them first, and presented his case for the film," Wise said. "I can't recall the exact words he said, but I've never seen him give a better performance—he really charmed the hell out of them."

Judgment came the next day: the film could be released, with some judicious editing. "The next day I got a list of changes that they all felt were necessary," Wise said. "They were all minor—a little trim here, a new loop of dialogue there. Orson didn't mind the changes—he was relieved."

The "minor changes" took six weeks to complete, with Wise coordinating the editing by telephone with assistant Mark Robson in Los Angeles, while Wise himself relooped the dialogue with actors who had already returned to New York. When the changes were completed, Robson recut a new work print and shipped it to Wise for a second showing for the studio representatives.

"The second time we screened it only for the lawyers," Wise said. "They said OK, and that was it."

The resulting compromise trimmed a scant three minutes and twenty-four seconds from the final print. Among the deletions were several references to Hearst in the opening newsreel (although the publisher's name still remained in the film), an assortment of comments about Kane's irresponsible journalism and Susan's drinking, and references to presidential assassinations (material about Kane's support of political assassination had featured prominently in Mankiewicz's early drafts, and had been whittled to a brief mention in the final print before it was cut entirely).

In addition, Paul Stewart looped in two new lines of dialogue: where Raymond the butler told Thompson on two occasions that Kane "was a little gone in the head," the dubbed-in lines were changed to the old man "acted kind of funny sometimes."

About the same time, RKO announced that the studio would proceed with a monstrous advertising campaign, a blitz that studio chief Schaefer called "one of the most far-reaching ever launched for an attraction by RKO Radio Pictures."

The campaign included two-color advertisements in, among other magazines, *Life, Look,* and the *Saturday Evening Post.* All three would later run large photo features about the film as well. RKO planned to reach fifty million readers with its promotion. The film would premiere at New York's preeminent movie theater, Radio City Music Hall.

Those opposed to the film should have realized they were fighting a losing battle. Thanks to Welles, most Hollywood insiders had seen *Citizen Kane,* as had most of the film industry press. To ensure positive talk about the film, Welles had screened it privately at every opportunity.

The talk about *Citizen Kane* was good; by now, hundreds of people, including some of the film industry's most important critics, had seen *Citizen Kane* and knew it delivered everything that Welles promised. To destroy the film or shelve it would have caused the biggest flap in Hollywood history. Besides, RKO desperately needed to release its high-profile picture. The studio had already invested nearly $1 million in production costs, advertising, and advances to Welles. As one of the studio's most expensive productions of the year—and certainly its most highly publicized—*Citizen Kane* needed to appear in theaters, bringing in box office receipts.

Further, RKO couldn't destroy the negative, even if its board had insisted; the studio's contract with Welles gave the director almost complete control of the fate of the film, including, possibly, the film's distribution. If RKO refused to release the film, Welles could have bought it and distributed it himself—a step he most certainly would have been willing to take (as it turned out, Welles also had such complete control of his production that his contract extended beyond his death to protect it, an issue that would emerge nearly fifty years after the release of the film).

On January 21, 1941, the ban on RKO in Hearst papers was lifted—but not against *Citizen Kane.* For more than eight months, one of the most highly touted films ever released, a film which even then was recognized as a landmark achievement, received no review or news coverage in any of Hearst's publications.

The next time the picture would "appear" was in RKO advertisements when the film went into general release in the fall of 1941. Even then, the hated name was excluded from advertisements in Hearst papers; readers only saw that a "Big Screen Attraction" would be opening in local theaters. Not until February 1942, when *Citizen Kane* was nominated for nine Academy Awards, did Hearst papers print the name of the film again in an article—and then only because they were forced to include it in a news story.

*   *   *

Schaefer and Welles had won—*Citizen Kane* survived. The studio chief braved the pressures of the rest of Hollywood and one of the world's most formidable corporate powers.

But still the film had not been released, and a threat continued to loom from the Hearst organization. As if exacting a penance for RKO's sins, Hearst newspapers kept attacking the studio on the most trivial of issues, just to keep the battle in the public eye.

It was no wonder that all at RKO felt besieged. RKO's plan to premiere the film in Radio City Music Hall in Rockefeller Center collapsed, thanks in large part to pressure from Parsons on the Rockefellers—even though the family's stake in RKO meant it had everything to gain by showcasing the film in its own theater.

The scheduled release date—Valentine's Day 1941—came and went; the premiere was postponed two weeks. Meanwhile, attacks by the Hearst press continued. When RKO found itself entangled in a trivial lawsuit for breach of contract, with a mere $7,000 awarded to producer Joseph Ermolieff, the decision was splashed across the front page of virtually all of the seventeen Hearst dailies. "Under ordinary circumstances," said *Variety,* "it wouldn't have rated a mention."

In the *New York Mirror,* Hearst's flagship paper, film critic Lee Mortimer blasted Hollywood in general and RKO in particular for its business practices, primarily an alleged unethical practice that Mortimer never explained but called "The Hollywood Runaround." In addition, the trade press, covering Parsons and other contacts in the Hearst organization, continued to publish rumblings about lawsuits and pressure on theater owners.

Welles himself was investigated. Mysterious "government investigators" poked around the studio to check on whisperings of his alleged Communist sympathies. Welles was asked directly if he was a Communist. When Welles asked his inquisitor to define his terms, he was told that a Communist was someone who gives his money to the government. "In that case," Welles replied, referring to his tax bracket, "I'm eighty-seven percent communist. The other thirteen precent of me is pure capitalist." In addition, his draft status was checked by Hearst reporters (Welles was unfit for military service, due to, among other things, severe allergies).

Later, Hearst papers tried to drum up support against Welles' radio and stage productions with the American Legion, Veterans of Foreign Wars, and other patriotic groups. When *Citizen Kane* eventually opened in Los Angeles, rumors circulated the night of the premiere that celebrities who attended the opening would somehow "incur the wrath" of the Hearst organization.

The message was clear. Hearst factions ensured that any theater owner who wanted to show the picture would feel the heat, although the form of the pressure never solidified into an actual attack. Concern among theater owners continued, as did resistance to booking *Citizen Kane.*

The pressure hurt—and going into March, Schaefer and RKO remained silent about *Citizen Kane*'s future. That silence was viewed as a lack of support and a clear signal of the possibility that the film might be destroyed. "Optimism of a few weeks ago has greatly subsided," a reporter for *Variety* wrote in March, "and a lot of insiders are willing to believe that an $800,000 bonfire of prints and negatives is not impossible."

Schaefer may have been silent only because he had nothing new to say—

eamup by Welles
n Kane' Release;
Now May Be Stalled

Hearst Papers' Anti-'Citizen Kane' Gripe Takes It Out on Welles-CBS

Welles' Threat to Raise 'Kane' Puts Him in Spot Between Odlum-Schaefer

N. Y. Legiter to House 'Citizen Kane' Day-and-Date With RKO Palace, B'way

Wednesday, May 7, 1941

RKO's Watchful Waiting on Hearst Papers' Further Reaction to 'Kane'

Scare 'Em Off?

Hollywood, May 6.
Motion picture celebs are being bluntly told that they will incur enmity in certain quarters by attending the Coast preem Thursday (8) night of 'Citizen Kane' at El Capitan.

Understood that those who disregard the warning will be tabbed by spotters and reported to headquarters.

RKO Radio is skedding Orson Welles for personals with 'Citizen Kane' in cities where Hearst press is strong.

New York, Chicago and Los Angeles are being used as test arenas for Orson Welles' 'Citizen Kane' and RKO will seek no engagements outside of those and a few other cities until editorial and legal reaction of William Randolph Hearst interests is determined. No selling on the film until 1941-42.

Court test is not anticipated by the distributing company, although a suit on the 'invasion of privacy' charge that Hearstians have suggested would not come as a surprise. RKO fully anticipated, however, that the Hearst press would let loose with a campaign of vituperation.

Hearst papers apparently now figure they can do Welles and the picture more harm by a campaign of silence. They neither mentioned nor printed reviews of the New York opening and apparently have allowed their campaign against Welles as a 'Communist' to lag. Drive, in which

on RKO-Schaefer;
Release Still Indef

All Film Cos. May Suffer Because
Of Hearst's Peeve at Welles' 'Kane'

Luce's Time-Life
To Force 'Citi
$800,000 Prod

RKO, Despite Hearst's Ire, Announces
Huge National Campaign for 'Kane'

4   PICTURES

Welles, As 25% Owner of 'Kane',
Would 'Force' RKO to Release Pic

Add: Hearst Vs. Welles ('Citizen
Kane'); More Newspaper Attacks

**'CITIZEN KANE'
RELEASE DATE
NOT YET SET**

WELLES EAST TO TALK 'CITIZEN KANE' FUTURE

Hollywood, Jan. 28.
Orson Welles and his publicity chief, Herbert Drake, left for New York to huddle with George Schaefer and other RKO execs on the future of 'Citizen Kane,' which is, more or less, stymied by threats of blackouts by the Hearst newspapers.
Drake is shoving off for the east with plenty of evidence that there is vast public attention drawn to the picture before its premiere, scheduled for Feb. 14.

With release date of Orson Welles' 'Citizen Kane' the day after tomorrow (Friday), not a single playdate, roadshow or otherwise, has been set for the film. That's taken to indicate trouble ahead on the picture which William Randolph Hearst alleges too closely parallels his own life. Hearst is reported bringing much pressure on the RKO directorate to shelve the film.

Welles Suing RKO on 'Citizen Kane'
In Effort to Force Pic's Release

Hearst Opens Bla..
'Citizen Kane

═══ WILSHIRE—HOLLYWOOD ═══

Admiral Free Cont. Park 12 — SCOTLAND YARD / I WANTED WINGS / Come Early
Hollywood at Vine

CAMPUS OL. 4466 — Prices Including Tax 10c AND 20c / I WANTED WINGS
Verm't-Sta. Monica

Great American Broadcast
SPECIAL ATTRACTION

Cinema-18c NI. 6266 — Come - Early / LANCER SPY
1122 No. Western

WALT DISNEY
RELUCTANT DRAGON

COLONY Cont. 12:30 — Bride Came C.O.D. / SCOTLAND YARD
6523 Hollywood nr. Wilcox

GORDON WH. 1151 — Greer Garson / Walter Pidgeon / Year's Finest Picture
La Brea at Melrose

BLOSSOMS IN THE DUST

Don Ameche-Mary Martin-"Rochester"
Kiss the Boys Goodbye
SPECIAL ATTRACTION

LAUREL WA. 5601 — LOST HORIZON / Star of Midnight
Beverly at Laurel

Hitching Post HI. — Roy Rogers / JESSE JAMES AT BAY / O'Brien-Arizona Legion
Holly at Vine

Marcal HE. /500 — Wallace Beery / BARNACLE BILL / FORCED LANDING
Hollywd. Blvd. at Gower

Movie Parade GL. 3911 — Constance Talmadge in / A Pair of Silk Stockings / Clara Bow-Dancing Mothers
1737 N. HIGHLAND

Hunley-25c Plus OL. Tax 4616 — Shepherd of the Hills / TOM, DICK & HARRY / COME EARLY
5115 Hollywood Blvd.

Oriental Free Park HI. 1146 — Come Early Nite / DANCE HALL
7425 SUNSET

ONE SHOWING — 8:50
INTERMEZZO

HAWAII HO. 2273 Free Park — FIRST POPULAR / PRICE L. A. RUN
5630 Hollywd. Blvd.

BIG SCREEN ATTRACTION

VISTA-20c OL. 5204 — MAN HUNT / BLONDE IN SOCIETY / Come Early
4473 SUNSET

Melvan-20c Fr. Prk HI. 9465 — COWBOY & BLONDE / I'LL WAIT FOR YOU / Special Attraction
Melrose at Van Ness

Sunset GR. 9151 — SUNNY / DARK JOURNEY
Sunset at Western

═══ PASADENA—MONROVIA—MONTEBELLO ═══

MONROVIA — Sheriff of Tombstone / THIS WOMAN IS MINE
MONROVIA

VOGUE Cont. 1 P.M. — TIME OUT for RHYTHM / Broadway, Limited / Come Early
MONTEBELLO

BARD'S 398 E. Colorado RY. 16502 — B. Davis-J. Cagney / BRIDE CAME C.O.D. / BARNACLE BILL
Pasadena

THE EXAMINER affords you the largest, most complete entertainment directory in America.

═══ BURBANK ═══

BURBANK — ROBBERS OF RANGE / MELODY FOR 3
BURBANK

LOMA Cont. 1 P.M. — Ann Miller-Rudy Vallee / TIME OUT FOR RHYTHM
BURBANK

ERROL FLYNN - FRED MacMURRAY
DIVE BOMBER

MAGNOLIA — Anniversary Week / CHAN IN RIO
BURBANK — DOROTHY LAMOUR - JON HALL
ALOMA of SOUTH SEAS

NEW MAJOR — Gentleman From Dixie / Sun Valley Serenade
BURBANK

═══ GLENDALE—SAN FERNANDO—EAGLE ROCK ═══

San Fernando — TOO MANY BLONDES / RICHEST MAN

TEMPLE-10c 31500 — Victor Mature / CAPTAIN CAUTION

although in retrospect, Schaefer no doubt regretted this low-key public support for his embattled director. Instead, he was busy trying to rally forces the studio needed to exhibit the film. RKO vainly tried to find top-flight theaters to premiere *Citizen Kane.* One theater after another refused; eventually the Palace in New York was enlisted, but not without RKO incurring massive renovation costs to outfit it for a showcase engagement. The El Capitan in Hollywood was converted from a venue of stage productions to host the Los Angeles premiere.

But where, during the furor of the early spring, was Orson Welles? He too was staying

The Hearst newspapers' first "mention" of Citizen Kane *after the film was banned from their pages appeared in October 1941 and was in the form of this advertisement for a "Big Screen Attraction." Note also the ad on the same page for* The Little Foxes—*apparently Warners liked RKO's slogan "It's Terrific!" for* Citizen Kane, *because the studio used "It's Great!" to describe its new Bette Davis vehicle.*

behind the scenes, but even so he was doing his best to promote his film's cause.

All along, Welles had denied and denied and denied that *Citizen Kane* was the story of Hearst. However, he didn't make the fight easier on himself when time and again he credited Hearst and other captains of industry for inspiring Kane's personality. "*Citizen Kane* is not based upon the life of Mr. Hearst, or anyone else," Welles said when the tempest began to rise. "On the other hand, had Mr. Hearst and other similar financial barons not lived during the period we discuss, *Citizen Kane* could not have been made." But when the Hearst ban slammed down on RKO, Welles was as mystified as anyone about what happened. "It looks," he told a reporter for *Newsweek*, "like my throat has been cut."

There were some signs that Welles enjoyed the fuss—to a point. On January 27, he told an authors' club luncheon in Los Angeles, "When I get *Citizen Kane* off my mind, I'm going to work on an idea for a great picture based on the life of William Randolph Hearst." But Welles' concern for his film's survival was earnest, and he stayed busy fighting off the Hearst onslaught. He reacted with fury to the *Friday* article and called publisher Dan Gillmor himself to demand space to reply. The conversation must have sizzled; in Welles' letter to Gillmor, which accompanied the rebuttal, he cracked, "As you can see, I'm just as ill-tempered as I promised to be."

Welles' reply, titled "*Citizen Kane* Is Not About Louella Parsons' Boss," was brief but scathing, and featured captions on the photographs in Welles' own words.

"*Citizen Kane* is the portrait of a public man's private life," Welles wrote. "I have met some publishers, but I know none of them well enough to make them possible as models.

"*Friday* ran a series of stills from *Kane*, whose captions were inaccurate descriptions of the action of the picture. Constant reference was made to the career of William Randolph Hearst. This is unfair to Hearst and to Kane.

"Worst of all," Welles said, referring to comments about Louella Parsons, "*Friday* puts these words into my mouth: 'Wait until the woman finds out that the picture's about her boss.' This is not a misquotation. *Friday*'s source invented it. *Citizen Kane* is not about Louella Parsons' boss. It is the portrait of a fictional newspaper tycoon, and I have never said or implied to anyone that it is anything else. The easiest way to draw parallels between Kane and other famous publishers is not to see the picture."

But it was too little too late. Welles' reply didn't appear until nearly a month after *Friday*'s original story, and by then, the distortions had already done their worst. And, as Welles himself pointed out in his rebuttal, "Retractions are notoriously valueless."

Instead, Welles played his strongest card: *Citizen Kane* itself. Far more effective in turning Hollywood opinion in Welles' favor were his private screenings of his film. In January and February, Welles showed the picture to everyone in Hollywood's inner circles who cared to sit through a screening. During some weeks, he showed it several nights in a row, or even twice a night.

Hundreds of prominent actors, producers, and directors saw the film in Hollywood; the film industry press, by now rallying to Welles' cause, reported that at one March 6 screening, guests included no less than Cary Grant; producers David O. Selznick and Walter Wanger; studio executives Harry Cohn, Roy Disney, Sam Goldwyn, and Jesse Lasky; and directors Leo McCarey and William Wyler.

When Welles went to New York to drum up support for *Citizen Kane* with the board of directors of RKO, he screened it on the East Coast as well. Among the prominent guests at his New York viewings were Henry Luce, publisher of *Time* and *Life,* and several of his editors (Luce thoroughly enjoyed the *News on the March* sequence, fully appreciating the recreation of his own *March of Time*).

With no love lost in his organization for Hearst and his high-pressure tactics, Luce ordered his staff to, as *Variety* put it, "unleash their guns to get the film released." Soon, several stories appeared in *Time* in support of Welles, and a lavish photo feature about *Citizen Kane* in *Life,* where it was showcased as "Movie of the Week."

As March passed, word began to leak out: *Citizen Kane* was something special—something *very* special. *Time* captured the sentiment felt in much of Hollywood when it reported that "to most of the several hundred people who have seen the film at private showings, *Citizen Kane* is the most sensational product of the U.S. movie industry."

By now, it was clear that if the pressure continued, the anti–*Citizen Kane* forces would have a fight on their hands from every critic who had seen the film, along with a large faction within the motion picture industry. No longer was the Hearst organization trying to prevent a libel against its chief executive; now it was viewed as a diabolical suppressor of a stunning work of cinematic achievement. Popular momentum began to swing in favor of *Citizen Kane.*

However, none of this pressure produced public release of the picture. February passed, as did the new release date of March 11, with no word from RKO about the fate of the film. Meanwhile, Hearst newspapers extended their ban on Welles to include reviews of or features about his new play, *Native Son,* which he was preparing to open on Broadway, with John Houseman producing. Later, the publications would attack his radio programs on CBS, until it became obvious that the repeated assaults on Welles' broadcasts in Hearst newspapers were actually helping to *increase* his ratings.

Finally, Welles was fed up. On March 11, he called reporters to his suite at the Ambassador Hotel in New York and announced he would sue RKO for breach of contract if the studio didn't release *Citizen Kane* within three months. Welles said:

>   I believe that the public is entitled to see *Citizen Kane*. For me to stand by while this picture was being suppressed would constitute a breach of faith with the public on my part as a producer. I have at this moment sufficient financial backing to buy *Citizen Kane* from RKO and release it myself.
>
>   Under my contract with RKO, I have the right to demand that the picture be released and to bring legal action to force its release. RKO must release *Citizen Kane*. If it does not do so immediately, I have instructed my attorney to commence proceedings.
>
>   I have been advised that strong pressure is being brought to bear in certain quarters to cause the withdrawal of my picture *Citizen Kane* because of an alleged resemblance between incidents in the picture and incidents in the life of Mr. William Hearst. Any such attempts at suppression would involve a serious interference with freedom of speech and with the integrity of the moving-picture industry as the foremost medium of artistic expression in the country.
>
>   There is nothing in the facts to warrant the situation that has arisen. *Citizen Kane* was not intended to have nor has it any reference whatsoever to Mr. Hearst or to any other living person. No statement to the contrary has ever been authorized by me. *Citizen Kane* was scrutinized and approved by both RKO Radio Pictures and the Hays Office. No one in those organizations nor anyone associated with me in the production of the picture believed that it represented anything but a psychological analysis of an imaginary individual. I regret exceedingly that anyone should interpret *Citizen Kane* to have a bearing upon any living person, or should impugn the artistic purposes of its producers.

Where this "sufficient backing" would come from is unknown; most likely, the phrase was only another Wellesian bluff to show RKO that he was serious about his plan. But it's also possible that a powerful backer did exist; Henry Luce would most certainly have been a likely candidate.

Welles' threats turned out to be unnecessary. He and Schaefer eventually calmed the waters and settled the dispute once and for all. *Citizen Kane* would be shown to the critics in formal press showings in early April and its premiere was slated for May 1 at the Palace Theater in New York.

5. Mr. Hearst

Considering the firestorm of controversy that arose over *Citizen Kane* before the film received even a single public viewing, the question which still eludes a completely satisfactory answer may be worth asking yet again: Was Charles Foster Kane really William Randolph Hearst?

Curiously, as much discussion and ink have been devoted to this question as to any other about *Citizen Kane*. Yet trying to determine if Kane's origins lie in Hearst—for some reason, long a subject of scholarly and journalistic pursuit—remains as difficult as explaining why it is worth knowing. There could be no denying that the parallels were many; however, in terms of the film's impact and legacy, whether or not Kane was Hearst doesn't matter one whit in appreciating the film's merits.

However, for a few anxious weeks in 1941, the question of Kane's possible link to Hearst was one of vital importance to the actual survival of *Citizen Kane*. While *Citizen Kane* weathered the storm, the result of that conflict severely damaged not only the film's chances for success, it also forever destroyed RKO president George Schaefer's grand plan for creating high-quality films at his struggling studio. Without doubt, Orson Welles' credibility as a potentially profitable producer-director was damaged as well—a setback which altered the course of his career.

For those reasons, the issue of Kane's origins still fascinates—however, it is not so much the relationship between Kane and Hearst that retains relevance; instead, exploring the reasons why so many people were driven nearly to the point of hysteria over the film makes a far more intriguing story.

There were unquestionably many similarities between the fictional Kane and the real-life Hearst. In his youth, William Randolph Hearst did take over

155

the reins of a struggling newspaper purchased by his father, the *San Francisco Examiner,* and led it into the black in only two years. When he entered the New York newspaper business with the *Morning Journal,* he raided the competition just as Kane did, stealing staff away from no less than Joseph Pulitzer's *New York World* (among Hearst's acquisitions was Richard Outcault, who invented the color Sunday funnies).

Hearst did strongly support in print, nearly to the point of mania, the entry of the United States into the Spanish-American War, and was a leader among those who verbally attacked President McKinley for being a pawn of corporate trusts (Kane chose to pick on his banker-guardian, Walter Thatcher).

In 1905, Hearst lost the election to become mayor of New York, not because of a personal scandal like the one that brought down Kane, but because corrupt political bosses literally stole victory from him by dumping legitimate ballot boxes from pro-Hearst neighborhoods into New York Harbor (Mankiewicz originally included this issue in his first draft of *American,* but the circumstances of Kane's political failure was changed as soon as Welles began to revise the script).

Hearst newspapers carried editorials supportive of political assassination only a few months before President McKinley was killed in Buffalo. Similarly, in *American,* Kane papers launched a print assault against President James Norton before he was wounded. This ongoing feud between Kane and the President of the United States featured prominently in early versions of *Citizen Kane,* but dwindled to a few brief mentions in the final draft. These scenes were deleted in New York when the lawyers for RKO and the other studios reached a compromise on the final cut.

During Hearst's most severe financial crisis, his banks and a "Conservation Committee" took partial control of his organization; both Kane and Hearst were left figureheads—ambitious men with financial power stripped from them, who in their declining years were left to tinker with the remains of their empires. Kane and Hearst both had insatiable appetites for Old-World treasures and filled warehouses with expensive but mostly unappreciated antiques. When to raise money, Hearst sold hundreds of art items to pay for the construction of San Simeon and the losses of the Depression, it was discovered that many items had never been uncrated from their original shipping boxes.

Those close to Hearst assuredly harbored private feelings about his personality that Kane seemed to echo. They saw in Kane the same overbearing behavior that they knew from personal experience with the real-life publisher: the misuse of power, the incredible possessiveness, the extravagant spending that led him to the brink of financial ruin, the blatant disregard for responsible journalism when his own desires were at stake, and—perhaps most revealing

William Randolph Hearst

—his transformation from a publisher perceived as a champion of the working man into narrow-minded elitist.

Finally—and perhaps the parallel that was most damning—Kane, like Hearst, constructed a gigantic private hilltop hideaway that served as much to provide him with a refuge from the world as it did a place to entertain his guests. Kane built his Xanadu on Florida's Gulf Coast; Hearst constructed a real-life version in the hills of central California, a one-hundred-room Mediterranean Revival–style enclave with two swimming pools—one indoor and one outdoor—which he called San Simeon (better known today as Hearst Castle).

Hearst inherited most of the 250,000-acre estate from his mother, and over the years he continued to add to the property by buying small parcels of land from local farmers. One legend recalls that Hearst was obsessed with owning the land for as far as the eye could see from his estate—no easy feat when your house sits on a mountainside—and Hearst supposedly dickered for years with one local farmer who would never sell the final piece needed to fulfill the publisher's baronial dream.

But there the similarities end. The most substantive difference between Kane and Hearst, of course, was that in 1941, Hearst was alive and Kane was dead. Hearst, seventy-eight at the time of *Citizen Kane*'s release, died in 1951 at age eighty-eight.

In addition, Hearst had a happy home life, both as a child, and later in the company of Marion Davies, his devoted mistress for more than thirty years. While Hearst's single marriage soured (both of Kane's relationships went bad), he remained a close and devoted father to his five sons. His wife, Millicent, refused to divorce him, and they remained "married" for forty-seven years. Had she divorced Hearst, Davies, thirty-four years his junior, would have married him.

Davies, whom Hearst supported in an acting career, was no flop in Hollywood as Susan Alexander was in her brief fling with grand opera—in fact, some Hollywood observers noted that Davies might have gone farther in the picture business without Hearst's constant meddling in her career.

Davies maintained a perfectly respectable career in both silent and sound films, appearing in more than forty pictures. During Hearst's financial crises, it was in part money from Davies' personal fortune—and her volunteering to sell some of her jewelry—that kept the publisher afloat. (Years later, Welles was asked to write the foreword of the reprint of Davies' memoirs. His brief commentary not only reviewed the differences between Hearst and Kane, but also praised both Davies' acting talents and her loyalty to Hearst.)

Hearst, unlike Kane, had been elected to public office, and served two uneventful terms in Congress before he ran against the Tammany bosses for mayor of New York City.

Unfortunately for Welles, two brief vignettes included in the final print of the film *did* have specific and public origins in incidents involving Hearst. Early in the film, when Kane's banker-guardian Walter Thatcher warns Kane that he's losing a million dollars a year on the *New York Inquirer,* Kane replies, "Do you realize that at that rate, I'll have to close this place in sixty years." The line, quite famous in newspaper lore, came from a comment by Hearst's mother, Phoebe, who when asked about her son losing a million dollars a year on his *Examiner* and *Journal,* replied, "At that rate, he could last thirty years."

Even more damaging was dialogue in the same scene which included Kane's response to a cable from his correspondent in Cuba, who can find no signs of a military uprising against Spanish rule. "You provide the prose poems," Kane said, "I'll provide the war." Again, it was practically word for word a rehash of the oft-quoted exchange between Hearst and artist Frederic Remington in 1896, who at the time was Hearst's correspondent in Cuba before Hearst's urgings contributed to the United States declaring war on Spain.

When Remington could find no bloodshed or atrocities, he wired to Hearst, "Everything quiet. There is no trouble here. There will be no more. I wish to return." Instead of recalling him, Hearst wired back, "Please remain. You furnish the pictures and I'll furnish the war."

However, outside of the Hearst organization, there were others who were positive that Kane was modeled after someone other than the publisher. For every accounting that "proved" Kane was modeled after Hearst, an equally solid rationale could point to another person. The list of prospects was nearly endless: some cited other newspaper executives besides Hearst as better models, such as Joseph Pulitzer, owner of the *New York World,* or *New York Herald* editor and publisher James Gordon Bennett, two of the most controversial publishers during the late years of the nineteenth century. Other candidates from the world of journalism included *New York Sun* publisher Charles A. Dana and newspaper chain owner Frank Munsey.

Even someone in Hearst's own "family," Charles Lederer, Marion Davies' nephew and a screenwriter who created such classics as *His Girl Friday* and *Kiss of Death,* thought Kane's character more closely resembled Robert Mc-Cormick and Joseph Patterson, former publishers of the *Chicago Tribune,* than Hearst. In fact, Harold McCormick, from another branch of the publishing family, actually did finance the opera career of his wife, Ganna Walska.

Other captains of industry outside the world of journalism were also nominated as models for Kane. Kodak chairman Jules Brulatour funded his wife Hope Hampton's aspirations in grand opera; she, like Susan Alexander, did not fare very well, but she certainly sang better than Susan did. For those who pointed to Xanadu as a key indicator of Kane's source, the Florentine

Renaissance estate built in Florida by John Ringling North, the founder of Ringling Bros. and Barnum & Bailey Circus, offered a suitable alternative inspiration to Hearst's San Simeon. North's mansion, like Hearst's, eventually became a state-owned museum.

From the beginning, of course, Welles and Mankiewicz denied that Kane was based on Hearst, or on any one person, for that matter. Later, when Welles was sued for allegedly using Ferdinand Lundberg's book *Imperial Hearst* as the basis for *Citizen Kane,* Welles testified under oath as to where the inspiration for Kane had come from.

"As in the case of a great deal of fiction, we drew to some extent on our observations of certain aspects of American life, and our knowledge of certain types among influential Americans," Welles testified. "It was intended to be the study of the character and psychological motivations of a fictional character who, of course, could never have been invented had not certain types of personalities of an equal position appeared in the American scene."

At the time of *Citizen Kane*'s release, there was some speculation, even among Welles' own staff, that the director did model Kane after Hearst in an effort to capitalize on the publicity; if so, he could have picked an easier target, and one with less clout—at the height of Hearst's influence, an estimated one in four Americans read Hearst publications—and a better reputation for clean dealing. More than forty years later, Welles still denied the connection, but he did acknowledge drawing dialogue from the exchange between Remington and Hearst. "In fact," Welles recalled, "it is the only purely Hearstian element in *Citizen Kane*. Except for the telegram and the crazy art collection (much too good to resist), in *Kane* everything was invented."

Mankiewicz, a favored visitor to the Hearst camp, had no reason to offend his host, or to chance incurring his wrath with an insulting screen portrayal —no single script, no weekly salary would have been worth the trouble it would cause. While Mankiewicz took incidents from his own background in newspaper work when he wrote the script, modeling Leland's drinking problem on his own—including the vignette based on his experience of being too drunk to write a review for the *New York Times*—it would have been senseless for him to base a script entirely on Hearst's life.

Even before *Citizen Kane* was released, fellow screenwriter Ben Hecht said that Mankiewicz had no intention of caricaturing Hearst. "Do you think . . . that Willie Hearst will figure it's about him?" Mankiewicz asked Hecht in March 1941. "I didn't write it about him, but about some of our other mutual friends—a sort of a compendium." Considering how many true incidents about "Willie" were included in early drafts of the script, it seems that Mankiewicz's "compendium" leaned more heavily toward Hearst than the writer realized.

Welles had indeed told Parsons and Hopper the truth: As far as he was concerned, Kane was a fictional publisher. However, Kane was a publisher who owned a castle on a hill overlooking a huge tract of land, he urged America's entry into the Spanish-American War, he acquired a huge art collection . . . and on and on. The similarities were too much for either Parsons or Hopper—both only too anxious to jump to conclusions—to take lying down. Their fury blinded them to other alternatives; in their minds, Charles Foster Kane was indeed William Randolph Hearst.

Whether or not Kane was modeled on Hearst, the fact that Parsons, easily the most powerful journalist in Hollywood, was "horrified" by a film that was at most, a mild caricature of her boss, shows just how rashly she reacted to the film. Hopper, her chief rival, reacted no better. While they didn't destroy *Citizen Kane,* the unyielding pressure they exerted scared off hundreds of potential film exhibitors and sank any opportunity RKO might have had to make money on the picture. In the long run, they also ruined George Schaefer's ambitious dream of supporting similar projects, and derailed Welles' chance to break into the picture business with a big score. Simply, Louella Parsons and Hedda Hopper believed that they saw Hearst in Kane; their power in the press did the rest.

Of course, none of the explanations from the Welles camp had any effect on the reactions of Hearst supporters who were early viewers of the film. It was the first moments of *Citizen Kane* that caused the most damage, and in the darkness of the screening room, Xanadu provided the best evidence for those willing to believe that Kane was Hearst. The fuss over the Hearst-Kane link no doubt started because the opening of the film concentrates so heavily on the single closest link between Kane and Hearst: Xanadu and its superficial similarities to San Simeon.

One can only imagine how Louella Parsons—a frequent visitor to San Simeon, the columnist who had been coolly assured by the young director that the film was not a slam at her employer—must have felt when the first thing she saw on screen was a virtual travelogue about an incredible hilltop mansion with its own private zoo, followed by brief clips of huge swimming pool parties and around-the-world antique gathering.

Then, Parsons witnessed the first speaking appearance of Kane—who is featured as a grinning old codger, nearly the same age as Hearst.

All of this was followed within minutes by the conversation between Kane and Thatcher, which includes the dialogue about Cuba, and the newspaper losing a million dollars a year. After that brash introduction, it's no wonder Parsons walked out of the screening; in her mind, Welles could have stuck a neon sign on the roof of Xanadu that read "San Simeon."

San Simeon was indeed referenced by RKO designers as one of the models

The gloomy Gothic vision of Kane's Xanadu is a far cry from Hearst's sunny Mediterranean Revival estate, San Simeon (far right).

for Xanadu (examples of privately owned American castles in the twentieth century are, after all, hard to find), but it was used primarily to establish the position of a large estate on a hillside setting. The design for Xanadu was inspired by combination of both fantasy and real buildings, among them Mont-St.-Michel and the Queen's castle in *Snow White*.

Hearst insiders—at least those who stayed through an entire screening of *Citizen Kane*—should have noticed immediately that the most important elements of San Simeon's charm are missing from Xanadu. Photos of San Simeon give it an extraordinary grandeur, a royal magnificence unlike anything else in the United States (much the same aura that the White House is often given in motion pictures).

But no one on RKO's design staff had ever visited San Simeon—at the time of *Citizen Kane*'s production, Hearst still used the estate; it was not the California public landmark that it is today. A visit to San Simeon reveals a high regard for intimacy and a surprising warmth in even the largest rooms of the mansion. While its Greek sculptures and medieval tapestries give the mansion a stately quality, the rooms are not particularly large or palatial, like those of Xanadu. Nor do San Simeon's largest rooms exude the antiseptic sterility of Xanadu's great hall, which was featured so prominently in *Citizen Kane*.

The presentation of Xanadu in the film may have been incredibly dramatic and effective, but Xanadu was no San Simeon. If Hearst loyalists assumed that Xanadu was their boss' house, it was only because they accepted Kane's house as the grossest caricature; it should be to their discredit, not Welles', that the confusion occurred.

*   *   *

What surprised early viewers of *Citizen Kane* was that the exteriors of Xanadu weren't actually shot at San Simeon. The images of Xanadu blaze across the screen so quickly during *News on the March* that many viewers simply assumed that Welles had pulled a fast one on Hearst and actually shot footage of San Simeon on the sly for his on-screen palace. Actually, the shots of Kane's home used in the newsreel came from a variety of stock sources or footage of the RKO back lot—outdoor footage shot specifically for *Citizen Kane* was filmed in Balboa Park in San Diego—and none of them showed San Simeon.

Another point missed during the early fuss over the film was that Hearst is actually mentioned in *Citizen Kane*. In the early part of the picture, when the screening of the newsreel ends, Rawlston, the head of the news company,

CITIZEN

The barren sterility of Xanadu's Great Hall . . .

who seems not unlike Henry Luce, asks his staff
about Kane, "But how is he different from Ford?
Or Hearst, for that matter? Or John Doe?" Rawlston's line flys by so fast in Welles' breakneck
pacing of the screening room dialogue that few
hear the reference on first viewing.

Strangely, it never occurred to those who
sought to "protect" Hearst that by attempting
to suppress *Citizen Kane,* they created a far larger
public issue than ever would have emerged if the
film had been allowed to run its natural course
without interference. Hearst's organization,
more than anything Orson Welles shot on film,
was responsible for creating the links between
Hearst and Kane.

That confusion remains today. At Hearst
Castle—one of the most popular public attrac-

tions in California, drawing more than 1 million visitors each year—some tourists assume that not only was Kane modeled after Hearst, but they were actually the same man. "People still come up here," said a Hearst Castle staff member nearly fifty years after *Citizen Kane* was released, "and want to know where the sled is."

But the ultimate irony about the battle between the Hearst organization and Orson Welles remains that Hearst himself may never have seen the film that caused all of the fuss. Over the years, Hearst's biographers and family members have reported that he absolutely saw the film, or he absolutely did not—both with equal certainty.

From the first, Hearst was handed the opportunity to view *Citizen Kane.* As an attempted

peace offering during the height of the fight, George Schaefer himself sent a print of *Citizen Kane* to Hearst at San Simeon. When the film was returned to RKO, the protective seals on the cans were not broken. However, no comments or letter of "thanks-but-no-thanks" came back with the film, so it's possible that Hearst's overprotective staff returned the print without letting their employer know it had arrived.

Charles Lederer recalled years later that he was positive that his aunt, Marion Davies, had never seen the film, and he was convinced that Hearst never saw it either. Lederer may have been the best source of inside information on the subject; he married Welles' ex-wife Virginia soon after the couple divorced (Virginia Nicholson Welles filed for a divorce in December 1939). Lederer visited Hearst at San Simeon along with both his wife and Welles' own daughter, Christopher.

While Lederer was positive, years after *Citizen Kane*'s release, that Hearst had not seen the film, his wife remembered the opposite. Virginia Nicholson told biographer Frank (*Citizen Welles*) Brady that a group hosted by Hearst and Davies viewed the film at San Simeon.

"When the film ended and the lights came up, we all looked over in Hearst's direction," Nicholson said. "He had a slightly scampish smile but didn't say anything. We were all afraid to utter a word. Then, he and Marion simply got up and went upstairs, in his private elevator, to retire. Although I saw him many times after that, I never heard him mention a word about the film."

However, John Tebbel, who wrote a biography of Hearst the year after he died, says categorically that Hearst and Davies saw *Citizen Kane* at the Geary Theater in San Francisco, soon after the film opened there. While no proof exists that Hearst saw the film then, as Orson Welles himself was to find out, the publisher was indeed in San Francisco at the time. Tebbel wrote that when a friend of Hearst's asked him how he liked *Citizen Kane*, "He looked away thoughtfully and replied, 'We thought it was a little too long.' "

It is even possible that at one time Hearst owned a copy of *Citizen Kane* and kept it in his film collection at San Simeon (first-run screenings were standard evening fare for Hearst and his guests). W. A. Swanberg, yet another biographer of Hearst, wrote that a year after *Citizen Kane* was released, the publisher noted the film's existence in his collection. He reportedly told Louis Shainmark, the managing editor of Hearst's *Chicago Herald-American* and a guest at San Simeon, "We have it here. I must run it off again sometime." Marion Davies, Swanberg reported, described *Citizen Kane* as "grotesque."

Hearst was probably only joking about owning a copy of the film. The inventory of San Simeon's contents conducted in 1957 after the property was given to the State of California—a year-long real-life project not unlike the reporters' rummaging at Xanadu—showed that several motion pictures remained in Hearst's vaults, but not *Citizen Kane*.

Whether or not Hearst saw *Citizen Kane* may never be known. What is certain is that in a chance encounter in a San Francisco hotel elevator, Welles actually offered Hearst the opportunity to see the film. Welles, a colorful raconteur, who by his own admission often modified stories as the occasion suited him, told two different versions of this story. But in each, he had the last word on the subject.

"I found myself alone with him in an elevator in the Fairmont Hotel on the night *Citizen Kane* was opening in San Francisco," Welles recalled more than twenty-five years later. "So I introduced myself and asked him if he'd like to come to the opening of the picture. He didn't answer. And as he was getting off at his floor, I said, (or, as Welles sometimes recalled, "I thought to myself . . .") 'Charles Foster Kane would have accepted.' No reply . . . And Kane would have, you know. That was his style—just as he finished Jed Leland's bad review of Susan as an opera singer."

6. Release

eeing [*Citizen Kane*], *it's as if you never really saw a movie before; no movie has ever grabbed you, pummeled you, socked you on the button with the vitality, the accuracy, the impact, the professional aim, that this one does.*

—Excerpt from Cecelia Ager's review of *Citizen Kane* in *PM* magazine

The web of suppression spun by the Hearst organization produced marvelously counterproductive results with the other press outlets across the country. The public furor over the attempts to scuttle *Citizen Kane* created a frenzy of requests for passes to the press screenings; for reporters, admission to an advance screening of *Citizen Kane* was the hottest ticket in New York. "Newspapermen wanting ducats seem to be climbing out from under every table," sighed one RKO press aide.

Finally, on May 1, *Citizen Kane* premiered at the RKO Palace in New York City. The film debuted in Chicago on May 6—Orson Welles' twenty-sixth birthday—and in Los Angeles on May 8. The rumored wrath of Hearst, which supposedly would descend on Hollywood notables who dared turn out for the premiere, never materialized; instead, the Los Angeles opening at the El Capitan was attended by one of the largest gatherings ever of Hollywood's finest.

With the premieres came an outpouring of accolades and commentary unlike anything ever written about a motion picture. The press screenings and the reviews that followed confirmed the rumors generated by Welles' private showings: by any measure, *Citizen Kane* was an astounding critical success, and by most accounts, one of the greatest films in Hollywood history (for a selection of complete reviews of *Citizen Kane,* see Compendium).

"Now that the wraps are off," said *New York Times* critic Bosley Crowther, "it can be safely stated that suppression of this film would have been a crime. *Citizen Kane* is far and away the most surprising and cinematically exciting motion picture to be seen here in many a moon. As a matter of fact, it comes close to being the most sensational film ever made in Hollywood."

Time wrote, "*Citizen Kane* has found important new techniques in picture-making and story-telling. Artful and artfully artless, it is not afraid to say the same thing twice if twice-telling reveals a fourfold truth."

One critic summed up the feelings of most in the film business who were fed up with the fuss caused by the Hearst organization. "After you've seen Orson Welles' first film, you'll wonder what all the controversy was about," said William Boehnel of the *New York World-Telegram*. "Because it doesn't make the slightest bit of difference whether it is or isn't about William Randolph Hearst or any other individual. What matters is that *Citizen Kane* is a cinema masterpiece."

Leo Mishkin of the *New York Morning Telegraph*, practically predicted the film's destiny when he wrote, "*Citizen Kane* will be around, will be remembered, will be followed and copied and imitated and reprinted, so long as the movies, as we now know them, exist."

Cecelia Ager in *PM* magazine was among the first to note that beyond the film's singular excellence, *Citizen Kane* was a benchmark by which the next generations of film would be measured. "Before *Citizen Kane*," Ager wrote, "it's as if the motion picture was a slumbering monster, a mighty force stupidly sleeping, lying there sleek, torpid, complacent—awaiting a fierce young man to come kick it to life, to rouse it, shake it, awaken it to its potentialities, to show it what it's got. Seeing it, it's as if you never really saw a movie before; no movie has ever grabbed you, pummeled you, socked you on the button with the vitality, the accuracy, the impact, the professional aim, that this one does."

Even more important were notices from film industry trade papers, which reported not only on the quality of a motion picture, but also its potential earning power at the box office. *Variety*'s critics not only raved about the film but predicted that it would be a ticket-selling smash as well. *Daily Variety* called the film "a box office explosion establishing Orson Welles as an overnight film click. *Citizen Kane* is a film possessing the sure dollar mark, which distinguishes every daring entertainment venture that is created by a workman who is master of the technique and mechanics of his medium. *Citizen Kane* is a triumph for Orson Welles, who overnight, so to speak, joins the top ranks of box-office film personalities."

At the offices of the *Hollywood Reporter*, publisher W. R. Wilkerson was gladly eating crow after seeing the picture. "When George Schaefer came along with Orson Welles and the latter's authority to produce, write, direct and star, we believed it too much to ask of any individual and suggested that Mr. Schaefer was just plain nuts," Wilkerson wrote in his column. "However, the nearest approach that anyone ever came to a batting average of 1,000 in the

Finally, after months of delays, Citizen Kane *premiered at New York's Palace Theater on May 1, 1941. Note the running news bulletin board describing the war in Africa above the gigantic* Kane *display; moviegoers could not escape the news about the escalating war in Europe and Africa, which grew worse by the day.*

delivery of an entertainment for the screen, Orson Welles accomplished with *Citizen Kane.*

"We criticized George Schaefer, we condemned Orson Welles, we ridiculed even the thought of what they attempted to do; we must now retract much of it. Where there was criticism, we now come to praise. Where there was condemnation, we now feel compelled to eulogize."

The reviews weren't unanimous—some critics crabbed slightly, calling the picture, among other things, "cold," "unemotional," and "unsatisfying." However, the vast majority lined up solidly behind Orson Welles in their praise of *Citizen Kane.*

All of the positive reviews and the applause in the trade press came as good news to film exhibitors across the country, who were still nervous about both the film's box office appeal and the potential wrath of the Hearst papers. And at first, it looked like *Citizen Kane* would be a big winner. In New York, the house at the Palace was nearly sold out for every performance during the first week.

Unfortunately, the lines at the box office didn't last. The early returns from New York couldn't be maintained, not even in Hollywood, where interest in the film still ran high. The theaters selected in Chicago and Los Angeles weren't appropriate for the kind of showcase presentation that a top-flight run required, and by the end of its first week of showings, *Citizen Kane* was pulled from the Hill Street, one of the two theaters where it was playing in Los Angeles. Receipts at the El Capitan, reported *Variety,* were "very disappointing."

Strangely, considering the curiosity raised by the Hearst controversy, lavish advertising purchased by RKO, and mountains of free publicity generated by the nation's critics, public interest couldn't be converted into big sales at the box office. Controversial or not, it was soon apparent that in 1941, *Citizen Kane* simply wasn't a film for the masses. The film continued to play in limited run for several months, with only mild success.

Although RKO came through as promised with its plans for a massive advertising campaign to back *Citizen Kane,* the studio's promotion never captured the spirit of the film or excited the potential audience as much as it could have. RKO may have had the cash, but it definitely didn't have the imagination; in an era when snappy slogans sold a film, the best RKO's advertising department could manage for *Citizen Kane* was "It's Terrific!"

Accompanying the slogan on much of the advertising material was a portrait of Kane as a young man, standing tall and defiant; the drawing barely resembles Welles. RKO chose to ignore the controversy in its advertising, and the studio did not capitalize on the cinematic innovation that Welles, his cast and crew strived so hard to achieve. Instead, the studio left the film without a hook for the public to grab, and the box office returns showed it.

The same painting of Welles used in the print advertising was used in an animated sign above the marquee of the Palace theater when the film debuted. The display included nine neon-rimmed images of Kane stacked one in front of the other, and each larger than the one before it. It was a dazzling display, but it captured neither the spirit nor the importance of the picture.

And still the pressure from Hearst loomed. Theaters—or in at least one case, entire theater chains—still felt that potential litigation hung over the head of any exhibitor who dared show *Citizen Kane.*

The biggest problem for the film was that once the Hearst threat was rolling, it was extremely difficult to stop. Because of the long and public battle over release of the film, some Hearst papers continued to either ignore or downplay RKO pictures.

The mere threat of Hearst action was disastrous; the Fox—West Coast theater chain actually paid the distribution fee for *Citizen Kane* but refused to show it when the film was included in an RKO block for general release in September 1941. The studio earned its rental fee, but because the film languished unviewed, there were no box office receipts to split.

In spite of the rumors and continued rumblings, the Hearst organization never acted against any theater that exhibited *Citizen Kane.* What publicity-hungry theater owners never considered was that if Hearst attacked, the resulting scuffle would have increased interest in the film among potential patrons. Apparently that sort of stunt was reserved for more proven Hollywood talent. "After all," said one theater owner, "the star of *Citizen Kane* may be *the* Orson Welles, but he's no Clark Gable."

The trend was only too clear. RKO couldn't boast the resources or the huge theater chains that MGM or Warner Bros. or Paramount could command; to be sure, RKO had many screens at its disposal, but not enough to resurrect *Citizen Kane* as a real money-maker. Eventually, the studio was forced to give up.

However, theaters in larger cities did report moderate business, and in more cosmopolitan areas, *Citizen Kane* played with great success for several months. But theaters in smaller communities reported an endless series of horror stories of dismal turnouts; their woes and triumphs in the exhibition business were included in the "What the Picture Did for Me" section of *Motion Picture Herald* magazine, and *Citizen Kane* was the favorite subject for gripes in late 1941 and early 1942.

It was somewhat gratifying to note, that even in the depths of exhibitor angst, the same theater owners who complained about *Citizen Kane*'s poor box office performance, time and again, also said that the film was a creative masterpiece—even in remote communities not known for their appreciation of films outside the norm.

"An artistic triumph, but not a small town picture," said one correspondent from the Paramount Theater in Dewey, Oklahoma. "It may be a classic, but it's plumb nuts to your show-going public," reported the manager of the Iris Theater in Velva, North Dakota. "While this picture was very pleasing to me and to a few of our better-informed patrons, it was very disappointing from the box office viewpoint," came a comment from the State Theater in Big Timber, Montana.

The limited public enthusiasm for *Citizen Kane* didn't affect the continuing accolades for the film. At the end of 1941, the *New York Times* ranked *Citizen Kane* among its top ten motion pictures of the year. The National Board of Review named the film its Best Picture. And, on the last day of the year, *Citizen Kane* was voted the outstanding production of 1941 by the New York Film Critics Circle, during the shortest voting session in the organization's history.

Welles also featured strongly in the New York critics' balloting for best director; through five ballots, he was tied with John Ford, who eventually won on the sixth vote for his sensitive direction of *How Green Was My Valley*. Curiously, Welles' astounding acting performance was virtually ignored, but he was in good company among those unnoticed by the critics—along with Cary Grant, Robert Montgomery, and a host of other fine actors with first-rate performances in 1941. By far the favorite acting performance of the year among both the critics and the public was Gary Cooper's low-key portrayal of the title role in *Sergeant York*. It was an omen of things to come.

While *Citizen Kane* continued to play sporadically across the nation, the last hope to save it as a box office success was the Academy Awards, where a strong showing would have breathed new life into the film's box office potential. *Citizen Kane* was nominated for nine Academy Awards: Best Picture; Direction (Welles); Actor (Welles); Original Screenplay (Mankiewicz and Welles); Art Direction (Perry Ferguson and company); Black-and-White Cinematography (Toland); Musical Score for a Dramatic Picture (Herrmann); Editing (Wise); and Sound Recording (RKO Studio Sound Department, John Aalberg, sound director). Had a category for achievement in makeup existed at the time, Maurice Seiderman would have been a certain nominee.

Regardless of the final outcome, it must have been tremendously gratifying to Welles—who no doubt still burned from his early grilling by the Hollywood establishment as the bearded bad boy—to be nominated personally in four categories (in addition to the actor, director, and the original screenplay categories, as producer, Welles would have received the Oscar if *Citizen Kane* had won the Best Picture award).

Nevertheless, the final results of the actual voting were no doubt a blow. With most of the Hollywood powers and virtually all of the press on Welles' side, *Citizen Kane* seemed like a shoo-in to win a bushel of statuettes. But when Oscar night came on February 26, 1942, other films took most of the top honors. While Welles did share an Oscar victory with Mankiewicz for Best Original Screenplay (in the process, becoming the youngest writer before or since to win the screenplay award), *Citizen Kane* was shot down in all of the other categories.

As expected after the New York critics' vote, Welles and everyone else was overlooked in the Best Actor category by runaway crowd favorite Gary Cooper. John Ford again surpassed Welles for best direction of *How Green Was My Valley,* and the same film nipped both Perry Ferguson in the Art Direction category and Gregg Toland for cinematography.

Strangely, *Citizen Kane's* spectacular achievement in sound was surpassed by *That Hamilton Woman,* a moderate Alexander Korda production, and Robert Wise's editing was bested by William Holmes' for *Sergeant York.* Bernard Herrmann also lost—but to himself; he picked up his first Oscar for his score for *The Devil and Daniel Webster* (at the time called *All That Money Can Buy*). And finally, with four other Academy Awards in its corner, it was no surprise when *How Green Was My Valley* was named Best Picture of 1941.

This time, it had been a Hollywood establishment of a different sort that plagued Welles and *Citizen Kane.* A new nemesis had reared up; scuttlebutt in Hollywood pointed an accusing finger at the screen extras, who voted disapproval of Orson Welles by casting their ballots for other films.

The voting rules for the Academy Awards in its early years were entirely different than those in force today. At the time, the Academy of Motion Picture Arts and Sciences opened a large part of the balloting not only to its own membership, but to screen extras and various union guilds as well. At some points in Academy history, the policy covering who could vote changed from year to year; in 1941, more than 6,000 screen extras were eligible to vote for best picture, all of the acting categories, and best song. The extras clearly held a strong hand in six categories; almost 10,000 ballots were mailed, and more than eighty percent were marked and returned.

Welles figured strongly in the nominations because the committees that chose the nominees included the cream of the Hollywood crop—those who rallied to Welles' support when the Hearst papers closed in. However, that backing wasn't enough when the final ballots were counted. The extras took up the anti-Welles cause that had festered since his arrival in Hollywood, and by sheer weight of numbers, destroyed his Oscar hopes. "There is no dissent," *Variety* said of Welles' losses, "that the extra vote scuttled him. The mob didn't like the guy personally, and took it out on him at the polls."

It is quite likely that the technical committees that awarded the other Oscars were also affected in much the same way; *Citizen Kane* was overlooked in several categories—in particular in sound and editing—in favor of clearly less impressive efforts. Or, when the choice came to an artist nominated twice in the same category and one of them was *Citizen Kane,* the committee chose the other; Herrmann's score for *The Devil and Daniel Webster,* while rousing and imaginative, is no match for the incredible complexity and haunting beauty of his composition for *Citizen Kane.*

It wasn't until 1957 that Academy Award nominations and final voting were limited solely to the Academy members—a rule that stands today. Taking nothing away from *How Green Was My Valley,* one of John Ford's finest screen achievements, there can be little doubt that had current voting rules been in force in 1941, the Academy Award winners that year would have been quite different. If *Citizen Kane* had won several Oscars, the film no doubt would have received a longer and larger screen run, shoring up Welles' already weakening position at RKO and making his career in Hollywood quite different.

Finally, in the spring of 1942, *Citizen Kane* was withdrawn from general circulation with barely a whimper. After its first run, it was listed on RKO's books at a loss of more than $150,000—all things considered, not a bad showing, when the problems of distribution, and the hundreds of theaters that refused outright to show the film, are factored into the accounting. If some of the larger chains had stiffened their resolve against the perceived Hearst threats and presented *Citizen Kane* for even a short run, the film might have shown a profit.

Through 1950, *Citizen Kane* played here and there, principally in the scattered revival theaters in larger cities that showed "oldies." But that was all. *Citizen Kane* disappeared in the United States almost entirely, and it didn't emerge again for more than five years.

7. Triumph

Amerca had not heard the last of *Citizen Kane* and in the late 1940s, the legend of Welles' motion picture was just beginning outside the United States. It was in France—where the postwar study of film as an art form was flourishing—that the first serious appreciation emerged to acknowledge *Citizen Kane* as a work of cinematic art.

The Nazi occupation of Europe prevented the importing of American films, so *Citizen Kane* didn't reach France until 1946. There, a cadre of young film writers, including André Bazin and later François Truffaut, sang the film's praises in a blend of appreciation for the film itself with a near-euphoric hero worship for the man who had produced so extraordinary a film at such a young age. "To shoot *Citizen Kane* at twenty-five years of age," sighed François Truffaut of Welles. "Is this not the dream of all the young habitués of the cinémathèques?"

Several French film magazines printed reviews and articles about Welles and his film, but it was *La Revue du Cinéma* (now *Cahiers du Cinéma*) that became the standard bearer of acclaim for *Citizen Kane*. The magazine printed articles in a succession of issues analyzing Welles' direction, Toland's photography, and the overall influence of *Citizen Kane* on film as an artistic medium, rather than as a purely commercial enterprise. For the first time, now years after its initial release, *Citizen Kane* was beginning to be viewed as a work of art.

That attitude had not yet taken hold in the United States. At the height of the American studio system, motion pictures—even the best ones—were merely fodder for the grist mill of endless production, distribution, and exhibition. With few revival theaters, and the convenience of videotape and laser discs still decades away, even the top-notch box office pictures dropped from sight in between widely spaced rereleases. Such was the case for *Citizen Kane* —and it had no gold-plated box office record to fall back on to ensure regular rerelease.

For the first half of the 1950s, the film was practically a nonentity in the United States; even though it was well remembered for its contributions to the screen, it wasn't shown *anywhere* in America—at least not where the public could buy tickets—once it faded away in 1950. It wasn't until 1956, fifteen years after the film's initial release, that *Citizen Kane* was reissued, in part to capitalize on Orson Welles' rousing return to Broadway in *King Lear*.

Meanwhile, the study of film in the United States had begun to grow throughout the fifties; although in America, it was not the film critics and cinema clubs, as in France, but rather institutions such as the Museum of Modern Art in New York, the growing number of revival theaters, and the just-emerging university film schools that led the way. Chief among the subjects for resurrection was *Citizen Kane*.

Ironically, the steady diet of films available on television—one of the chief villains in the fall of the Hollywood studios—helped establish classic films as works to appreciate among a new postwar audience of young film viewers. When the studios began to sell or lease their film catalogues for broadcast, RKO's was among the first to go on the block. In December 1955, 740 films were sold to C&C Super Corp. Within months, *Citizen Kane* aired on television for the first time.

By the mid-1950s, *Citizen Kane* had not as yet become enshrined, but its reputation was growing. The film had never strayed far from the limelight among those who appreciated cinema most; as early as 1952, a poll of film critics conducted by *Sight and Sound,* the British film magazine, ranked *Citizen Kane* as a runner-up in its listing of the top ten best films ever made.

The rise of film appreciation as a discipline, plus the growing stature of Orson Welles as both a director of and actor in many other projects, further enhanced *Citizen Kane*'s place in the film rankings. In 1962, a second poll by *Sight and Sound* voted *Citizen Kane* the best film of all time; it has stayed number one with the critics ever since. It must have been mildly amusing for Welles to note that both Louella Parsons and Hedda Hopper lived to see the motion picture they hated so much elevated to the ranks of the best films ever produced.

But what must have been particularly satisfying for Welles was that not only had *Citizen Kane* risen to the top of the heap in surveys of critics and academics, it had also acquired a position no less solid with the public—the film's time had finally come with the general audience that had not appreciated it when it was first released. Several polls of film fans placed *Citizen Kane* at top of the picks of screen favorites.

A publicity poster from the 1956 rerelease of Citizen Kane. *RKO had no better luck choosing a catchy slogan for the picture the second time around than it did for the original release.*

Some called him a hero.... Others called him a heel

ORSON WELLES

CITIZEN KANE

THE MERCURY ACTORS Joseph Cotten · Everett Sloane
George Coulouris · Paul Stewart · Erskine Sanford · Dorothy Comingore
Ray Collins · William Alland · Ruth Warrick · Agnes Moorehead
RE-RELEASED by RKO RADIO PICTURES

The film that routinely tops all critical polls, the motion picture used most frequently in film classes to show young filmmakers how to create their art, is now also first in the minds of film fans who have grown to love it. For Orson Welles and *Citizen Kane,* the triumph was, at last, complete.

The Sight and Sound Surveys: The Best Films of All Time

1952

1. *The Bicycle Thief* (Vittorio De Sica, 1949)
2. *City Lights* (Charles Chaplin, 1930)
   The Gold Rush (Charles Chaplin, 1925)
4. *Battleship Potemkin* (Sergei Eisenstein, 1925)
5. *Louisiana Story* (Robert Flaherty, 1947)
   Intolerance (D. W. Griffith, 1916)
7. *Greed* (Erich Von Stroheim, 1924)
   Le Jour Se Leve (Marcel Carné, 1939)
10. *Brief Encounter* (David Lean, 1945)
    Le Million (René Clair, 1930)

Runners-Up

1. *Citizen Kane* (Orson Welles, 1941)
   La Grande Illusion (Jean Renoir, 1937)
   The Grapes of Wrath (John Ford, 1940)
4. *The Childhood of Maxim Gorki* (Mark Donskoi, 1938)
   Monsieur Verdoux (Charles Chaplin, 1947)

1962

1. *Citizen Kane* (Orson Welles, 1941)
2. *L'Avventura* (Michelangelo Antonioni, 1960)
3. *La Règle du Jeu* (Jean Renoir, 1939)*

4. *Greed* (Erich Von Stroheim, 1924)
   Ugetsu Monogatari (Kenji Mizoguchi, 1953)
6. *Battleship Potemkin* (Sergei Eisenstein, 1925)
   The Bicycle Thief (Vittorio De Sica, 1949)
   Ivan the Terrible (Sergei Eisenstein, 1943–46)
9. *La Terra Trema* (Luchino Visconti, 1948)
10. *L'Atalante* (Jean Vigo, 1933)

* Released in the United States as *The Rules of the Game.*

Runners-Up

1. *Hiroshima Mon Amour* (Alain Resnais, 1959)
   Pather Panchali (Satyajit Ray, 1955)
   Zéro de Conduite (Jean Vigo, 1933)
4. *City Lights* (Charles Chaplin, 1930)
   The Childhood of Maxim Gorki (Mark Donskoi, 1938)

1972

1. *Citizen Kane* (Orson Welles, 1941)
2. *La Règle du Jeu* (Jean Renoir, 1939)*
3. *Battleship Potemkin* (Sergei Eisenstein, 1925)
4. *8½* (Federico Fellini, 1963)
5. *L'Avventura* (Michelangelo Antonioni, 1960)
   Persona (Ingmar Bergman, 1967)
7. *The Passion of Joan of Arc* (Carl Dreyer, 1928)
8. *The General* (Buster Keaton/Clyde Bruckman, 1926)
   The Magnificent Ambersons (Orson Welles, 1942)
10. *Ugetsu Monogatari* (Kenji Mizoguchi, 1953)
    Wild Strawberries (Ingmar Bergman, 1957)

* Released in the United States as *The Rules of the Game.*

Runners-Up

1. *The Gold Rush* (Charles Chaplin, 1925)
   Hiroshima Mon Amour (Alain Resnais, 1959)
   Ikiru (Akira Kurosawa, 1952)

Ivan the Terrible (Sergei Eisenstein, 1943–46)
Pierrot le Fou (Jean-Luc Godard, 1965)
Vertigo (Alfred Hitchcock, 1958)

1982

1. *Citizen Kane* (Orson Welles, 1941)
2. *La Règle du Jeu* (Jean Renoir, 1939)*
3. *Seven Samurai* (Akira Kurosawa, 1954)
4. *Singin' in the Rain* (Gene Kelly/Stanley Donen, 1952)
5. *8½* (Federico Fellini, 1963)
6. *Battleship Potemkin* (Sergei Eisenstein, 1925)
7. *L'Avventura* (Michelangelo Antonioni, 1960)
8. *The Magnificent Ambersons* (Orson Welles, 1942)
9. *Vertigo* (Alfred Hitchcock, 1958)
10. *The General* (Buster Keaton/Clyde Bruckman, 1926)
    The Searchers (John Ford, 1956)

* Released in the United States as *The Rules of the Game.*

Runners-Up

1. *2001: A Space Odyssey* (Stanley Kubrick, 1968)
   Andrei Roublev (Andrei Tarkovsky, 1966)
   Greed (Erich Von Stroheim, 1924)
   Jules and Jim (François Truffaut, 1961)
   The Third Man (Carol Reed, 1949)

8. After the End

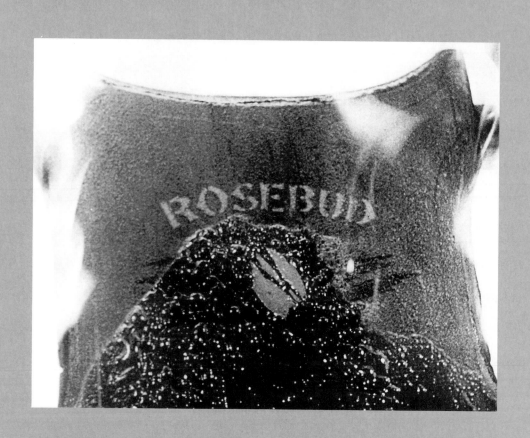

Following *Citizen Kane,* Orson Welles went on to develop a fruitful yet stormy motion picture career, creating a body of work that was as controversial as the film which began it. Welles' time in residence at RKO was fraught with controversy; control of the final cut for his next production, *The Magnificent Ambersons,* was taken from him, the film drastically reedited when the director's version proved unacceptable to preview audiences.

In June 1942, barely a year after *Citizen Kane* premiered, George Schaefer was forced to resign as president of RKO, when the studio's fortunes once again fell into disarray. Two weeks later, the Mercury staff was summarily ejected from the RKO lot, the space supposedly needed for other production companies. That the expulsion followed Schaefer's dismissal by only a few days was, of course, purely coincidental.

The extraordinary union forged between a young director and a forward-thinking studio chief may not have turned out as successfully as all had hoped in the summer of 1939. Nevertheless, *The Magnificent Ambersons,* even in its recut form, together with *Citizen Kane,* form a permanent legacy to demonstrate the tremendous achievement possible when filmmakers take the risk often viewed as the greatest in Hollywood: bucking the system to attempt something new. *Citizen Kane* remains a fabulous aberration, the potent proof that a film of greatness could be produced within the Hollywood studio system by an individual whose ideas and methods ran contrary to all of the conventions.

While misfortune may have plagued the early success of *Citizen Kane,* the sole injustice which remained from those early days of Welles' career was the perception that he created his most brilliant success almost before his career began, and his efforts that followed were somehow lessened by his first achievement. "After Welles' success with *Citizen Kane*," the Associated Press once summed up far too simply, "his dealings with Hollywood studios deteriorated, although he continued to turn out films, appear on talk shows, promote wine and act as a narrator."

True, Welles may have had only one opportunity to achieve such an astounding feat—a young director, creating his first film, who produced a

Statues from the great hall of Xanadu rest in a warehouse on the studio lot that once housed RKO-Pathé; fifty years after the filming of Citizen Kane, *the studio was owned by GTG Entertainment, a partnership between producer Grant Tinker and the Gannett Corp. Some of the statues are still crated in wood frames tagged "Xanadu, Florida."*

masterpiece—yet over the four decades that followed *Citizen Kane,* he developed a vibrant career in motion pictures that transcended any single film. Welles' true monument remains the extraordinary diversity he accomplished in his work, as he directed or performed in more than forty films in Europe and America, a life's achievement of filmmaking more varied and daring than any of his contemporaries.

Always in demand as an actor—yet reluctant to devote his energies solely to performance when he could produce and direct instead—Welles' life was an unending quest to create innovative motion pictures and secure financing to produce them. He took acting roles directed by others so he could earn money to fund his own projects; Welles' films sometimes failed miserably, often succeeded brilliantly, but were always notable for their imaginative approach to filmmaking. For those who could look beyond his early success with *Citizen Kane,* Welles became acknowledged for what he had always hoped to become: the innovative, productive maverick, ever working against the grain.

Welles remained as well known later in his career for his unorthodox production methods as when he started: he shot *Macbeth* in little more than two weeks; his *Othello,* produced when he could devote the time and money to the project, required years of sporadic work to complete. Yet Welles and his films—*Lady from Shanghai, Chimes at Midnight, Touch of Evil, The Stranger, The Trial,* and *F for Fake,* among them—always pushed the creative envelope, for better or worse, to explore new cinematic directions and bold ideas in filmmaking.

* * *

Welles appeared in a motion picture for the final time in a captivating role as the commentator of Henry Jaglom's *Someone to Love.* The film, shot shortly before Welles' death but not released until three years later, provides a pleasant but eerie memorial to Welles—a last stand, seemingly from beyond the grave, for him to probe once more the questions of life, love, and relationships.

However, *Someone to Love* would not mark the last time Welles surfaced in the news after he died. He turned out to be something of a soothsayer, because in his last days, he fully understood that yet another threat loomed for his greatest work.

Welles knew that an emerging technology, video colorization, might be used one day to alter *Citizen Kane.* Colorization—which with a computer palette adds color to a video transfer of black-and-white film—provides what some programmers consider a necessary marketing boost to entice viewers who are supposedly uninterested in watching movies originally shot in black and white.

Recalled director Henry Jaglom, "Orson said to me at lunch, about two weeks before he died—I remember this vividly—'Please do this for me. Don't let Ted Turner deface my movie with his crayons.' "

It was an impressive bit of clairvoyance. The conversation in September 1985 occurred nearly a year before Turner Entertainment acquired MGM/United Artists, the studio which then owned the rights to *Citizen Kane*. In 1986, Turner sought the incredible celluloid treasure trove in the studio vaults; he sold the studio itself, but retained the broadcast rights to more than 3,600 motion pictures and other properties in the studio's inventory. The company began to colorize some of Hollywood's most popular films, despite protests from the motion picture industry's creative talent.

Colorization affects only the video version of a motion picture; the original film is not affected. However, for those who are exposed to classic films on television, at best colorization represents a pallid attempt to attract their interest. At the same time the process overwhelms the artistic intentions carefully placed on film by a director working painstakingly with his production designer, photographer, and lighting experts.

With films such as *Casablanca, It's a Wonderful Life,* and *The Maltese Falcon* already colorized, the announcement in mid-January 1989 that *Citizen Kane* would undergo the same computerized treatment became a battle cry to gather Hollywood's most powerful forces to stop the colorization. Many of Hollywood's artisans rallied in support; among them a host of directors who were weaned on *Citizen Kane*.

The uproar lasted barely two weeks. In mid-February, Turner Entertainment canceled its plans to colorize *Citizen Kane*. The reasons were not artistic or aesthetic—rather, they were legal. *Citizen Kane* had been protected, firmly and finally, by Orson Welles' original 1939 contract with RKO. The fifty-year-old contract that Hollywood had so despised saved the film that the entire motion picture industry grew to consider its greatest treasure.

"Our attorneys looked at the contract between RKO Pictures, Inc., and Orson Welles and his production company, Mercury Productions, Inc., and, on the basis of their review, we have decided not to proceed with colorization of the movie," said Roger Mayer, president of Turner Entertainment.

"While a court test might uphold our legal right to colorize the film, provisions of the contract could be read to prohibit colorization without permission of the Welles estate," Mayer said. "We have completed restoration of a printing negative which now enables us to show first-rate black-and-white prints of this masterpiece."

* * *

Orson Welles died on October 10, 1985, at age seventy. To the end, he was still the plotting producer, planning to bring his projects before the cameras;

*Welles in his mid-sixties,
still the plotting producer.*

at his death, he was working on a number of projects, not the least of which was a film production of *King Lear*—with himself in the title role.

Welles may have been a maverick, but the film world grew to acknowledge his artistry even though he didn't fit any of the standard molds. Welles had bestowed on him the highest awards for film achievement that the motion picture industry could offer: the Directors Guild gave Welles its D. W. Griffith Award in 1984 (he had already received an honorary Oscar in 1971 for his lifelong contributions to the art of cinema). Perhaps most notably, he was presented with the Lifetime Achievement Award of the American Film Institute in 1975, joining the likes of John Ford, Alfred Hitchcock, Bette Davis, and others, who were all products of the Hollywood studio system—a rogue among the establishment.

It was the creative rogue, Welles knew, who could provide a powerful motivating spirit that the finely honed but stodgy machinery of the studio system could never hope to inspire. The regret voiced time and again by many film veterans of Hollywood's golden era has been the frustration they felt over their lack of control of their work; scripts were shuttled from one writer to another, studio chiefs would order actors' performances radically reshaped, directors' individual creativity was often neutralized in the editing room for the sake of the studio's style. The eventual products were, indeed, marvelous films, but with only a few exceptions, an individual's claim over any measure of a motion picture was in large part diluted by the studio's unyielding control over its production methods.

The motion picture industry was not inherently flawed by its iron-clad rule over production of its films; the system worked superbly for decades to produce entertainment loved worldwide. However, the studios, with their production-line methods, were no safe harbor for individual creativity—they were never designed to operate smoothly with individuals rocking the boat—which is precisely why Welles' original contract with RKO caused such an uproar.

The most experienced directors and popular stars in Hollywood couldn't ensure, as they moved from one production to the next, that they would receive even a few slivers of the creative freedom that Welles' contract guaranteed. One can only imagine how many more *Citizen Kane*s might have been possible if the studio production chiefs who ran Hollywood in its heyday had been willing to unleash their veteran technical and creative forces, granting them but a portion of the creative control that Welles acquired as a novice.

For a few brief months during the summer of 1940, Orson Welles was granted the power to create a motion picture precisely as he wanted to film it, and he shared the artistic liberties of his no-strings contract with his cast and crew. Welles created an exacting personal vision for *Citizen Kane,* but he reached his goal by encouraging the people around him to take the lead and show him what they could accomplish together. They demonstrated in *Citizen Kane* the creative possibilities that could be achieved when a studio operating during the height of the motion picture industry's power was willing to let its artists work unencumbered by the system that dictated the norm.

"I owe it to my ignorance," Welles said of his success with *Citizen Kane,* twenty-five years after the film debuted. "If this word seems inadequate, replace it with innocence.

"I said to myself: this is what the camera should be really capable of doing, in a normal fashion. When we were at the point of shooting the first sequence, I said, 'Let's do that!' Gregg Toland answered that it was impossible. I came back with, 'We can always try; we'll soon see. Why not?' "

Compendium

THE CAST OF
CITIZEN KANE

This cast list for *Citizen Kane* is reprinted from RKO's complete roster of performers hired for Production #281. This list has been edited and revised somewhat: On RKO's original cast list, Dorothy Comingore was identified as "Linda Winters," her stage name. Al Eben, who had the brief speaking role as Solly, the Inquirer's production foreman, was originally supposed to be named Mike in the film. Alan Ladd's name was misspelled as "Allan."

The first ten actors in the cast are listed here in the same order they were showcased in cameos at the end of *Citizen Kane*. The cameos were part of Welles' efforts to highlight his players as much as possible: "Most of the principal actors in *Citizen Kane* are new to motion pictures," the film's credits read. "The Mercury Theatre is proud to introduce them."

The next grouping of eight performers appeared on screen in a standard cast list which followed the cameos (note where Welles placed himself). The remaining players—"small parts and bits," as they were called—are uncredited in the film.

THE CAST OF CITIZEN KANE

Jed Leland	Joseph Cotten
Susan Alexander	Dorothy Comingore
Kane's Mother	Agnes Moorehead
Emily Norton	Ruth Warrick
"Boss" Jim W. Gettys	Ray Collins
Carter	Erskine Sanford
Bernstein	Everett Sloane
Thompson	William Alland
Raymond	Paul Stewart
Thatcher	George Coulouris

Matiste	Fortunio Bonanova
The Headwaiter	Gus Schilling
Mr. Rawlston	Philip Van Zandt
Miss Anderson	Georgia Backus
Kane's Father	Harry Shannon
Kane III	Sonny Bupp
Kane, age eight	Buddy Swan
Kane	Orson Welles

SMALL PARTS AND BITS

Solly	Al Eben
Miss Townsend	Ellen Lowe
Entertainer	Charles Bennett
Dr. Corey	Irving Mitchell
Jennings	Joe Manz
Reporter	Alan Ladd
Reporter	Louise Currie
Reporter	Eddie Coke
Reporter	Walter Sande
Reporter	Arthur O'Connell
Reporter	Richard Wilson
Reporter	Katherine Trosper
Reporter	Milt Kibbe
Newsman	Bruce Sidney
Newspaper Man	Lew Harvey
Reporter	Louis Natheaux
Teddy Roosevelt	Tom Curran
Civic Leader	Ed Peil
Civic Leader	Charles Meakin
Politician	Mitchell Ingraham
Politician	Francis Sayles
Narrator	William Alland
Maid	Louise Franklin
Bit Nurse	Edith Evanson
Orchestra Leader	Arthur Kay
Chorus Master	Tudor Williams
Prompter	James Mack
Stagehand	Gohr Van Vleck
Stagehand	Jack Raymond
City Editor	Herbert Corthell
Hireling	Shimen Ruskin
Hireling	George Sherwood
Hireling	Eddie Cobb
Bit	Edward Hemmer
Bit Expressman	Olin Francis
Ethel	Frances Neal
Bit Photographer	Bob Dudley
Copy Boy	George Noisom
Boss Printer	Jack Curtis
Bit Investigator	Landers Stevens
Ward Heeler	John Dilson
Ward Heeler	Walter James
Male Secretary	William O'Brien
Housemaid	Donna Dax
Big Governess	Myrtle Rischell
Male Secretary	Joe North
Newswoman	Petra De Silva
Bit Man	Gino Corrado
French Maid	Suzanne Dulier
Shadowgraph Man	Major McBride
Jetsam	Karl Thomas
Flotsam	Glen Turnbull
Bit	Carmen La Roux
Portugese Laborer	Harry Vejar
Reporter	Harriet Brandon
Bit General	Captain Garcia
Bit Speaker	Art Yeoman
Politician	Phillip Morris
Insert Bit	Marie Day
Gorilla Man	Albert Frazier
Bit Man	Guy Repp
Bit Copy Boy	Tim Davis
Bit Man	Buck Mack
Bit Butler	Jack Morton

THE PRODUCTION OF
CITIZEN KANE

A Mercury Theatre Production for RKO Radio Pictures, Inc.

First public screening in New York City at the Palace Theater, May 1, 1941. Premiered in Los Angeles at the El Capitan Theater on May 8, 1941.

Director	**Orson Welles**
Assistant Directors	**Eddie Donahoe**
	Freddie Fleck
Producer	**Orson Welles**
Associate Producer	**Richard Baer**
Assistant Producers	**William Alland**
	Richard Wilson
Screenplay	**Herman J. Mankiewicz**
	Orson Welles
Editorial Supervision	**John Houseman**
Continuity	**Amalia Kent**
Cinematography	**Gregg Toland**
Camera Operator	**Bert Shipman**
Gaffer	**Bill McClellan**
Grip	**Ralph Hoge**
Assistant Cameraman	**Eddie Garvin**
Cameraman for Early Makeup and Wardrobe Tests	**Russell Metty**
Retakes and Additional Shooting	**Harry Wild**
Original Musical Score	**Bernard Herrmann** **(Herrmann also arranged the score, and conducted its recording.)**
''Charlie Kane'' Lyrics	**Herman Ruby** **(Music from the Mexican song, "A Poco No")**
Art Director	**Perry Ferguson**

Assistant Art Director	**Hilyard Brown**
Principal Sketch Artist	**Charles Ohmann**
Sketches and Graphics	**Al Abbott**
	Claude Gillingwater, Jr.
	Albert Pyke
	Maurice Zuberano
Art Department Head	**Van Nest Polglase**
Set Decoration	**Darrell Silvera (Department Head)**
Assistant Set Decorator	**Al Fields**
Prop Manager	**Charles Sayers**
Makeup	**Maurice Seiderman**
Assistant Makeup Artist	**Layne Britton**
Makeup Department Head	**Mel Berns**
Costume Design	**Edward Stevenson**
Wardrobe	**Earl Leas**
	Margaret Van Horn
Special Effects	**Vernon L. Walker (Department Head)**
Optical Printing	**Linwood G. Dunn**
Effects Cameraman	**Russell Cully**
Montage Effects	**Douglas Travers**
Matte Artist	**Mario Larrinaga**
Editor	**Robert Wise**
Assistant Editor	**Mark Robson**
Sound Department Head	**John Aalberg**
Sound Production Mixer	**Bailey Fesler**
Boom	**Jimmy Thompson**
Rerecording	**James G. Stewart**
Sound Effects	**Harry Essman**
Still Photography	**Alexander Kahle**
Publicity for Mercury Theatre	**Herbert Drake**
Dance Choreography	**Arthur Appel**

THE BUDGET

These budget figures are RKO's budget tabulations for *Citizen Kane* dated March 8, 1941. Although there were other expenses associated with the film during its original release, this tabulation constitutes the budget for the actual production of the motion picture.

In spite of RKO's ongoing concerns about finances, Welles remained remarkably close to budget during production of *Citizen Kane*—an amazing feat, considering his lack of experience as a producer-director and the intensely complicated nature of his first project.

In fact, the single largest budget category in the budget of *Citizen Kane* was "Indirect Costs," the studio's own charges for overhead and administration that it automatically tacked on to every production. Even with indirect costs included, Welles' spending on *Citizen Kane* exceeded his target by only 12 percent.

Category	Budget Estimate	Actual Costs
Supervision	$ 81,493.00	$ 83,015.27
Songs	5,000.00	362.00
Screenplay	34,317.00	34,195.24
Directors	—	458.33
Cast	68,048.00	87,633.68
Extras	13,557.00	16,943.53
Production Staff	$ 16,376.00	$ 18,183.20
Camera Staff	24,270.00	26,684.58
Sound Recording	6,752.00	9,400.74
Film and Laboratory	18,117.00	20,988.94
Set Design and Art Work	12,000.00	15,350.13
Set Construction	58,775.00	59,206.23
Set Maintenance	4,000.00	3,981.17
Set Standby Labor	12,500.00	14,653.71
Set Striking	6,500.00	6,541.43
Properties and Drapery	21,913.00	29,355.18
Lighting	19,895.00	24,171.60
Wardrobe	15,766.00	17,241.64
Makeup	15,586.00	13,675.10
Transportation	14,782.00	11,189.98
Location	1,759.00	1,845.77
Special Effects	2,698.00	5,493.79
Cutting	9,560.00	12,132.33
Musical Score	22,464.00	35,435.86
Scoring: Sound and Laboratory	1,788.00	3,582.43
Rerecording	7,288.00	16,761.37
Process	24,465.00	38,048.74
Inserts	4,780.00	7,905.84
Main and End Titles	750.00	970.40
Checkup and Master Prints	1,000.00	1,902.88
Tests	20,000.00	16,425.18
Stills	2,463.00	2,854.26
Special Taxes	13,000.00	14,405.28
Insurance	9,000.00	7,952.31
Royalties and Code Certificate	7,005.00	—
Miscellaneous	25,500.00	24,811.07
Labor Adjustments	—	2,274.19
Total Direct Costs	$603,167.00	$686,033.38
Indirect Costs (20% studio overhead)	$120,633.00	$137,206.67
Total Picture Cost	$723,800.00	$823,240.05

GREGG TOLAND AND BERNARD HERRMANN

Soon after *Citizen Kane* was produced, two of the artists most vital to its production, cinematographer Gregg Toland and composer Bernard Herrmann, were each asked to write articles about their experiences working on the motion picture. Their recollections provide a rare glimpse at the role of these two immensely talented artists in the process of filmmaking—and in particular, how they responded to the unusual and energizing circumstances which collaborating with Orson Welles brought to their work.

"HOW I BROKE THE RULES IN *CITIZEN KANE*"

BY

Gregg Toland

POPULAR PHOTOGRAPHY
JUNE 1941

There's been a good deal of gratifying discussion recently about the photography of Orson Welles' first movie, *Citizen Kane*. The gist of the talk has been that the cinematography in that film was "daring" and "advanced," and that I violated all the photographic commandments and conventions in shooting the picture.

Right away I want to make a distinction between "commandment" and "convention." Photographically speaking, I understand a commandment to be a rule, axiom, or principle, an incontrovertible fact of photographic procedure which is unchangeable for physical and chemical reasons. On the other hand, a convention, to me, is a usage which has become acceptable through repetition. It is a tradition rather than a rule. With time, the convention becomes a commandment, through force of habit. I feel that the limiting effect is both obvious and unfortunate.

With these definitions in mind, I'll admit that I defied a good many conventions in filming *Citizen Kane*. Orson Welles was insistent that the story be told most effectively, letting the Hollywood conventions of movie-making go hang if need be. With such wholehearted backing, I was able to test and prove several ideas generally accepted as being radical in Hollywood circles.

Welles' use of the cinematographer as a real aid to him in telling the story, and his appreciation of the camera's story-telling potentialities, helped me immeasurably. He was willing—and this is very rare in Hollywood—that I take weeks to achieve a desired photographic effect.

The photographic approach to *Citizen Kane* was planned and considered long before the first camera turned. That is also unconventional in Hollywood, where most cinematographers learn of their next assignments only a few days before the scheduled shooting starts. Altogether, I was on the job for a half year, including preparation and actual shooting.

Although it was Welles' first effort in movies, he came to the job with a rare vision and understanding of camera purpose and direction. It was his idea that the technique of filming should never be evident to the audience. He wanted to avoid the established Hollywood conventions, most of which are accepted by audiences because of their frequent use. And this frequent use of conventions is dictated by pressure of time and reluctance to deviate from the accepted.

As a case in point, depth of field nearly always is sacrificed in Hollywood productions. The normal human eye sees everything before it (within reasonable distance) clearly and sharply. There is no special or single center of visual sharpness in real life. But the Hollywood cameras focus on a center of interest, and allow the other components of a scene to "fuzz out" in those regions before and beyond the focal point.

The attainment of an approximate human-eye focus was one of our fundamental aims of *Citizen Kane*. It took a great deal of doing, but we proved that it can be done.

We solved the depth-of-field problem by means of preproduction testing and experiment. We built our system of "visual reality" on the well-known fact that lenses of shorter focal length are characterized by comparatively greater depth, and that stopping down a lens increases the depth even further.

The tendency in Hollywood has been to stop down to f3.5 occasionally in filming interiors. More often the working aperture is between f2.3 and f3.2. The use of the f3.5 aperture is still uncommon enough to be cause for conversation in the film capital. Yet any professional or amateur who has used short-focus lenses knows that the increase in depth obtained by stopping down from f2.3 to f3.5 can make quite a difference.

But we wanted to stop down considerably further. By experimenting with high-speed films, we discovered that lens aperture could be reduced appreciably, but that we still weren't able to stop down enough for our purposes. This meant that an increased illumination level had to be obtained. And since we were already violating Hollywood tradition by using ceilinged sets, we were unable to step up illumination by means of extra lights mounted on catwalks or strung above the scene.

The Vard "Opticoating" system developed at the California Institute of Technology proved to be one factor in the eventual solution of our lighting problems. Being essentially a method of treating lens surfaces, Opticoating eliminates refraction, permits light to penetrate instead of scattering, and thus increases lens speed by as much as a full stop. Our coated lenses also permitted us to shoot directly into lights without anything like the dire results usually encountered.

Another aid in solving our small-aperture problem was the twin-arc broadside lamp, developed for Technicolor work. We began to employ these lamps before we hit upon the use of the high-speed film which we eventually chose. The combination of coated lenses, arc broadside lamps, and the fastest available film made it possible to photograph nearly all interior scenes at an aperture of f8 or even smaller. I shot several scenes at f11 and f16. That's a big jump from f2.3 and it's certainly unconventional in Hollywood filming.

Even the standard 47 and 50-mm. lenses afford great depth of field when stopped down to f11 or f16. And the shorter-focus wide-angle lenses act virtually like human eyes, providing almost universal focus at such small apertures. In some cases we were able to hold sharp focus over a depth of 200 feet.

I referred previously to the unconventional use of ceilinged sets. The *Citizen Kane* sets have ceilings because we wanted reality, and we felt that it would be easier to believe a room was a room if its ceiling could be seen in the picture. Furthermore, lighting effects in unceilinged rooms generally are not realistic because the illumination comes from unnatural angles.

We planned most of our camera setups to take advantage of the ceilings, in some cases even building the sets so as to permit shooting upward from floor level. None of the sets was rigged for overhead lighting, although occasionally necessary backlighting was arranged by lifting a small section of the ceiling and using a light through the opening. The deep sets called for unusually penetrating lamps, and the twin-arc broadsides mentioned earlier filled the bill. The ceilings gave us another advantage in addition to realism—freedom from worry about microphone shadow, the bugaboo of all sound filming. We were able to place our mikes above the muslin ceiling, which allowed them to pick up sound but not to throw shadows.

There were other violations of Hollywood tradition in the photographic details of *Citizen Kane*. One of them resulted from Welles' insistence that scenes should flow together smoothly and imperceptibly. Accordingly, before actual shooting began, everything had

been planned with full realization of what the camera could bring to the audience. We arranged our action so as to avoid direct cuts, to permit panning or dollying from one angle to another whenever that type of camera action fitted the continuity. By way of example, scenes which conventionally would require a shift from closeup to full shot were planned so that the action would take place simultaneously in extreme foreground and extreme background.

Our constant efforts toward increasing realism and making mechanical details imperceptible led eventually to the solution of all the problems we had created for ourselves. As we avoided direct cuts, so we steered clear of traditional transitions. Most of the transitions in *Citizen Kane* are lap dissolves in which the background dissolves from one scene to the next shortly before the players in the foreground are dissolved. This was accomplished rather simply with two light-dimming outfits, one for the actors and one for the set.

The dissolve is begun by dimming the lights on the background, eventually fading it out entirely. Then the lights on the people are dimmed to produce a fade-out on them. The fade-in is made the same way, fading in the set lights first, then the lights for the people.

Intercutting was eliminated wherever possible, with the idea of achieving further visual simplification. Instead of following the usual practice of cutting from a close-up to an "insert" (which explains or elaborates upon the close-up), we made a single, straight shot, compressing the whole scene into a single composition.

Here's an example. Where the idea is to show an actor reading something, we don't show a close-up of the actor and then follow it with a cut to the reading matter "insert." We simply compose the shot with the actor's head on one side of the frame and the reading matter on the other. In one such case in the filming of *Citizen Kane,* the actor's head was less than 16 inches from the lens, the reading matter was about three feet away, and a group of men in the background was 12 to 18 feet away. Yet all three components of this scene—actor in foreground, reading matter, and group—are sharp and clear to the audience.

My focusing was based on the principle of depth of field. Knowing the focal length and other characteristics of the lenses we were using, I worked out the various focal points as I came to them. By following a depth-of-field table in using any lens, you can always tell just where to set your focus in order to attain overall sharpness within required limits. It's an important fact, however, that much depends upon the properties of the lens in use at the time—and its characteristics should be determined carefully before any attempt is made to use this zone-focusing technique.

Such differences as exist between the cinematography in *Citizen Kane* and the camera work on the average Hollywood product are based on the rare opportunity provided me by Orson Welles, who was in complete sympathy with my theory that the photography should fit the story. I have been trying to follow that principle for some time in an effort to provide visual variety as well as a proper photographic vehicle for the plot. Fitting *Wuthering Heights* and *Grapes of Wrath* and *Long Voyage Home* to an identical photographic pattern would be unfair to director, writer, actors, and audience.

Style too often becomes deadly sameness. In my opinion, the day of highly stylized cinematography is passing, and is being superseded by a candid, realistic technique and an individual approach to each new film subject.

You will accomplish much more by fitting your photography to the story instead of limiting the story to the narrow confines of conventional photographic practice. And as you do so you'll learn that the movie camera is a flexible instrument, with many of its possibilities still unexplored. New realms remain to be discovered by amateurs and professionals who are willing to think about it and take the necessary time to make the thought a reality.

* * *

"SCORE FOR A FILM"

BY
Bernard Herrmann

NEW YORK TIMES
MAY 25, 1941

"Citizen Kane" was the first motion picture on which I had ever worked. I had heard of the many handicaps that exist for a composer in Hollywood. One was the great speed with which scores often had to be written—sometimes in as little as two or three weeks. Another was that the composer seldom had time to do his own orchestration. And again—that once the music was written and conducted, the composer had little to say about the sound levels or dynamics of the score in the finished film.

Not one of these conditions prevailed during the production of "Citizen Kane."

I was given twelve weeks in which to do my job. This not only gave me ample time to think about the film and to work out a general artistic plan for the score, but also enabled me to do my own orchestration and conducting.

* * *

I worked on the film, reel by reel, as it was being shot and cut. In this way I had a sense of the picture being built, and of my own music being a part of that building. Most musical scores in Hollywood are written after the film is entirely finished, and the composer must adapt his music to the scenes on the screen. In many scenes in "Citizen Kane," an entirely different method was used, many of the sequences being tailored to match the music.

This was particularly true in the numerous photographic "montages," which are used throughout the film to denote the passing of time. When I first saw the picture I felt that it might be interesting to write complete musical numbers for these montages. In other words, instead of a mere atmospheric or rhythmic cue, a brief piece would be written. Welles agreed, and once the music was set, cut many of his sequences to match the length of the pieces.

* * *

The most striking illustration of this method may be found in the "breakfast montage" between Kane and his first wife. Here, in the space of three or four minutes, Welles shows the rise and fall of affection between two married people. The setting is a breakfast table. The young couple enters, gay and very much in love. They talk for a few seconds, then the scene changes. Once more we see them at the breakfast table, but the atmosphere has changed. Discord is beginning to creep into the conversation. Brief scene after brief scene follows, each showing the gradual breakdown of their affection, until finally they read their newspapers, opposite each other, in silence.

For this montage, I used the old classic form of the theme and variations. A waltz in the style of Waldteufel is the theme. It is heard during the first scene. Then, as discord crops up, the variations begin. Each scene is a separate variation. Finally, the waltz theme is heard bleakly played in the high registers of the violins.

Earlier in the film the scenes in the office showing Kane's newspaper activities are treated in a similar way. This part of the picture takes place in the 1890s, and, to match its mood, I used the various dance forms popular at that time. Thus, the montage showing the increase of circulation of the Inquirer is done as a can-can scherzo. The Inquirer's campaign against the traction trust is done in the form of a gallop. Kane and his friend Leland arrive at the office to the rhythm of early ragtime. This whole section, in itself, contains a kind of ballet suite in miniature.

* * *

Leitmotifs are used in "Citizen Kane" to give unity to the score as a whole. I am not a great believer in the leitmotif as a device for motion picture music—but in this film its use was practically imperative, because of the story itself and the manner in which it is unfolded.

There are two main motifs. One—a simple four-note figure in the brass—is that of Kane's power. It is given out in the very first two bars of the film. The second motif is that of Rosebud. Heard as a solo on the vibraphone, it first appears during the death scene at the very beginning of the picture. It is heard again and again throughout the film under various guises, and if followed closely, is a clue to the ultimate identity of Rosebud itself.

The motif of power is also transformed, becoming a vigorous piece of ragtime, a hornpipe polka, and at the end of the picture, a final commentary of Kane's life.

In handling these motifs I used a great deal of what might be termed "radio scoring." The movies frequently overlook opportunities for musical cues which last only a few seconds—that is, from five to fifteen seconds at the most—the reason being that the eye usually covers the transition.

On the other hand, in radio drama, every scene must be bridged by some sort of sound device, so that even five seconds of music becomes a vital instrument in telling the ear that the scene is shifting. I felt that in this film, where the photographic contrasts were often so sharp and sudden, a brief cue—even two or three chords—might heighten the effect immeasurably.

In addition to all this psychological and structural music, "Citizen Kane" is full of incidental music of all kinds. There is a large section of newsreel music, bands and hurdy-gurdy tunes, there is even an opera recitative and aria. All of these are realistic music. The newsreel music during the "News on the March" sequence was selected from the RKO files, and used in typical newsreel manner. The opera aria, "Salammbo," was composed in the style of the 19th-century French Oriental operatic school.

* * *

In orchestrating the picture, I avoided, as much as possible, the realistic sound of a large symphony orchestra. The motion picture soundtrack is an exquisitely sensitive medium, and with skillful engineering a simple bass flute solo, the pulsing of a bass drum, or the sound of muted horns can often be far more effective than half a hundred musicians playing away. Save for the opera sequence, some of the ballet montages, and a portion of the final scene, most of the cues were orchestrated for unorthodox instrumental combinations.

Sound effects were blended many times in "Citizen Kane," with the music, to add intensity to certain scenes. This also was a carryover from radio technique. The best example of this may be found in the "suicide" montage, which portrays the chaos of the second Mrs. Kane's operatic career. Here, soundtracks of her voice were blended with a rhythmical musical motif to produce an effect of mounting hysteria.

Music also was used in place of an actual sound effect, as in the jigsaw puzzle scenes at Xanadu, where it simulates the endless ticking of a clock.

* * *

Finally, a word about the "dubbing" of the music—that is, the recording of the score into the final soundtrack. Too often, in Hollywood, the composer has little to say about this technical procedure, and the result is that some of the best film music is often submerged to scarcely audible levels. Welles and I felt that music which was intended only as atmospheric background should be originally written for that purpose, and not toned down in the dubbing room. In other words, the dynamics of all music in the picture should be planned ahead of time so that the final dubbing is merely a transference process.

With this in mind, two full weeks were spent in the dubbing room, and music under our supervision was often re-recorded six or seven times before the proper dynamic level was achieved. The result is an exact projection of the original ideas in the score. Technically, no composer could ask for more.

* * *

THE REVIEWS

Here is a selection of the original reviews of *Citizen Kane*, including commentary from the general press, as well as views from the motion picture industry publications.

Clearly, most of the critics who covered Hollywood films in 1941 stood staunchly behind *Citizen Kane*—perhaps too staunchly. Several of these reviews are laced with overdoses of hyperbole blended with the legitimate praise; more than a few reviews, for example, gushed about the point that the "entire cast" of *Citizen Kane* was new to motion pictures. Even RKO's publicity acknowledged that most—but not all—of the players were new to the screen.

Also, some reviews had more than a little trouble with other facts as well; those which attempted to reprint dialogue from the film— in particular the passage in which William Randolph Hearst's name is mentioned—couldn't get it quite right, even though they reprinted them as if they were transcription of actual quotes.

Finally, one publication decided that it should divulge the film's most important secret: the *Hollywood Reporter*, in the midst of its praise-filled review of *Citizen Kane*, gave away the meaning of Rosebud six weeks before the film premiered.

Beyond the hype, of particular interest is the distinct note of desperation that fills those reviews published in mid-March of 1941, when the threat against *Citizen Kane*'s survival seemed greatest. Today, with *Citizen Kane* such an integral part of American film history, it seems nearly inconceivable to imagine that the film might not exist. Yet because of the Hearst controversy, when some of these reviews appeared—in particular the articles published by *Time*, *Newsweek*, and the *Hollywood Reporter*—the distinct possibility remained that *Citizen Kane* would be destroyed or shelved forever without ever receiving public release.

The *Hollywood Reporter* may have summed up the feelings among all film writers in March of 1941, when in its otherwise lavish review, the publication glumly predicted, "we will be surprised if the picture ever hits a theater where admission is charged." To read the spectrum of overwhelmingly enthusiastic commentary for *Citizen Kane*, tinged with regret about the dark future which appeared to loom for the motion picture, provides an fascinating sidelight into the unique circumstances behind the controversy, as several of the film world's most influential writers wrote about the uncertain future of the film they knew was one of Hollywood's finest achievements.

THE NEW YORK TIMES

The review of *Citizen Kane* by Bosley Crowther, film critic for the *New York Times*, was one of the most insightful—and praise-filled—appraisals of *Citizen Kane* published following the film's premiere in New York.

After his original review was published on May 2, 1941, Crowther felt the film's unorthodox approach required additional commentary—a feeling also reinforced by his own "uneasy" ponderings that some of the original reviews may have gone a bit too far in their praise. After viewing the film a second time, Crowther wrote another appraisal more than twice the length of his original review.

Crowther's refusal in both articles to mention the name of "an eminent publisher" sums up his distaste for the Hearst organization's interference in the release of *Citizen Kane*.

Here are both of Crowther's articles.

NEW YORK TIMES REVIEW
BY
Bosley Crowther
MAY 2, 1941

Within the withering spotlight as no other film has ever been before, Orson Welles' "Citizen Kane" had its world premiere at the Palace last evening. And now that the wraps are off, the mystery has been exposed, and Mr. Welles and the RKO directors have taken the much-debated leap, it can be safely stated that suppression of this film would have been a crime. For, in spite of some disconcerting lapses and strange ambiguities in the creation of the principal character, "Citizen Kane" is far and away the most surprising and cinematically exciting motion picture to be seen here in many a moon. As a matter of fact, it comes close to being the most sensational film ever made in Hollywood.

Count on Mr. Welles; he doesn't do things by halves. Being a mercurial fellow, with a frightening theatrical flair, he moved right into the movies, grabbed the medium by the ears and began to toss it around with the dexterity of a seasoned veteran. Fact is, he handled it with more verve and inspired ingenuity than any of the elder craftsmen have exhibited in years. With the able assistance of Gregg Toland, whose services should not be overlooked, he found in the camera the perfect instrument to encompass his dramatic energies and absorb his prolific ideas. Upon the screen he discovered an area large enough for his expansive whims to have free play. And the consequence is that he has made a picture of tremendous and overpowering scope, not in physical extent so much as in its rapid and graphic rotation of thoughts. Mr. Welles has put upon the screen a motion picture that really moves.

As for the story which he tells—and which has provoked such an uncommon fuss—this corner frankly holds considerable reservation. Naturally we wouldn't know how closely—if at all—it parallels the life of an eminent publisher, as has been somewhat cryptically alleged. But that is beside the point in a rigidly critical appraisal. The blamable circumstance is that it fails to provide a clear picture of the character and motives behind the man about whom the whole thing revolves.

As the picture opens, Charles Kane lies dying in the fabulous castle he has built—the castle called Xanadu, in which he has surrounded himself with vast treasures. And as death closes his eyes, his heavy lips murmur one word, "Rosebud." Suddenly the death scene is broken; the screen becomes alive with a staccato March-of-Time-like news feature recounting the career of the dead man—how, as a poor boy, he came into great wealth, how he became a newspaper publisher as a young man, how he aspired to political office, was defeated because of a personal scandal, devoted himself to material acquisition and finally died.

But the editor of the news feature is not satisfied, he wants to know the secret of Kane's strange nature and especially what he meant by "Rosebud." So a reporter is dispatched to find out, and the remainder of the picture is devoted to an absorbing visualization of Kane's phenomenal career as told by his boyhood guardian, two of his closest newspaper associates, and his mistress. Each is agreed on one thing—that Kane was a titanic egomaniac. It is also clearly revealed that the man was in some way consumed by his own terrifying selfishness. But just exactly what it is that eats upon him, why it is there and, for that matter, whether Kane is really a villain, a social parasite, is never clearly revealed. And the final, poignant identification of "Rosebud" sheds little more than a vague, sentimental light upon his character. At the end Kubla Kane is still an enigma—a very confusing one.

But check that off to the absorption of Mr. Welles in more visible details. Like the novelist Thomas Wolfe, his abundance of imagery is so great that it sometimes gets in the way of his logic. And the less critical will probably be content with an undefined Kane, anyhow. After all, nobody understood him. Why should Mr. Welles? Isn't it enough that he presents a theatrical character with consummate theatricality?

We would, indeed, like to say as many nice things as possible about everything else in this film—about the excellent direction of Mr. Welles, about the sure and penetrating performances of literally every member of the cast and about the stunning manner in which the music of Bernard Herrmann has been used. Space, unfortunately, is short. All we can say, in conclusion, is that you shouldn't miss this film. It is cynical, ironic, sometimes oppressive, and as realistic as a slap. But it has more vitality than 15 other films we could name. And, although it may not give a thoroughly clear answer, at least it brings to mind one deeply moral thought: For what shall it profit a man if he shall gain the whole world and lose his own soul? See "Citizen Kane" for further details.

* * *

"THE AMBIGUOUS 'CITIZEN KANE' "

BY

Bosley Crowther

MAY 4, 1941

Orson Welles, in his first motion picture, creates a titanic character, which does everything but explain itself.

Now that the returns are in from most of the local journalistic precincts and Orson Welles' "Citizen Kane" has been overwhelm-ingly selected as one of the great (if not the greatest) motion pictures of all time, this department rather finds itself with the uncomfortable feeling of a cat regarding a king. For we, in spite of the fact that we cast our vote in favor of it, frankly went to the polls with our fingers dexterously crossed and came away vaguely uneasy about the absolute wisdom of the choice. Mr. Welles has made an absorbing, exciting motion picture, and there is no question but what, compared with the average, it is vastly superior.

But is it, as some of the more enthusiastic votecasters have called it, the greatest film ever made? Is it, indeed, a great picture—saying "great" with awe in one's voice? And does it promise much for the future of its amazing young producer? We, a minority feline, are not altogether certain, and a careful consideration of those questions will form the burden of these allegedly second thoughts.

One fact cannot be disregarded in an estimation of this film: when "Citizen Kane" had its world premiere at the Palace on Thursday evening, it was riding the crest of perhaps the most provocative publicity wave ever to float a motion picture. The circumstances of the case are too familiar for more than capsule repetition. Mr. Welles had made the picture in the greatest secrecy—had written it, produced it, directed it, and acted in it with carte blanche from RKO, his apparently self-satisfied sponsor. Furthermore, the aura of mystery was rendered even more formidable by the fact that Mr. Welles was an enfant terrible of note, had created quite a murmur with his well-advertised oddities and had already taken a bye on two previously projected films.

Then suddenly the word got around as to what "Citizen Kane" was all about—the story of a newspaper publisher who rules a chain of aggressive journals and lives in baronial splendor surrounded by treasures of art. Immediately folks got suspicious that it might bear a close parallel to the life of an eminent publisher now living in much the same way. Certain ones saw the picture and allegedly pulled strings to have it squelched. The matter at once became news. Would "Citizen Kane" be released? Would RKO dare to fly in the face of assumed improvidence? Many folks became considerably disturbed, so when finally the picture was presented, it had an audience waiting breathless and alert.

This fact is very important for one particular reason: regardless of what the film actually showed upon the screen, this extraordinary advance publicity preordered a mental attitude. Folks who are generally familiar with the history of yellow journalism in America and with its more notorious exponents were prepared to see in "Citizen Kane" an archetype of ruthless publisher. Further, they were ready to respond with quick and prescient recognition to even the slightest implication. And although the film fails completely to state a case against Publisher Kane, to identify him except by vague suggestion with the flagrant tactics of yellow journalism, it is the belief of this department that most of the people who have seen the picture so far have come away with the solid conviction that they have beheld the image of an unscrupulous tycoon.

Yet at no point in the picture is a black mark actually checked against Kane. Not a shred of evidence is presented to indicate absolutely that he is a social scoundrel. As a matter of fact, there is no reason to assume from what is shown upon the screen that he is anything but an honest publisher with a consistently conscientious attitude toward society. This is a surprising realization after you've seen the film, but it is a fact. We saw it twice just to make sure. And because there is this lack of positive characterization, because the real significance of Kane depends entirely upon one's personal preconceptions, we are inclined to feel that Mr. Welles is slightly hoodwinking the public. Or rather, we should say that circumstances have made it possible for him to do so.

Of course, one might reasonably argue that Mr. Welles, as an expert showman, has simply taken advantage of an established attitude and that the picture anyhow is not concerned so much with the importance of Kane to society as it is with the importance of the man to himself. In a measure this is true. But the entire significance of Kane to himself and to those around him is predicated upon the assumption that he is a sort of monster, that he has betrayed everything that is decent in his mania for wealth and power. And this the picture does not show.

We hate to discover a inconsistency in a film which is so beautifully made—and beautiful is a temperate word for Mr. Welles' "Citizen Kane." Everything about it, from a technical point of view, is surpassingly magnificent. With the able assistance of Gregg Toland, whose contribution was obviously great, he has made use of all the best devices of pure cinema which have been brought out through the years. And he has invented a few of his own. Mr. Welles and Mr. Toland have used the camera not only to record a story but to comment upon it, to compose by visual contrasts and sharp glimpses caught from unusual points an overpoweringly suggestive film.

The music of Bernard Herrmann is applied with incomparable effect; Mr. Welles has directed the whole with the sureness and distinction of a seasoned master, and the entire cast—but especially Joseph Cotten, Dorothy Comingore, Everett Sloane, and Mr. Welles himself—perform it in a manner which puts to shame the surface posturings of some of our more popular stars.

But this corner is inclined to suspect that the enthusiasm with which Mr. Welles made the film—the natural bent of a first-class showman toward eloquent and dramatic effects—rather worked against the logic of his story. And the accomplishment of his purpose has been so completely impressive that it tends to blind the audience to the holes in the fabric. "Citizen Kane" opens with the imposing death of the main character, an old man tucked away in a fabulously ornate castle. And as he dies, his heavy lips mutter one word, "Rosebud." Suddenly the mood changes. On the screen is flashed a newsreel feature, which recounts in "March of Time" style the highlights of the dead man's career—this strange, unfathomable man who ruled an empire of newspapers, industries and such, but whom no one apparently understood.

The news feature ends, and its editor, dissatisfied with its superficiality, dispatches a man to discover the meaning of that dying word, "Rosebud." In it may lie the secret to Kane's heart. Thus the remainder of the picture is taken up with the story of Kane's life as it is told to the reporter by four of the man's closest associates. It reveals Kane as an egomaniac, a colossus who bestrides the world, from his poor and humble beginnings to his death in a secluded pleasure-dome. But the enigma of his life is never solved, either by the newsreel reporter or by Mr. Welles for the benefit of the audience. And when the significance of "Rosebud" is made apparent in the final sequence of the film, it provides little more than a dramatic and poignant shock. It does not clarify, except by sentimental suggestion, the reason for Kane's complexity.

As so we are bound to conclude that this picture is not truly great, for its theme is basically vague and its significance depends on circumstances. Unquestionably, Mr. Welles is the most dynamic newcomer in films and his talents are infinite. But the showman will have to acquire a good bit more discipline before he is thoroughly dependable. When he does—and let's hope it will be soon—his fame should extend to Mars.

* * *

Bosley Crowther's irritation about William Randolph Hearst is restrained; while the *Newsweek* review by John O'Hara doesn't mention Hedda Hopper and Louella Parsons by name, his contempt for the two columnists practically leaps off the page.

"CITIZEN KANE"

BY
John O'Hara

NEWSWEEK
MARCH 17, 1941

It is with exceeding regret that your faithful bystander reports that he has just seen a picture which he thinks must be the best picture he ever saw.

With no less regret, he reports that he has just seen the best actor in the history of acting.

Name of picture: *Citizen Kane*.

Name of actor: Orson Welles.

Reason for regret: you, my dear, may never see the picture. (From now on, it's *I*.)

I saw *Citizen Kane* the other night. I am told that my name was crossed off a list of persons who were invited to look at the picture, my name being crossed off because some big shot remembered I had been a newspaperman. So, for the first time in my life, I indignantly denied that I was a newspaperman. Nevertheless, I had to be snuck into the showing of *Citizen Kane* under a phony name. That's what's going on about this wonderful picture. Intrigue.

Why intrigue? Well, because. A few obsequious and/or bulbous middle-aged ladies think the picture ought not to be shown, owing to the fact that the picture is rumored to have something to do with a certain publisher, who, for the first time in his life, or maybe the second, shall be nameless. That the nameless publisher might be astute enough to realize that for the first time in his rowdy life, he had been made a human being did not worry the loyal ladies. Sycophancy of that kind, like curtseying, is deliberate. The ladies merely wait for a chance to show they can still do it, even if it means cracking a femur. This time I think they may have cracked off more than they can chew. I hope.

The story is that of a publisher, from his whippersnapper to-his doting days. His origin is humble, and most likely not acceptable to the quarreling ladies, whose origin is not for a second in question here. A fresh punk out of various colleges, the publisher walks into a newspaper office as a not quite legitimate heir, and thereupon enjoys himself and power. At a rather late date it is shown that his sybaritic pastimes and his power are incomplete, for he can buy or produce anything but love. He doesn't give love; he lacks love. With everything in the world that you and I might expect to bring happiness, the publisher is a lonely, unwanted, feared, tragicomic man. He dies, speaking one mysterious word, a female name. At the end of this wonderful picture you get to know what the name was. You also (later) realize how silly women can be, especially obsequious women.

Look in vain here for any but obscure hints as to the story of *Citizen Kane*. My intention is to make you want to see the picture; if possible, to make you wonder why you are not seeing what I think is as good a picture as was ever made. Up to now I have thought that the very best talking picture ever made was *M*. I have seen *M* at least eight times. As a movie writer and press agent I used to have them run off the attack sequence in *The Big Parade*, the one in the woods where the boys don't know where the sharpshooter's going to hit next, every time I had a chance. One of my very favorite silents was that beautiful job, "The Great Gatsby." And if you want to settle bets on any phase of *The Birth of a Nation*, call me. But *Citizen Kane* is Late 1941. It lacks nothing.

And aside from what it does not lack, *Citizen Kane* has Orson Welles. It is traditional that if you are a great artist, no one gives a damn about you while you're still alive. Welles has had plenty of that. He got a tag put to his name through the Mars thing, just as Scott Fitzgerald, who wrote better than any man in our time, got a Jazz Age tag put to his name. I say, if you plan to have any grandchildren to see and to bore, see Orson Welles so that you can bore your grandchildren with some honesty. There never has been a better actor than Orson Welles. I just got finished saying there never has been a better actor than Orson Welles, and I don't want any of your lip.

Do yourself a favor. Go to your neighborhood exhibitor and ask him why he isn't showing *Citizen Kane. Then* sue me.

* * *

"KANE CASE"

TIME MAGAZINE
MARCH 17, 1941

As in some grotesque fable, it appeared last week that Hollywood was about to turn upon and destroy its greatest creation. That creation was Citizen Kane, the film which Orson Welles and his Mercury players had spent more than a year talking and thinking about and 70 days shooting with $750,000 of Radio-Keith-Orpheum's money.

The film was in the cans. A magazine advertising campaign had begun. But no release was set by RKO for the picture to be shown to the public, and it seemed very likely that none would ever be. Old Mr. William Randolph Hearst, who had only heard reports of the picture through his cinematic eyes, ears and tongue, Columnist Louella Parsons, thought the life of Kane was too close a parallel to the life of Hearst.

The picture. The objection of Mr. Hearst, who founded a publishing empire on sensationalism, is ironic. For to most of the several hundred people who have seen the film at private showings, *Citizen Kane* is the most sensational product of the U.S. movie industry. It has found important new techniques in picture-making and story-telling. Artful and artfully artless, it is not afraid to say the same thing twice if twice-telling reveals a fourfold truth. It is as psychiatrically sound as a fine novel but projected with far greater scope, for instance, than Aldous Huxley was inspired to bring to his novel on the same theme. It is a work of art created by grown people for grown people.

The story begins with the death of Charles Foster Kane (Orson Welles), at one time the world's third richest man, overlord of mines and factories and steamship lines, boss of newspapers, news services and radio chains, possessor of a vast castle in Florida, a staggering agglomeration of art, two wives, millions of enemies. The "March of Time" is running off rushes of its Kane biography in its projection room. But when they are shown, the editor does not think the facts reveal the man. "It might be any rich publisher—Pulitzer, Hearst or John Doe," he complains. "Get me something that will show it is Kane. Find out his last words. Maybe they meant something."

Kane's last word was "Rosebud." Thompson (William Alland), the newsreel reporter, spends two feverish weeks in interviewing five people. Thompson talks to Kane's trollopish second wife (Dorothy Comingore), whom he tried to make a singer, finally established in the castle. There she passed the years assembling jigsaw puzzles until she walked out in boredom. Then there is Kane's rich guardian (George Coulouris) whom Kane hated; Kane's general manager (Everett Sloane), the sad, loyal, philosophical Jew who stuck by to the end; his former drama editor and best friend (Joseph Cotten) with whom Kane broke after Kane's disastrous try for the Governorship of New York; Kane's butler (Paul Stewart). None knew the meaning of "Rosebud."

But each in his way understood a little of the man: he was not cruel, but he did cruel things; he was not generous, but he did generous things; he was willful, capricious, and he wanted to be loved—on his own terms. The March of Time never finds the meaning of "Rosebud," nor the key to Kane's frustrations, but, almost by accident, the audience does.

So sharply does *Citizen Kane* veer from cinema cliche, it hardly seems like a movie. There are some extraordinary technical novelties through which Welles and wiry, experienced little Photographer Gregg Toland have given the camera a new eloquence—for example, the "stolen" newsreels, the aged and streaked documentary shots. When Susan makes her disastrous operatic debut, the camera tells the story by climbing high up among the flies to find two stagehands—one with his hand pinching his nose in disgust.

Always the camera seems to be giving the narrative a special meaning where it will help most: picturing a small bottle beside a tumbler when Susan Kane is lying drugged with an overdose of sedatives, exploring the love nest and the family breakfast table like a pair of prying eyes and ears.

Orson Welles treats the audience like a jury, calling up the witnesses, letting them offer the evidence, injecting no opinions of his own. He merely sees that their stories are told with absorbing clarity. Unforgettable are such scenes as the spanning of Kane's first marriage in a single conversation, the silly immensity of the castle halls which echo the flat whines of Susan.

Hollywood claimed Welles never would make the grade. From the moment he arrived there, its citizens resented him and his Martians and his youth and his talent. When he grew a beard for his first film, a sporty press agent sent him a bearded ham for Christmas; while he was dining out one evening, a playful actor cut off his tie with a table knife; columnists dubbed him with nicknames like "Little Orson Annie." At announcements that his first two productions had been called off, the town nodded knowingly. He was just a big bag of publicity.

But whatever Orson Welles did do, Hollywood was pretty sure it would break all the rules. Hollywood was right.

* * *

"MR. GENIUS COMES THROUGH; 'KANE' ASTONISHING PICTURE"

HOLLYWOOD REPORTER
MARCH 12, 1941

MANKIEWICZ, TOLAND GIVE GREAT AID FILM LIFTS PROD. INTO TOP RANKING

"Citizen Kane" is a great motion picture. Great in that it was produced by a man who had never had any motion picture experience; great because he cast it with people who had never faced a camera in a motion picture production before; great in the manner of its story-telling, in both the writing of that story and its unfolding before a camera; great in that its photographic accomplishments are the highlights of motion picture photography to date, and finally great, because technically, it is a few steps ahead of anything that has been made in pictures before.

From the point of entertainment, this reviewer chooses again to qualify it as great. An audience might not think so because they might not understand its technical perfections, or will be astonished, as we were, at the acting of a cast that had never been in a studio before. Nor will they credit the fact that this entertainment was really brought to the screen on a low budget—under $800,000—and, in order to accomplish that, things had to be done that no brain or set of brains had ever before accomplished.

These items interested us, made the entertainment much greater, and how much an audience's ignorance of these facts will discount the actual entertainment, we can't tell. But we'll venture the opinion that no ticket buyer, if he ever has the opportunity of buying a ticket to see "Citizen Kane," will leave the theater mad at his buy, because he will be entertained, although probably not as much as those knowing the inside of this whole production.

Whether the story was inspired by the life of William Randolph Hearst is of little interest to this reviewer; that's for others to determine and act as they see fit. However, we might express our opinion that we will be surprised if the picture ever hits a theater where admission is charged, and if that is finally the case, audiences will lose the opportunity of seeing a fine motion picture produced in a most adult fashion and one that should lift Orson Welles right up to the top of producers and actors.

VIOLATES TRADITION

Welles has made his Hollywood debut in such an astonishingly unconventional production that it is difficult to criticize "Citizen Kane" along the customary lines. Time after time, as the life of Charles Foster Kane is unfolded, Welles violates cinema tradition in acting, writing and photography, and gets away with it all magnificently.

He wastes no time in introducing his different technique. The film begins with a mythical two-reel "News on the March," obviously based on the "March of Time," since the commentator's phraseology is unmistakable "Time" talk. It is a short on the life of the great publisher, Charles Foster Kane, who has just died, and it touches the highlights of his career from the day he acquires "The New York Inquirer" until his death.

As Kane succumbs, he is heard to mutter one word, "Rosebud," and it is this one word which holds together the succeeding episodes of the film. As the short ends, it becomes apparent that this was a screening of the subject for its producers. They are dissatisfied with it, because the short has not brought out the hidden motivations which make Kane such a fabulous character, nor has it explained the meaning of the cryptic reference to "Rosebud."

HEARST MENTIONED ONCE

It is in this scene at the end of the "News on the March" sequence that the name of Hearst is mentioned for the only time in "Citizen Kane." One of the actors is overheard saying: "It could have been any publisher, could have been Pulitzer, could have been Hearst." Another responds, "Yes, and it could have been John Doe."

A reporter from "News on the March" then begins the monumental task of checking Kane's life, beginning with his infancy in the West when he inherits a fortune, the arrival of the estate's lawyers to take young Kane to school finds him sledding in the snow and fighting against leaving this pastime to accompany the attorneys. To obtain his information, the reporter interviews the five persons who knew Kane best: his lawyer; his right hand man in the Kane publications; his former dramatic critic; and his second wife, whom he meets as a penniless flighty girl and attempts to make the public accept as a great singer; and the butler who manages his farflung estate on the Gulf of Mexico.

WIFE SUPPLIES DRAMA

The drama critic, the lawyer, the butler, and his publishing aide all contribute their bits to the Kane saga, but the dramatic high spots come mostly from the memory of the press tycoon's second wife, by this time a drunken derelict, still trying to be a singer in an Atlantic City dive. When she meets Kane, he is already married to the niece of a mythical U.S. president, and so bored that he rarely comes home. Their meeting is just a "pick-up" on a rainy street, but it progresses so fast that, in no time, the illicit amour becomes

public knowledge through exposure by a politician he is fighting, and Kane loses a sure election as governor of New York.

His first wife divorces him, he marries the singer, and then inaugurates a campaign in all his papers to establish her as a star. She is a desperately incompetent performer, and his efforts to put her over make him a laughing stock and cost him his best friend, the dramatic critic.

Finally, shorn of most of his journalistic power by the 1929 crash, an embittered old man, he retires to his incredible Gulf Coast palace. There the second wife does jigsaw puzzles in the vast living room and grows to hate him. She leaves him, and Kane's death follows very soon afterwards. He is broken, friendless, and all he has left behind him are the palace and its grounds—which include a private zoo—his untold art treasures, and a string of papers actually controlled by banks.

Not until the final scene is the mystery of "Rosebud" explained, and, though it is done with utter simplicity, it provides a chill and a lump in anyone's throat.

"ROSEBUD" EXPLAINED

The camera pans over the limitless expanse of paintings, sculpture, and all his other useless possessions. Appraisers are sorting it out, and the worthless items burned. Into the flames go all manner of knickknacks, and at last the wreckers begin burning odds and ends from his mother's home out west, which Kane had collected after she died. Suddenly the flames are seen licking over a little boy's sled. The camera picks it out from the rest of the fire, and on it is written the one word "Rosebud."

Welles' performance is nothing less than astonishing. He begins as a youth of 21, goes through middle age to his death, and makes every moment believable in voice, walk, and gesture. Even in his love scenes is Welles effective.

The support he gets from the cast, every one of whom is a completely new face to picture audiences, is downright amazing. There isn't a weak member of the troupe, and though space doesn't permit praise for all of them, a few must be selected for special mention. Dorothy Comingore, as the singer, is put through a range of emotions that would try any actress one could name, but she delivers without a second's let-down. "Citizen Kane" should make this girl a star. Joseph Cotten, who played in "Philadelphia Story," is splendid as the drama critic, as are Everett Sloane in the role of Bernstein, Kane's faithful aide, and Ruth Warrick, as his first wife.

Gregg Toland's camera has never performed such miracles. He has caught the players from daringly unusual angles. He produced effects so novel in some scenes that they cannot be described here. The musical score by Bernard Herrmann is also worthy of commendation.

* * *

Copyright © 1941 by the *Hollywood Reporter*. Reprinted by permission.

ORSON WELLES

Citizen Kane

AN RKO-RADIO PICTURE

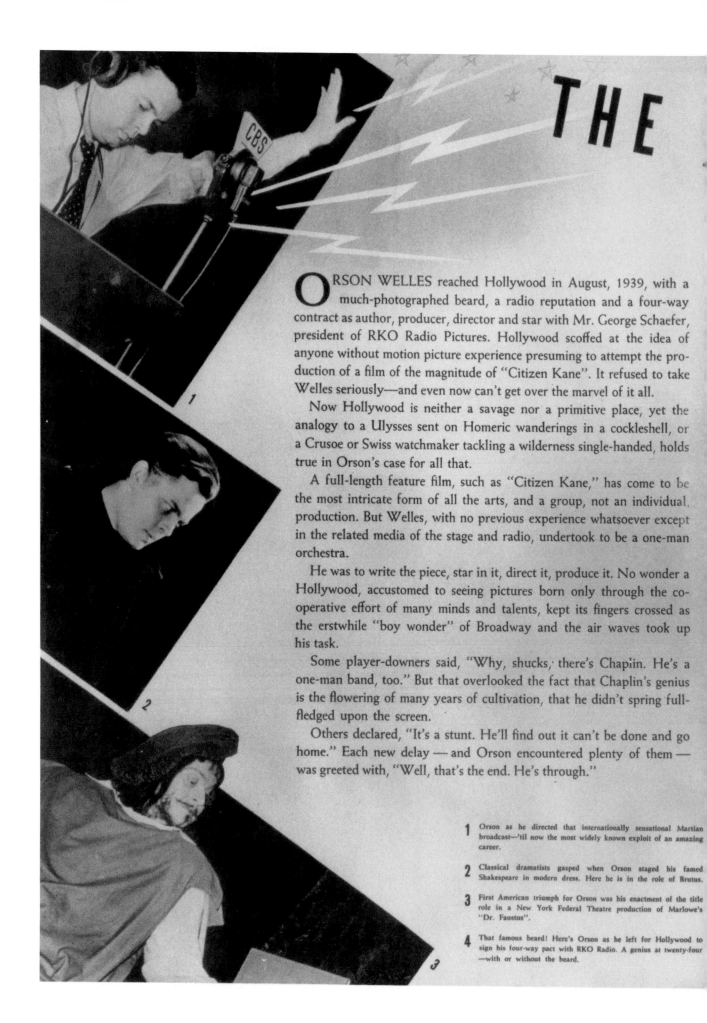

THE

ORSON WELLES reached Hollywood in August, 1939, with a much-photographed beard, a radio reputation and a four-way contract as author, producer, director and star with Mr. George Schaefer, president of RKO Radio Pictures. Hollywood scoffed at the idea of anyone without motion picture experience presuming to attempt the production of a film of the magnitude of "Citizen Kane". It refused to take Welles seriously—and even now can't get over the marvel of it all.

Now Hollywood is neither a savage nor a primitive place, yet the analogy to a Ulysses sent on Homeric wanderings in a cockleshell, or a Crusoe or Swiss watchmaker tackling a wilderness single-handed, holds true in Orson's case for all that.

A full-length feature film, such as "Citizen Kane," has come to be the most intricate form of all the arts, and a group, not an individual, production. But Welles, with no previous experience whatsoever except in the related media of the stage and radio, undertook to be a one-man orchestra.

He was to write the piece, star in it, direct it, produce it. No wonder a Hollywood, accustomed to seeing pictures born only through the cooperative effort of many minds and talents, kept its fingers crossed as the erstwhile "boy wonder" of Broadway and the air waves took up his task.

Some player-downers said, "Why, shucks, there's Chaplin. He's a one-man band, too." But that overlooked the fact that Chaplin's genius is the flowering of many years of cultivation, that he didn't spring full-fledged upon the screen.

Others declared, "It's a stunt. He'll find out it can't be done and go home." Each new delay — and Orson encountered plenty of them — was greeted with, "Well, that's the end. He's through."

1   Orson as he directed that internationally sensational Martian broadcast—'til now the most widely known exploit of an amazing career.

2   Classical dramatists gasped when Orson staged his famed Shakespeare in modern dress. Here he is in the role of Brutus.

3   First American triumph for Orson was his enactment of the title role in a New York Federal Theatre production of Marlowe's "Dr. Faustus".

4   That famous beard! Here's Orson as he left for Hollywood to sign his four-way pact with RKO Radio. A genius at twenty-four —with or without the beard.

AZING MR. WELLES

Six-feet-two Orson, however, strangely stuck along. Like Swiss Robinson on his island, he was learning how to do things as he progressed. He was in Hollywood, but not of it. Parties of the stars knew him not. Where you could find him, however, was on the RKO Radio lot, often at night, nosing into every department, learning how movies are made.

No Cook's tour this, and no Hollywood-in-ten-easy-lessons. It went on month upon month, more than a year, before Welles was ready to launch into production. That prolonged delay itself drew criticism from Doubting Thomases, "Aw, he'll never get started."

But Welles went right along, learning how to put Sound into pictures, how to cut 'em to eliminate dud footage and point up the drama, how to make the camera as fluid in its observations as the eyes of another party in the room. He studied lighting, set designing, special effects — those tricks with which movie wizards make things seem what they aren't.

Finally he went to work producing "Citizen Kane" from his own story of an American colossus striding across sixty years of living history. He directed it, starred in it, learned to dance for it, put all his recently acquired knowledge at work, picked up more as he went along. When it was finished, he supervised the scoring, too.

Sure, he was new to the movies. But the young Welles who stirred Broadway with his gangster-dictator version of "Julius Caesar," his All-Negro production of "Macbeth," was pretty new then to the stage, too. The Welles who scared the pants off the country with drama of an invasion by Martian monsters couched in terms of a newscast, was no ancient in Radio. You have to be pretty new to everything when you're still in the middle twenties.

MAN OF
ENDLESS
SURPRISES—

THIS is the story of Orson Welles, or the case history of one of America's most amazing young geniuses.

Genius is definitely the word for Mr. Welles, who at the ripe old age of twenty-five can look back upon a successful career as an author, playwright, actor, broadway director and producer, radio star and painter.

Born in Kenosha, Wis., Orson was the son of Richard Head Welles, a well-known inventor and manufacturer. His mother was Beatrice Ives Welles, a concert pianist from whom he drew much of his artistic perception and sensitivity.

Orson at an early age exhibited the amazing precociousness that has characterized his entire career. At eleven, for example, he made a solitary walking tour of Europe. At an even younger age he staged his first theatrical venture —a backyard puppet show of Shakespeare!

Until the death of his mother, when he was eight years old, Orson's schooling had consisted largely of home tutoring, with a few months of formalistic training in a Madison, Wis., school.

His father, however, was resolved to make the process of education more systematic than it had been, so he enrolled young Orson at the Todd School in Woodstock, Ill.

There the future stage, screen and radio star first played at the drama for public consumption. Participating in the dramatic activities of the school, he staged an original version of Shakespeare's "Julius Caesar," enacting vigorously the parts of both Cassius and Marc Antony.

During this period, also, he exhibited a surprising proclivity for painting. He was so good, as a matter of fact, that his instructor predicted he would become America's greatest painter.

It was with this prediction in mind that, at the age of sixteen, Orson began a walking trip through Ireland to paint the sights he encountered.

And while in Dublin, he found his true vocation. He decided to become an actor. So he went to the manager of the famed Gate Theater and announced that he was Orson Welles, star of the New York Guild Theater.

The ruse worked—and Orson found himself starring in the next production of the theater. He remained there a full season, drawing universal acclaim for his superb work. During the period, also, he set a record by becoming the first American ever to act as a guest star with the world-famous Abbey Players of Dublin. His career was definitely launched!

RKO RADIO STUDIOS
Hollywood, California

Returning to New York in 1932, he found the producers there less susceptible to his blandishments than their colleagues in Ireland.

So, not daunted, he set sail for Africa to see what the dark continent was like. His explorations, however, were side-tracked in Morocco, when he decided to write a book.

The volume, "Mercury Shakespeare", is still a best-seller in its class.

A year later, Orson again found himself in New York. This time he managed to secure an introduction to Katharine Cornell, who thought so much of his ability that she gave him a place in a company she was then organizing to tour the hinterlands.

From the noted actress, Welles received a thorough grounding in the theatre. He appeared with her in such plays as "Candida," "Romeo and Juliet," and "The Barretts of Wimpole Street."

Then, in rapid succession, he became a Broadway Star, got himself a job impersonating The Shadow in the radio thriller serial, became commentator for the March of Time program on the air and was appointed producer for the Federal Theater in New York.

His success here led to the formation of the Mercury Theatre, which he organized with John Houseman. And from this group stemmed the Mercury Theater of the Air, under whose auspices Welles staged Radio's most sensational broadcast — The Martian Invasion.

This was the broadcast which frightened millions of listeners throughout the country into outright panic so widespread that a Congressional investigation was threatened!

When Welles signed his now-famous contract with RKO Radio Pictures, he insisted on a clause permitting him to continue his work with the Mercury Players.

Many of the actors of the company make their screen debuts with Orson in "Citizen Kane." Among the cast are such well-known stage and radio figures as Dorothy Comingore, Ruth Warrick, George Coulouris, Joseph Cotten, Paul Stewart and Harry Shannon.

As a matter of fact, you won't find a single familiar movie name in the group. Orson, with his customary disregard of tradition, has introduced fifteen new actors in this film — an unprecedented figure in Hollywood productions!

But then, setting new precedents has always been a Welles forte. And, from all indications, it will continue to be so.

1 The still-bearded Orson learns the intricacies of cutting and editing via the Moviola and technician, Fred Maguire.

2 Producer-Director Welles confers with himself and decides "they" don't quite like the way the turban designed for Dorothy Comingore looks.

3 Actor Welles and Director Welles slightly mixed up as he takes a look at a scene from the other end of the camera.

4 Author Orson dictating some bits of new business to be incorporated into the script before the cameras start turning. Only a day or two more left for that beard!

HIGHLIGHTS IN THE LIFE OF *Citizen Kane*

Orson Welles as he appears in the title role at one stage of the story, in which he portrays a fictional newspaper tycoon. The following photo sequence presents the highlights in the life of "Citizen Kane."

1 The boyhood of Charles Foster Kane is the only portion of his life which, for obvious reasons, Orson Welles does not enact in RKO Radio's "Citizen Kane." To make up for his absence, he cast in this part a seven-year-old actor whose resemblance to himself is astounding. The youthful double is Buddy Swan. Buddy in this scene is being introduced by his mother, Agnes Moorhead, to George Coulouris, who has just informed her that property she owns has been found to be worth millions of dollars. In the background is Harry Shannon, who is seen as Kane, Sr.

2 Three young men begin newspaper careers. They are Joseph Cotten, noted Broadway actor, Orson Welles and Everett Sloane. In this scene, Charles Foster Kane is manifestly young, enthusiastic, handsome. Welles' characterization from this youthful stage to that of an old man is an outstanding example of dramatic interpretation.

3 Spectacular highlight in the life of "Citizen Kane" is sequence depicting him as playboy. In this scene, Orson Welles proves that he can dance as well as act, write, produce and direct. He's chorus boy above!

4 Social peak in career of "Citizen Kane" was his marriage to niece of prominent statesman. Here Welles is shown with bride, Ruth Warrick, and wedding party on White House lawn. Depicted marriage is failure, ends in divorce.

5 Citizen Kane's second wife is a singer, portrayed by Dorothy Comingore. Here she is shown as she appears in opera Welles finances for her. Sequence is typical of colorful and elaborate settings in picture. For opera episode, Welles ordered original score written for mythical musical play.

6 Dramatic highpoint is the meeting between wife No. 1 and wife No. 2 in this scene. The actors are Ray Collins, Dorothy Comingore, Orson Welles and Ruth Warrick.

7 Excitement-packed chapter in life of "Citizen Kane" is his race for Governorship. He
Orson Welles is shown delivering oration in course of campaign. Note careful staging
unusual camera angle of this scene, in which Welles displays fiery qualities as politic
spieler.

8 Old age is darkened by rift between Kane and second wife. Here Orson Welles ar
Dorothy Comingore, are shown in tense moment. Welles is famed for his enactment
aged parts, such as that he played in his Broadway version of G. B. Shaw's "Heartbrea
House."

9 End of trail. In this scene his earthly belongings are being auctioned off. It's a powerfu
dramatic presentation. Shown in scene are Paul Stewart and William Alland, both wel
known New York actors. Stewart portrays Kane's butler, Alland a reporter.

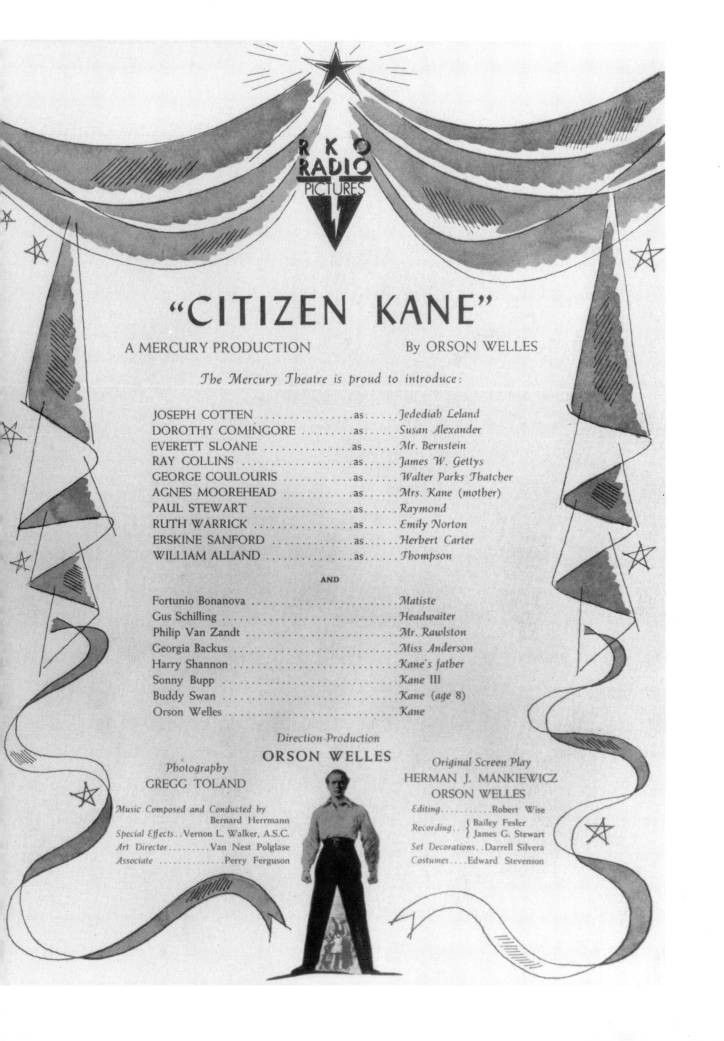

RKO RADIO PICTURES

"CITIZEN KANE"

A MERCURY PRODUCTION   By ORSON WELLES

The Mercury Theatre is proud to introduce:

JOSEPH COTTEN	as	*Jedediah Leland*
DOROTHY COMINGORE	as	*Susan Alexander*
EVERETT SLOANE	as	*Mr. Bernstein*
RAY COLLINS	as	*James W. Gettys*
GEORGE COULOURIS	as	*Walter Parks Thatcher*
AGNES MOOREHEAD	as	*Mrs. Kane (mother)*
PAUL STEWART	as	*Raymond*
RUTH WARRICK	as	*Emily Norton*
ERSKINE SANFORD	as	*Herbert Carter*
WILLIAM ALLAND	as	*Thompson*

AND

Fortunio Bonanova	*Matiste*
Gus Schilling	*Headwaiter*
Philip Van Zandt	*Mr. Rawlston*
Georgia Backus	*Miss Anderson*
Harry Shannon	*Kane's father*
Sonny Bupp	*Kane III*
Buddy Swan	*Kane (age 8)*
Orson Welles	*Kane*

Direction-Production
ORSON WELLES

Photography
GREGG TOLAND

Original Screen Play
HERMAN J. MANKIEWICZ
ORSON WELLES

Music Composed and Conducted by
Bernard Herrmann
Special Effects . . Vernon L. Walker, A.S.C.
Art Director . . . . Van Nest Polglase
Associate . . . . Perry Ferguson

Editing . . . . Robert Wise
Recording . . { Bailey Fesler
{ James G. Stewart
Set Decorations . . Darrell Silvera
Costumes . . . . . Edward Stevenson

QUICK-STEPPING THROUGH A FEW OF THE OUTSTANDING SCENES OF "CITIZEN KAN

IN HIS FIRST PRODUCTION AN UNUSUAL, COMPELLING, DRAMATIC ENTERTAINMENT—

NOW IT'S
ORSON WELLES
OF *Hollywood*

SCENES FROM HIS FIRST MOTION PICTURE PRODUCTION, "CITIZEN KANE"

THAT UNPREDICTABLE PERSONALITY, ORSON WELLES, WHO BRINGS TO THE SCREEN

DISTINCT NEW MOTION PICTURE TECHNIQUE THAT IS YEARS AHEAD OF ITS TIME!

* ORSON WELLES *

AUTHOR

THE
"FOUR-MOST"
PERSONALITY

* ORSON WELLES *

PRODUCER

★ ORSON WELLES ★

DIRECTOR

F MOTION PICTURES!

STAR

★ ORSON WELLES ★

MOST OF THE PRINCIPAL PLAYERS IN "CITIZEN KANE" ARE NEW TO MOTION PICTURES .. THE MERCURY THEATRE IS PROUD TO INTRODUCE

THE MERCURY ACTORS

RUTH WARRICK (Emily Norton) reached New York City as custodian of a live turkey which she carted up the steps of City Hall and presented to His Honor the Mayor, as part of some civic celebration which chose her "Miss Jubilesta." She remained in New York, where her radio work commended her to Welles. A screen test confirmed his opinion. She makes her film debut as the first Mrs. Kane in "Citizen Kane."

JOSEPH COTTON (Jedediah Leland) was leading man to Katharine Hepburn in the Broadway run of "The Philadelphia Story." His thespic talents were developed by understudying Lynn Overman in "Dancing Partner" and Melvyn Douglas in "Tonight Or Never." In his association with Welles he played the lead in "Shoemaker's Holiday" and appeared in "Julius Caesar," "Horse Eats Hat" and "Dr. Faustus." His performance in "Citizen Kane" brought him a long-term contract with RKO Radio.

DOROTHY COMINGORE (Susan Alexander) took two screen tests to attain a Hollywood foothold. Discovered by Charlie Chaplin at the Carmel Little Theatre, his praise won her a contract with a studio which terminated three months after without benefit of screen test. A second studio, more foresighted, gave her a screen test and then relegated her to crowd scenes. She smashed a Hollywood tradition by breaking her contract, refusing to appear unless permitted to act. Welles was introduced to her at a party. Her second screen test was rewarding. With her first big part as the second Mrs. Kane she embarks on her second Hollywood career.

EVERETT SLOANE (Mr. Bernstein) entered the theatre, after graduating from University of Pennsylvania, via Jasper Deeter's Hedgerow Theatre. Unable to find a Broadway engagement, he tried his hand in a Wall Street brokerage house, which collapsed in 1929. He next turned to radio acting and has been at it since, with the exception of some time out for plays, among them "Three Men on a Horse" and "Boy Meets Girl." He has taken part in every one of the Welles weekly radio broadcasts, including the famous "The War of the Worlds." He played Sammy Goldberg in the Goldberg family radio show for nine years, leaving when signed by Welles for "Citizen Kane."

ERSKINE SANFORD (Herbert Carter) was playing the title role in "Mr. Pim Passes By" nineteen years ago at Kenosha, Wis. Backstage he was introduced to a seven-year-old lad who startled him with the remark "an admirable performance, Mr. Sanford." It was Welles, who had just been taken to his first play! When Welles began his series of Broadway productions, Sanford left the Theatre Guild, with which he was associated for fifteen years, to join the Mercury Theatre players.

AGNES MOOREHEAD (Mrs. Kane, the mother) first met Orson Welles when he was a very grown-up young man of five years. He had just returned to the Waldorf Hotel from a concert and delivered a dramatic and rather rhetorical description of the evening's music. Only when Miss Moorehead joined the Mercury Players in Hollywood did she associate the precocious child with the man who was playing the title role in "Citizen Kane."

RAY COLLINS (James W. Gettys) has played upwards of 900 roles in the theatre and on radio. Even since he ran away from home when seventeen years of age, he has been one of the busiest of actors. He averages 20 to 25 radio shows each week, exclusive of theatrical engagements. After joining Welles' Mercury Theatre group at its start, he also played roles in Welles' phonographic recordings of Shakespearean plays.

PAUL STEWART (Raymond) currently in the cast of Orson Welles' Broadway production of "Native Son", seventh in his list of stage appearances, can look back upon the day when he recommended the giant Orson to radio director Homer Fickett as the ideal voice for the air version of "The March of Time". "Citizen Kane", Paul's film debut, finds the pair still together.

GEORGE COULOURIS (Walter Parks Thatcher) appeared in London as Sir Thomas Grey in "Henry IV," as Tybalt in "Romeo and Juliet," and in Noel Coward's "Sirocco." In New York he played in "The Apple Cart," with Pauline Lord in "The Late Christopher Bean," with Helen Hayes in "Mary of Scotland," with Philip Merivale in "Valley Forge," with Katharine Cornell in "Saint Joan," with Barry Fitzgerald in "The White Steed" and with Orson Welles as Marc Anthony in "Julius Caesar."

WILLIAM ALLAND (Thompson) makes his debut as a film actor in "Citizen Kane." At eighteen, with a semi-professional troupe of Baltimore, he edited, acted, directed and stage-managed the whole repertory. A scholarship at the New York Neighborhood Playhouse brought him to New York. To come to Welles' notice, he secured a humble part as one of the mob in Welles' modern-dress "Julius Caesar," intrigued with the stage manager till he was promoted to errand runner. In this capacity he marched into Welles' dressing room with a lunch tray, locked the door and read him the part of Marullus. He won the role.

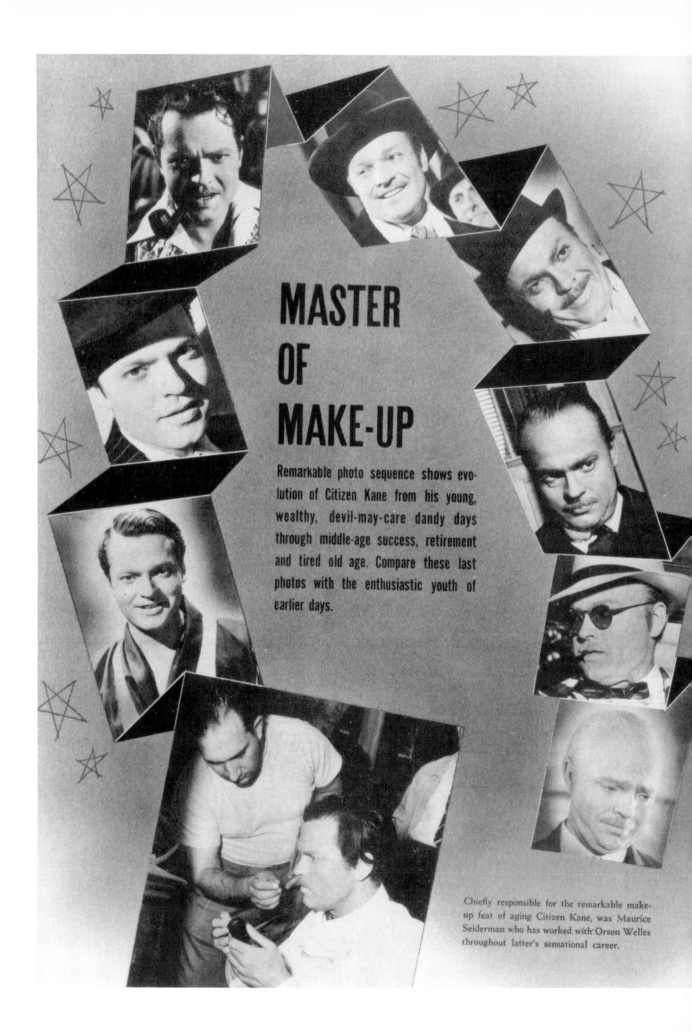

MASTER OF MAKE-UP

Remarkable photo sequence shows evolution of Citizen Kane from his young, wealthy, devil-may-care dandy days through middle-age success, retirement and tired old age. Compare these last photos with the enthusiastic youth of earlier days.

Chiefly responsible for the remarkable make-up feat of aging Citizen Kane, was Maurice Seiderman who has worked with Orson Welles throughout latter's sensational career.

Orson Welles, according to reputation, is wont to do things in the grand manner. And judging by the coldly scientific statistics gathered during the production of "Citizen Kane", the reputation is well deserved, indeed.

Now take the matter of illuminating gas. Some obscure genius has figured out that a set on "Citizen Kane", used more illuminating gas than any set of its size or kind in history. It's a fireplace 25 feet wide and 18 feet deep — statistics! — presumably burning logs, but actually consuming 2240 cubic feet of gas per hour. This is enough to warm the average home for at least three months in sub-zero weather.

Did you know that 215, 555 linear feet of raw 35-mm negative rolled through the cameras in the shooting of "Citizen Kane?" If shown continuously, this would take 2395.55 minutes, or 39.925 hours. No one looks at it that way, of course, but a statistician. It is not at all unusual in the movies, in fact, to use this much film.

Figures Unbelievable

Then there is the matter of the makeup man — always a sound source of strange information. According to Maurice Seiderman, who concocted the makeups that transform "Kane" players from young folks to venerable antiques of 75 during the course of the story, his initial outlay was for fourteen 300-pound barrels of casting plaster.

From there, Seiderman went on to make plaster casts of the players' heads, faces, noses, cheekbones, chins and what other anatomical tid bits would need working over as the characters aged. From these came latex moulds, which were glued on under the makeup. Just imagine — it took 75 gallons of the liquid latex (otherwise, and less scientifically, rubber) to make the makeup. Seiderman assures everyone that this amount of rubber would make seven or eight complete sets of auto tires.

Welles' Costumes Good for Statistics

Orson's costumes are always good for statistics. He wears 37 different ones in the film. This line could be pursued to the point where the number of needles dulled by frenzied tailors could be determined. What tossed the tailors into the sartorial dither was the fact that Orson ages from 25 to 75 in the film, and his figure alters along with the makeup (Sly Seiderman is in again with 20 sponge rubber gadgets for the figure alterations.) The tailors were particularly proud of a nifty little evening number in bright purple serge. Three of them saw spots before their eyes for seven days afterward.

The art director had his day of contributing statistics. His name is Perry Ferguson, and as he crawled out from under a six-foot pile of sketches, he announced that there were either 106 or 116 different sets for "Citizen Kane." His inaccuracy was due to the fact that his best previous score on a movie was around 65.

Great Days for the "Swing Gang"

It was the property department that really acquired a statistical wing-ding, though. Set Dresser Al Fields had to get furnishings for the biggest interior of a home ever seen in a movie. Twenty men—known to the trade as a "swing gang"— lugged stuff into the set, said stuff consisting of items ranging from antique snuff boxes to stray hunks of a 15th Century Shinto shrine from Japan. The man Kane, you'll gather, gathered antiques. You bet he did.

The prop boys were really proudest though about their packing cases. It seems that the new-fangled paper carton has made packing cases almost a collector's item. But never let it be said a prop man fell down—the RKO Radio boys dug up 72, count 'em, 72, and even six dozen assorted crates.

Lurching around in his numerical Sargasso, the statistician apparently overlooked one minor detail. There are also actors in the picture.

In fact, there are also 796 extras, 19 dancing girls, 84 bit players, 28 stand-ins (you won't see them), and 28 players of parts.

Among the players of parts is Orson Welles. He appears in the title role—and for the sake of statistics, he is also the producer, the director—and the guy who started off all the statistics.

STAR ORSON WELLES MAKES FLUID CAMERA THE STAR OF "CITIZEN KANE"

The camera boom loomed above the movie set, vaguely reminiscent of some prehistoric monster's articulated skeleton. It was a structure of steel lattice, anchored at one end, tilted sideward and ground up and down by a winch. At the end, sticking up in the air, was a movie camera, a saddle seat, and a bald-headed man occupying it. He kept squinting downward at the set through the camera range finder.

"Okay," he finally called. "Let me down now."

So the winch operator lowered him to stage level and he leaped out of the saddle — not only bald but gray-mustached. He was a large man. He was in his shirt sleeves. He leaped around very spryly at variance with his seeming age.

Well, that was as it should be, for the man was Orson Welles, who is only 25. So he had to apply makeup, for he was about to step into the picture and play the part of a man of 70.

Welles, who plays all ages of his titular hero over a range of fifty-odd years, in "Citizen Kane," had been busy figuring out camera angles for a scene. Now he turned the camera over to its legitimate operator, the famed Gregg Toland, and went about something else.

Startles Hollywood

It was like that all the time on the sets. If it wasn't like that it was something else. For Welles is the daring young man on the flying trapeze, if ever Hollywood saw one. What with being producer, director, writer and star of his first picture venture, he managed to keep pretty well occupied.

But he doesn't let it get him down. Perhaps back in New York, where on the stage he produced "Macbeth" with an all-Negro cast and "Julius Caesar" in modern dress, where in the radio world he played "The Shadow" and also the invader from Mars, scaring the life out of the populace in the hinterlands with that broadcast — perhaps back there they became used to his ebullience.

Hollywood, however, never saw any man float through the air with that greatest of ease which young Welles displays, violating just about all traditions of movie-making as he does so, and having a grand time for himself besides.

Unhampered by Precedent

Welles in dealing with his script is by Hollywood standards fantastic. He had never made a movie. So, despite a year's intensive study of all processes involved before he turned a wheel on production, he still wasn't hampered by facts.

That became apparent immediately he went to work. He started out with a script, but kept it carefully guarded. It is known, however, that he had slashed that script almost beyond recognition in the weeks he was at work on actual production. He revised, amended, augmented, deleted, as he went along.

Take, for instance, a notable sequence in which Welles, as publisher of a newspaper, hosts the staff. As originally written, the scene lasted just long enough to establish that Citizen Kane's best friend, played by Joseph Cotten, didn't want to take a certain job.

But when Welles came to shoot in actuality what earlier he had devised on paper, he decided a few items were lacking. He wanted to include things which would add both to delineation of his principal characters and to the entertainment values of his picture. Result: for a week they went on shooting, adding this and tossing in that, in the old "shooting off the cuff" style — a style which, incidentally, produced "Intolerance" and "Birth of a Nation."

It's Revolution!

Upshot was the scene as finally filmed included a lot of guests with lines to speak, a special song with a hoofer (type of the Nineties) to sing it, a chorus of can-can girls and Welles dancing with them. He even painstakingly learned the dance routine.

In the matter of lighting his sets, too, Welles has worked a revolution. Hollywood for years has been accustomed to light its sets from the top. That means, of course, no ceilings. But Welles blandly said a room wasn't a room without ceilings, and he wanted ceilings.

So something new in lighting effects can be looked for in "Citizen Kane."

Incidentally, of course, the use of ceilings necessitated new ways of recording sound. Not to become technical, sound engineers have been accustomed to poke the recording mike on the end of a long arm above the heads of actors. But how to do it with a ceiling in the room — a ceiling which would stop the mike, and also would record its shadow cast by the lights?

No wonder Hollywood was talking months in advance about "Citizen Kane" with a curiosity all but unparalleled. Only Selznick's "Gone With the Wind" when in the making, and Chaplin's "The Great Dictator," aroused comparable speculation.

Candid Shots around the lot during the filming of "Citizen Kane"

Sources for Illustrations

Academy of Motion Picture Arts and Sciences, Margaret Herrick Library

Cover, pages v, viii, xvi, 13, 35, 40, 41, 43, 44, 46, 48, 49, 51, 53, 58, 61, 62, 66, 76, 81, 85, 87, 88, 92, 93, 94, 95, 96, 97, 98, 99, 101, 102, 105, 112, 113, 114, 126, 137, 139, 154, 157, 164, 175, 195, 200, 202

Indiana University, Lilly Library

xxii, 9, 29, 30, 54, 74, 78, 79

Frame stills from the 35-mm print of *Citizen Kane*

2, 16, 38, 56, 65, 70, 71, 75, 86, 110, 118, 120, 121, 123, 124, 132, 162, 172, 182, 190, 238

UCLA Theater Arts Library

129, 217–236

University of Santa Barbara, Music Library

128

University of Southern California, Cinema-Television Library

21, 27, 33, 59, 82, 90, 106, 107, 109, 203, 208

The author would like to thank these people, publications, and organizations for providing material that is used in this book:

- *Cahiers du Cinéma*, the French cinema magazine, for granting permission to use excerpts of its publication.
- The Directors Guild of America, for granting permission to reprint material from its magazine's coverage of *Citizen Kane*.
- The *Hollywood Reporter*, for granting permission to reprint its review of *Citizen Kane*.
- The *New York Times*, for granting permission to reprint Bosley Crowther's reviews of *Citizen Kane*, as well as "Score for a Film" by Bernard Herrmann.
- *Popular Photography* magazine, for granting permission to reprint "How I Broke the Rules in *Citizen Kane*," by Gregg Toland.
- *Newsweek* magazine, for granting permission to reprint John O'Hara's review of *Citizen Kane*.
- *Time* magazine, for granting permission to reprint its review of *Citizen Kane*.
- *American Cinematographer* magazine, for granting permission to reprint exerpts of Gregg Toland's article from 1941.

The term "Academy Award" is a registered trademark and service mark of the Academy of Motion Picture Arts and Sciences.

241

Decide Future Of Welles' Pic By This Week

Welles, As 25% Owner of 'Kane', Would 'Force' RKO to Release Pic

Bovine Justice

Hollywood, Feb. 4.

Killing a toreador is less heinous than killing a bull, under the ruling of the Will Hays office, as applied to the 20th-Fox production, 'Blood and Sand.'

Actual slaying of beef on the hoof, including preliminary bandarillo sharpshooting, is banned, but Tyrone Power, the bullfighter who is ruined by a bull, is permitted to die on celluloid with the approval of the censor.

$2.60 Per Share On Par Common Stock in Sight

MULLS $2-ING 'NGS' AT ASTOR, N.Y.

'CITIZEN KANE' RELEASE DATE NOT YET SET

With release date of Orson Welles' 'Citizen Kane,' not a single playdate, roadshow or otherwise, has been set for the film.

Lyric, Indpls., Sale May Hasten Olson's Yen for Retirement

4 PIX

Hearst Papers' Anti-'Citizen Kane' Gripe Takes It Out on Welles-CBS

MEET PAR PROD. RUSH

Welles Suing RKO on 'Citizen Kane' In Effort to Force Pic's Release

Meyers' Remain Continue

Wednesday, May 7, 1941

RKO's Watchful Waiting on Hearst Papers' Further Reaction to 'Kane'

Scare 'Em Off?

Hollywood, May 6.

Motion picture celebs are being bluntly told that they will incur enmity in certain quarters by attending the Coast preem Thursday (8) night of 'Citizen Kane' at El Capitan.

New York, Chicago and Los Angeles are being used as test arenas for Orson Welles' 'Citizen Kane' and RKO will seek no engagements outside of those and a few other cities until editorial and legal reaction of William Randolph Hearst interests is determined. No selling on the film until 1941-42.

RCA's 1st Quarter Net Profit, $2,734,572; Sarnoff Reviews Biz

N. Y. Legiter to House 'Citizen Kane' Day-and-Date With RKO Palace, B'way

URGE STRAIGHT 10% TO STOP PRICE CUTS

Detroit, May 6.

MOJDEN

Nazis' New Said to Be To Cool O

Luce's Time To Force $800,00

F.D.R.'s Gag-Hint Ma Pix Ce

The Authors Club at luncheon.

"When I get 'Citizen Kane' off my mind, I'm going to work on an idea for a great picture based on the life of William Randolph Hearst."

WELLES EAST TO TALK 'CITIZEN KANE' FUTURE

Hollywood, Jan. 28.

Orson Welles and his publicity chief, Herbert Drake, left for New York to huddle with George Schaefer and other RKO execs on the future of 'Citizen Kane,' which is, more or less, stymied by threats of blackouts in the Hearst newspapers.

Drake is shoving off for the east with plenty of evidence that there is vast public attention drawn to the picture before its premiere, scheduled for Feb. 14.

FIDLER ASKS $250,000 LIBEL FROM WILKERSON

Los Angeles, Jan. 28.

Damages of $250,000 were asked by Jimmie Fidler, film columnist, in a libel complaint filed in Superior Court last Friday (24) against Wilkerson Daily Corp., publishers of Hollywood Reporter, trade paper, and William R. Wilkerson, editor and publisher. Two causes of libel action were specified, each of which seeks $75,000 compensatory damages and $50,000 punitive damages. Action was filed for Fidler by the law firm of Zagon & Aaron.

Suit was dismissed yesterday (Monday), but will be refiled when

---

Bernie Scrams Coast Nitery on the 'Bounce', $6,000 Payoff Dubious

Beverly Hills, Jan. 28.

It was a blunt 'no soh' that Ben Bernie tossed at the Victor Hugo nitery when asked to finish out his eight weeks at the grotto. Three weeks were enough, and that for $3,000, which he affectionately termed a 'bounceroo.' And if that didn't convince him, there was the

FLU REISSUE FLOPPING HOLLYWOOD FILMERS

Hollywood, Jan. 28.

Old man flu is putting on a return engagement in Hollywood, slowing up film production and knocking off players, execs, agents and directors with impartial abandon.

Among the victims last week were Edward Arnold, M-C Lever,

Irwin Dash, who put sidering publishing a ne

took it literally.

While visiting Jack E Jack replied, 'That's the

Another milton listens to ask her anything she sa Anyway, Tschaikowsl and many other immort is straightened out. Tl so often.

Lana Turner: Better Clark and Johnson: Ca Gable. Henny Youngman

Read an ad in a Lo panion to hitch-hiker.' I've got field glasses to n Eavesdropped at the detective I am.'

Eavesdropped at the detective his telephone number: 'As long as I'm leavin now a blotter for the team There's a bookmaker or on how long a marriage

Middleton & Spellme. Bessinger & White, Josie Clinton & Co

If you don't like this get stuck like you did.

L. A. to N

Mary Astor.
Jack Benny.
Wallace Beery.
Robert Benchley.

1941

Wednesday, January 22, 1941

VARIETY

H'WOOD BUYIN

RKO, Despite Hearst's Ire, Announces Huge National Campaign for 'Kane'

RKO last week openly flaunted William Randolph Hearst. At the same time it assured the film industry that it has no intention of withholding Orson Welles' 'Citizen Kane' despite the publisher's demand to do so. Film will be released at the end of February.

Studio, which has never taken any official cognizance of Hearst's ire or threats, has announced for the film a national advertising campaign that will be 'one of the most far-reaching ever launched for an attraction by RKO Radio Pictures.'

Hearst papers apparently will get their share of the big RKO budget, the publisher's edict against publicity for the company or its duct in his publications. Top ex RKO said last week

Penthouse Blues

Hollywood, Jan. 21.

'A Girl's Best Friend Is Wall Street' might have been a hot title back in the feverish days of 1928, but now the story detours north at Trinity Church and becomes 'A Girl's Best Friend Is Broadway.'

Picture rolls tomorrow (Wed.) at Columbia with Joan Bennett and Franchot Tone in the top spots, directed by Richard Wallace. 'Wall Street' title was ditched after the budget too trimming.

HAS HOLD ON OF 20 SH

Six Plays Definitely chased by Film Comp With Stakes in Two tain Buys — Heavy Plunging

HIGH PRICES

Welles' Threat to Raise 'Kane' Puts Him in Spot Between Odlum-Schaefer

Oscaring Their Own

Hollywood, March 18.

William Gargan missed out on an Academy award in the supporting player class but his film work for the past year hasn't gone entirely unrewarded. Last Saturday night he was gifted with a statue of St. Patrick by the Gaelic Society of America for being the 'outstanding' Irish actor.

Femme award went to Geraldine Fitzgerald, who was ku-dosed with a statuette of St. Bridget.

Immediate future for Orson

Welles' 'Citizen Kane' bleak, with indications that R planning to give it a brushoff Welles' threat of court a causes some other move. Prod er's announcement last week his attorney is preparing suit brought no official reaction fro RKO. However, George J. Schaefer RKO prez, is said to have called Welles from Hollywood Saturday (15) and told him:

'I'm coming to New York next week. Don't do anything legal until I arrive. I'll take it up once more with the board of directors when I get there.'

Schaefer is slated to plane into Manhattan tomorrow (Thursday). There's no board meeting scheduled, however, until March 31, which apparently means two more weeks of for 'Kane.' Delaying

When William of the West resigned the tes understood a fortune in

thereafter he oward Hughes n of theatres In 1930 he k to serve in for RKO and en the late S. withdrew as adio stood objections

---

LOEW'S $500,000 COUNTERCLAIM

God Bless America.................Berlin
Yes, My Darling Daughter............Feist
*Down Argentina Way ('Down Argentine Way')....Miller
* Filmusical.

Hearst Opens Blast on RKO-Schaefer; 'Citizen Kane' Release Still Indef

William Randolph Hearst got his first real opportunity last week since his burn at RKO to show how he feels about the company—and stuck the knife in deep. Both the studio and George J. Schaefer, its president, were lambasted mercilessly on front pages of Hearst papers from coast to coast. The news peg was a remote suit against Schaefer and RKO that even the trade papers relegated to inside pages.

Meantime, Orson Welles' 'Citizen Kane,' which it is said Hearst alleges too closely resembles his own life and is the cause of the publisher's ire at RKO, is getting close to its release date and still no engagements have been set for it. RKO maintains that the possibility the film will be soapboxes is delaying the opening, but it is known that lawyers have been busy and there's dissension within the company on the course to be taken. Hearst has allegedly demanded that the film be shelved.

Suit that caused the fireworks in the Heart dailies ended with a $7,000 decision against RKO, won by Joseph N. Ermolieff in Los Angeles court. Ermolieff is a European producer who

(Continued on page 18)

MRS. EMLYN WILLIAMS REMAINING IN U.S.

Mrs. Mollie Williams, wife of playwright-actor Emlyn Williams, is remaining in the U. S. indefinitely with their two children. She had planned to return to England after arranging with Herman Shumlin for the production of her husband's 'The Corn Is Green,' at the National, N.Y. But Williams, currently touring the English provinces in his new play, 'He Was Born Gay,' persuaded her to stay in the U. S., at least until after the expected Nazi invasion attempt this spring.

Sam Scribner III

Sam Scribner, former showman, has been in the Lawrence hospital, Bronxville, N. Y., for the past week. Veteran, who is 83, was reported ill with grippe, but the hospital declined to verify the ailment.

He is treasurer of the Actors Fund, where it was stated his condition is favorable, and chairman of Theatre Authority.

FDR Birthday Ball Spokesman Denies Actors 'Pushed Around'

Washington, Feb. 13.

Editor VARIETY:

Because Hollywood stars have contributed so generously to the success of the Washington Birthday Ball Celebrations, and because others who are eager to come in the future may get the wrong impression, may I challenge VARIETY's page one story of Feb. 12, to the effect that the guests contributed to the motion picture industry were 'pushed around,' or given unhospitable treatment.

Contrary to the vague charge of Mr. Alan Corelli, that those who made many personal appearances were denied White House luncheon invitations, and to participate in other activities, the facts are that all stars were included in every official event on the program, and this included, of course, presence at Mrs. Roosevelt's luncheon in the afternoon, and at the

(Continued on page 55)

BRITISH WAR RELIEF BENEFIT IN N. Y. SRO

Indicated that the 'Carnival for Britain,' benefit show at the Music Hall, Radio City, Friday (21) at midnight, will be over capacity. Over the weekend the theatre advised the American Theatre Wing of the British War Relief that no more tickets were on hand except front locations, priced at $10.

RUBINOFF
AND HIS VIOLIN
on Personal Appearance Tour
until May 15th. Dates in 125 cities.

Management:
PHIL RUBINOFF
Paramount Bldg. New York City

Music to Suit Audience Mood For 'Fantasia'

Hollywood, Feb. 18.

Recording of three musical numbers to be incorporated in Walt Disney's 'Fantasia' after the initial roadshowings of the cartoon opus are well under way, has been started here by Leopold Stokowski. Numbers will be switched and varied, under present plan, to provide evenings of light concerts or more dramatic compositions to suit all types of music lovers, and incidentally to bring repeat customers to the box-office.

Selections to hit the sound tracks under the Stokowski baton are 'Peter and the Wolf,' by Prokofiev; 'Flight of the Bumble Bee,' by Rimsky-Korsakov, and 'Swan of Tuonela,' by Sibelius.

Stokowski has completed music and animation is about two-thirds through on 'Clair de Lune,' by Debussy, which is also planned for insertion in the original picture.

Jackie Gleason, M.C., To Make Film for WB

Jackie Gleason, via agent

Wednesday, April 23, 1941

VARIETY

GOVT'S 'MORE T

Add: Hearst Vs. Welles ('Citizen Kane'); More Newspaper Attacks

Battle of the Hearst papers against Orson Welles continued on all fronts during the past week as RKO prepared for the roadshow preem of Welles' pic, 'Citizen Kane,' at the Palace, N.Y. May 1 and other cities throughout the country during the drumming month. Warfare included:

Steady bombardment from the heaviest editorial artillery in the Hearst press is faced by the entire film industry as a result of the fury which William Randolph Hearst had has been thrown by the revelation that 'Citizen Kane,' Orson Welles' first film, bears similarity to the life of the publisher.

Not only has Hearst forbidden any mention of the distributor, RKO, or product in any of his papers, but the studio publicity department has tipped that the Hearst press will keep up a continuous against the entire industry.

The threat is to put heavy emphasis on widescale employment of foreigners in picture production to the exclusion of idle Americans. Pot-shots are also threatened against all censorious situations or material in films.

Hearst, in addition, is going ahead with his threatened suit for an injunction to restrain RKO from releasing 'Kane,' according to word given by studio officials from Louella O. Parsons, motion picture Jeaditor of the Hearst newspapers. Lower street execs declared that was count the ultimatum, following a direct question as to the publisher's intention.

parent Hearst's objection to the release of 'Citizen Kane' is said to be based on

(Continued on page 55)

RKO's Holme Knighted

Randle F. Holme, chairman of RKO's British company, has been conferred a knighthood by the King of England for distinguished service to the crown.

Phil Reisman, RKO foreign chief, received notification in N. Y.

U.S. NEWS VIA AIR TO EUROPE VITAL NOW

Despite the recent publicity concerning short-wave radio propaganda from the United States to South America, the real importance of Yankee transmissions at this moment in history are the news programs in French, German and Italian beamed at Europe. News from the U. S. and especially news of preparations over here to spoil the dictators' push-over campaign, has enormous value just now.

President Roosevelt's inaugural speech will be shortwaved by NBC in French, German and Italian, leaving General Electric in Schenectady to beam the English definitely itself to the British Isles. In Great Britain the BBC will pick-up and longwave the President's address.

Joe College Goes Gaucho

Mania for rhumba tempo which has reached heavy proportions in metropolitan centers apparently is reaching the college proms.

Band booking agencies are beginning to sell proms name outfits coupled to Latin tempo dispensers, which work as relief crews much as they do in most New York hotel rooms.

All Film Cos. May Suffer Because Of Hearst's Peeve at Welles' 'Kane'

Hollywood, Jan. 14.

100 Newsreelmen to Use 50,000 Feet Covering Roosevelt's Inaugural

Newsreels are preparing the most postelaborate coverage ever given a presidential inauguration when President Roosevelt is sworn in for a third term this month in Washington.

Each newsreel will have 10 cameramen, five or more sound men and technicians, with the five reels represented by nearly 100 men at the chasing. Approximately 50,000 feet of film will be photographed on the event.

BURDENED S
BIZ'S NEW

Morgenthau's 'Larg
Bill' Warning Ca
ready Tax-Loaded
men to Flinch—
Hit Amusements
Front

20% GATE

EACH TIME
'WILL, WON

Comeback Barito
Grueling 'Ot
Saturday as
formance of
Private Melody
self

$500,000 TO

Lawrence Tibbett h
if somewhat cau
through his 'comeback
both on the radio and
politan Opera but he
great artistic risks, n
posing to sing this Sat
(18) the grueling ba
'Otello.' The result of
this dynamic sing

(Continued on

JJ.'s 'Love'
For New S
Attack o

Quickest operetta fl
son was 'Night of
stopped at the Hudson
day (11) after seven
It was a Shubert pro
J. was entirely in char
which played out-of-t
two months to such m
ance that the manag
not to open it on Bro
Showings out of tow
panied by a series of
tween Shubert and J
is reported having o
one reviewer in Bost
in Chicago barred

(Continued on

NOT ENOUGH